ENTERTAINING JUDGMENT

THE AFTERLIFE IN POPULAR IMAGINATION

GREG GARRETT

OXFORD
UNIVERSITY PRESS

OXFORD
UNIVERSITY PRESS

Oxford University Press is a department of the
University of Oxford. It furthers the University's objective
of excellence in research, scholarship, and education
by publishing worldwide.

Oxford   New York
Auckland   Cape Town   Dar es Salaam   Hong Kong   Karachi
Kuala Lumpur   Madrid   Melbourne   Mexico City   Nairobi
New Delhi   Shanghai   Taipei   Toronto

With offices in
Argentina   Austria   Brazil   Chile   Czech Republic   France   Greece
Guatemala   Hungary   Italy   Japan   Poland   Portugal   Singapore
South Korea   Switzerland   Thailand   Turkey   Ukraine   Vietnam

Oxford is a registered trade mark of Oxford University Press
in the UK and certain other countries.

Published in the United States of America by
Oxford University Press
198 Madison Avenue, New York, NY 10016

Author is represented by the literary agency of Alive Communications,
Inc., 7680 Goddard Street, Suite 200, Colorado Springs, CO 80920,
www.alivecommunications.com.

© Greg Garrett 2015

Library of Congress Cataloging-in-Publication Data
Garrett, Greg.
Entertaining judgment : the afterlife in popular imagination / Greg Garrett.
pages   cm
Includes bibliographical references and index.
ISBN 978-0-19-933590-9 (hardcover : alk. paper) — ISBN 978-0-19-933591-6 (ebook) —
ISBN 978-0-19-933592-3 (ebook)   1. Popular culture—Religious aspects.
2. Future life.   3. Popular culture—United States—History—20th century.
4. Popular culture—United States—History—21st century.   I. Title.
BL65.C8G38 2015
202'.3—dc23   2014011227

1 3 5 7 9 8 6 4 2

Typeset in Sabon LT Standard

Printed in the United States of America
on acid-free paper

For Jeanie, who makes my life Heaven.

CONTENTS

ENTERTAINING JUDGMENT

ENTERTAINING JUDGMENT

How We Understand the Afterlife

As the sun begins to set, a baseball player, John Kinsella, walks across a baseball diamond incongruously nestled within an Iowa cornfield. Beside him is Ray, the son he had never expected to see again. Things had ended badly between them, with pain and sadness on both sides, and now John can scarcely take his eyes off Ray, who not surprisingly seems just as amazed to see his father. After all, John died years ago, and Ray now appears older than this uniformed ballplayer who is a walking, talking version of those old photos of his dad before he married and settled into family life.

"It's so beautiful here," John says. "For me—well, for me, it's like a dream come true. Can I ask you something? Is this—is this heaven?"

Ray Kinsella shrugs a little and looks abashed. Strangely enough, it's not the first time a dead person has asked him this question about the ballpark he built in the middle of his cornfield.

"It's Iowa," he answers sheepishly.

"Iowa?"

"Yeah."

"I could have sworn it was heaven." John Kinsella turns away to gather up his baseball equipment, but his question has sparked an equally important one for Ray.

"Is—is there a heaven?"

John turns, gazes unblinking at his son, and says, without a shred of doubt, "Oh, yeah. It's the place dreams come true."

Is this heaven? *Is* there a heaven? The questions raised in the movie *Field of Dreams* are the ones we all ask about the afterlife. They haunt us because, unlike other knowledge we seek, they cannot be answered from our store of experience. No one living truly knows the answer to these mysteries: Where did we come from? What happens to us when we die? Is there another form of existence then? Are there consequences or rewards in that next life—if there is one—for the things we did in this life? If there are consequences, will we proceed directly to our final state of being, or will we be required (or permitted) to pursue some intermediary step first? Is there a God? A devil? Is anyone up there (or down there!) looking after, or over, us?

These questions express our deepest concerns about existence. We wonder if there is a guiding intelligence behind the universe. If there is, what does that intelligence feel about us? And all of this is our way of approaching the underlying question: Is the future to be longed for or feared?

Many believe that after this life our souls, perhaps in our resurrected bodies, will continue to exist. The concept of an afterlife is a part of most religious traditions, whether that next life is thought of as a place of reward, punishment, or transition, and almost all of us are familiar with some of these religious and cultural constructions of what might come next. Our sacred texts and religious traditions attempt to provide answers to our seemingly unanswerable questions, and they ask only that we accept them through the eyes of faith. What awaits us, religion teaches, may be heaven, hell, or purgatory—realms of the blessed, of the damned, and of the not-yet-worthy. These are dominant understandings of the afterlife in the West, all of them conditioned on our behavior in this life and on our efforts to be faithful to our beliefs, or, at the very least, to be good human beings. As Miles, the narrator of John Green's *Looking for Alaska*, notes in writing his final exam on the afterlife for his world religions class, "People, I thought, wanted security. They couldn't bear the idea of death being a big black nothing, couldn't bear the thought of their loved ones not existing, and couldn't even imagine themselves not existing. I finally decided that people believed in an afterlife because they couldn't bear not to."[1]

As we see from *Looking for Alaska*, cultural and narrative understandings can also help to shape our ideas about these future places or states of being; our perceptions of sacred as well as secular matters are always being informed by secular texts as well as by holy ones. Recalling Mark Twain's observation that people of his day learned more of their religion from plays, novels, and the Christmas story than from sermons, Lynn Schofield Clark notes that "today, as then, central beliefs concerning the realm beyond this world and the afterlife come from many, often unexpected sources."[2]

This is true whether we're talking about heaven, hell, or purgatory. It's true about our understanding of supernatural creatures like demons, angels, and spirits. It's even true about our ideas about God, the devil, and other divine or diabolical forces. We rely on this imaginative help because our holy books leave a lot to be desired as authoritative sources of information about the afterlife. The Bible and the Qur'an include some references to the realms of paradise and of eternal punishment, but not many. As New Testament scholar N. T. Wright has noted, there is almost nothing in the Bible about going to heaven and still less about hell. Although many Christians have placed their beliefs about the afterlife at the center of their faith, Wright argues that the frequent and somewhat confusing references to the kingdom of heaven in the gospels are not attempting to describe a place, heaven, but something else entirely: God's sovereign rule breaking through into the earthly realm.[3] Outside the wild apocalyptic vision of Revelation, biblical references to heaven and hell are few and far between. Today's Calvinists may talk a great deal about heaven and hell, but in his fifteen-hundred-page masterwork, *The Institutes of Christian Religion*, John Calvin devotes only a couple of passages to heaven, and a single paragraph to hell.

The word purgatory doesn't appear in the Bible. The concept of a place of punishment between this life and the next was extrapolated by theologians largely from a single verse in Matthew in which Jesus says, "Whoever speaks a word against the Son of Man will be forgiven, but whoever speaks against the Holy Spirit will not be forgiven, either in this age or in the age to come."[4] Much of what Christians believe about the afterlife does not come from the Bible, but through human imagination, whether theological or creative.

As Wright points out, our modern Western concepts of the afterlife have been largely shaped by such things as medieval images of heaven and hell and the *Divine Comedy* of Dante.[5] Art, literature, and other forms of culture represent visually and dramatically the sacred abstractions that we otherwise know only through the stories of our faith traditions. Sometimes our cultural imaginings reinforce the impressions we receive through our faith; sometimes they call them into question. They can encourage us to believe; they can cause us to doubt. But always these imaginings are a part of our process of creating meaning. This is the central premise of this book.

Stewart Hoover, who presided over a quantitative study about audience interactions with various forms of media, concluded that mass media play a "subtle, nuanced and complex role" in helping people create religious meaning and form their religious identities.[6] While the media might not necessarily constitute the primary influences on our beliefs (despite what generations of censorious religious leaders and concerned parents have said about novels, movies, and music), what we read, watch, listen to, and play is one avenue of our ongoing search for religious answers, and it is a broad and well-traveled avenue indeed. Consciously or not, we are taking in information when we encounter literary and media representations of the world to come. For example:

Kenny McCormick is not like other children. He's two-dimensional, for one thing (like the rest of the characters on the television show *South Park*). He's poor—the poorest kid in town, as his so-called friend Eric Cartman is fond of pointing out. He is also one of those rare individuals with direct experience of the afterlife, because Kenny dies, over and over again (more than one hundred times so far in sixteen seasons of the show), in ways both gruesome and ridiculous. He's visited hell, and as someone who has suffered so undeservedly perhaps deserves, he's been to heaven. At the end of the feature film *South Park: Bigger, Longer, and Uncut*, Kenny is permitted to enter heaven, passing through a phalanx of bare-breasted female angels, two of whom fit him with wings and a halo. Kenny flies directly toward the viewer and the closing credits roll. A similar vision of heaven appears in the Emmy-winning *South Park* episode "Best Friends Forever" from 2005. After his usual death, Kenny is chosen to lead the angelic forces in the fight against Satan on the grounds that he has mastered a video game, *Heaven versus Hell.* When he arrives in heaven, he enters a vision out of Christian art: a gleaming heavenly city, winged angels, the gatekeeper St. Peter, and the archangel Michael, who is in charge of heaven's defenses at least until Kenny takes over.

South Park's heavenly scenes parody hundreds of years of religious and cultural depictions, a "fluffy clouds" heaven like the one Colton Burpo told his father he had visited while having surgery for appendicitis: "Colton had climbed into the lap of Jesus, who was dressed in a white robe with a royal purple sash. The Son of Man then summoned winged angels and requested music. There were halos and bright colors, a rainbow horse and a throne for the Son at the right hand of the Father."[7] In this and many other of our most traditional and sentimental visions of a Christian heaven, a shiny, sparkling realm takes what we know about the valuable and the beautiful in this life and simply translates it into the next: jeweled crowns, streets of gold, golden harps.

In most of our versions of paradise, sacred or secular, heaven is a place where dreams come true—buxom angels for Kenny and a rainbow horse for little Colton. It is, as Leah Rozen writes, "a heaven bursting with fluffy clouds and angels strumming on harps." Whether we're talking about books or television or film, we should recognize this version of heaven to be, as Rozen writes, cheesy and clichéd.[8] In fact, one rarely sees the "fluffy cloud heaven" now unless it's used for comic effect, although it is no less recognizable for that as one possible vision of the afterlife.

Susie Salmon is also in heaven, or "her heaven," as she describes it. Although it has no fluffy clouds, her heaven may be equally stereotypical. A young girl brutally raped and murdered probably deserves a heavenly afterlife. In Alice Sebold's best-selling novel *The Lovely Bones* and the film adaptation directed by Peter Jackson, Susie looks down from heaven on an earth where she desperately wants her broken family to heal and her killer to be caught. Her heaven is both more prosaic than Kenny's, and more secular. You won't find archangels, or St. Peter, or even God in this heaven. But as Katherine Viner notes, "The view of heaven presented in *The Lovely Bones* is a familiar one—a place of happiness, without judgment, where you get what you desire as long as you know why you desire it."[9] In her heaven, Susie has a roommate named Holly, interacts with an intake counselor named Franny, and walks around a landscape that looks very much like the future into which she will never live:

> When I first entered heaven I thought everyone saw what I saw. That in everyone's heaven there were soccer goalposts in the distance and lumbering women throwing shot and javelin. That all the buildings were like suburban northeast high schools built in the 1960s. Large, squat buildings spread out on dismally landscaped sandy lots, with overhangs and open spaces to make them feel modern. My favorite part was how the colored blocks were turquoise and orange, just like the blocks in Fairfax High. Sometimes, on Earth, I had made my father drive me by Fairfax High so I could imagine myself there.[10]

These are only two of the many versions of heaven or paradise in literature and culture, surprisingly perhaps, given the difficulty of setting any dramatic story in a realm marked by bliss, lack of conflict, and stasis. Margaret Atwood describes the problem for storytellers in *The Blind Assassin*, where she writes that "happiness is a garden walled with glass: there's no way in or out. In Paradise there are no stories, because there are no journeys. It's loss and regret and misery and yearning that drive the story forward, along its twisted road."[11] It should be and is difficult to write of heaven without succumbing to sentiment or cliché. In my younger years as a fiction writer, my still-unfinished novel about Winston Churchill's adventures after death was stalled by my inability to imbue heaven with anything like reality. I found it impossible to write convincingly of a place I couldn't imagine with any freshness. Of course this has hardly deterred media from showing us heaven, whether traditional or radically different.

We encounter heaven in works ranging from classics like Dante's *Paradiso* and Milton's *Paradise Lost* to contemporary novels such as C. S. Lewis's *The Last Battle* and Leif Enger's best seller *Peace like a River*. We see it in the films *It's a Wonderful Life*, *What Dreams May Come*, and *Tree of Life*. We find images of heaven on television in *South Park*, *The Simpsons*, and *Charmed*. We enter heaven in comics and graphic novels, see it represented by the paradisaical planet Krypton in the Superman mythos, or by Asgard, the heavenly realm where Thor resides. Heaven is presented more literally as the realm of the blessed dead from which the hero Green Arrow is forced to return in *Quiver*, a story arc written by filmmaker Kevin Smith, or from which Ben Grimm (The Thing) is "rescued" by the other members of the Fantastic Four in a set of stories written by Mark Waid.

Heaven often appears in popular music, whether standards, pop, or hip hop. If we survey the charts from the 1920s to the present we find: "My Blue Heaven" ("Just Molly and me and baby makes three / We're happy in my blue heaven"), "Cheek to Cheek" ("Heaven / I'm in heaven…. When we're out together dancing cheek to cheek"), Belinda Carlisle's "Heaven Is a Place on Earth" ("They say in heaven love comes first / We'll make heaven a place on Earth"), Def Leppard's "Heaven Is" ("Heaven is a girl I know so well / She makes me feel good when I feel like hell"), Keyshia Cole's "Sent from Heaven" ("I wanna be the one who you believe / In your heart is sent from…heaven"), and Coldplay's "Hurts Like Heaven" ("Oh you use your heart as a weapon / And it hurts like heaven"). The use of heaven as a metaphor allows meaning to flow simultaneously in both directions. In each of these songs (and many others), the songwriter uses the idea of paradise to transcend an earthly reality. At the same time, the song's earthly associations flavor our understanding of heaven: dancing cheek to cheek is like heaven, but at the same time, heaven is like dancing cheek to cheek.

Hell too is a popular topic. It is often said that in John Milton's *Paradise Lost* God is perhaps the least interesting character while Satan is, by Milton's intention, the most dynamic and most compelling.[12] Hell is a place of driving ambition, of great conflict, of violence and abuse, and thus, naturally, of tremendous dramatic interest. As with heaven, we find hell used to flavor earthly settings and situations while earthly analogues help us understand something about the place of eternal punishment and separation. Death Valley is "hellish," for example, because of its deadly and unrelenting heat.

One familiar fictional setting, Gotham City, is hellish because it is full of unremitting evil, senseless mayhem, and violence perpetrated by and directed against its inhabitants. Despite Batman's never-ending efforts, Gotham is a dark, difficult, and wretched place, as close to hell on earth as we can imagine. In the graphic novel *Planetary/Batman: Night on Earth*, Elijah Snow describes Gotham City's history: "Old as New York, founded on the East Coast and originally designed by English masons on opium…exacerbated by absinthe-fiend local architects in the twenties, basically not fit for human habitation."[13] Frank Miller's *The Dark Knight Returns*, a mythic remaking of the Batman story from the 1980s, opens with images of hellish flames and heat: Bruce Wayne (the secret identity of Batman, that fearsome figure of the night) is involved in a fiery crash of the race car he is driving. We cut immediately to images of Gotham suffering under a heat wave, its yellow sky heated beyond endurance.

In this city, violence and atrocities are part and parcel of the superheated environment, and as Bruce walks through the streets, he muses that he and perhaps all those he passes are dead and doomed: "I'm a zombie, a flying Dutchman, a dead man, ten years dead," while a street protester in the same frame carries a sign that could be a commentary on Bruce's interior monologue. It simply says: "We are damned."[14]

Whether in comics like *The Dark Knight Returns*, *Batman: Year One*, or *The Joker: Death of the Family*, in the cinematic versions of Gotham brought to the screen by Tim Burton (*Batman* and *Batman Returns*) and Christopher Nolan (*Batman Begins*, *The Dark Knight*, and *The Dark Knight Rises*), or the Gotham City with which you can interact in best-selling video games such as *Arkham Asylum*, *Arkham City*, and *Arkham Origins*, few settings in popular culture proffer so powerful a vision of hell on earth. As in the traditional theological understandings of hell, the residents of Gotham are far removed from God, from beauty, from justice, from peace, and from joy.

Unlike Metropolis, that lovely, well-lit, we might even say heavenly city of the future and home to the godlike Superman, Gotham feels to its inhabitants like a place of eternal punishment. Perhaps unsurprisingly, only a seemingly demonic force, that of Batman, can prevail in the location of such evil. Only greater violence can prevent violence, greater determination overwhelm that of devilish villains like The Joker, Mr. Freeze, and the Penguin. In *Batman Begins*, Batman (Christian Bale) consciously fashions himself into a demonic creature of the night to make his enemies fear him. Christopher Nolan depicts Batman breaking up a warehouse drug deal by using elements common to horror films—traveling Steadicam, dramatic musical stings to make the audience jump, moving shadows, sudden bursts of violence. It is the central irony of the Batman mythos: our hero is trying to clean up hell using many of hell's own methods—which might be, incidentally, why Batman's hard-fought peace never ever seems to last for long.

Hell can also be played for humor, however, particularly now that many doubt its actual existence. In "Pancakes," a two-page strip from Mike Mignola's comic series *Hellboy*, the young title character, the red-hued son of a demon prince and a human witch, is getting ready for his breakfast at the army base where he has been taken after crossing over from hell. General Norton Ricker, of the Bureau for Paranormal Research and Defense, is in charge of feeding him. Hellboy wants noodles, but when he arrives at the table the general informs him that he can't have noodles for breakfast. He is going to eat pancakes.

"But I don't like pancakes!" Hellboy protests.

Tough, the general responds. You're trying them—at least one bite.

The general cuts and spears some pancake on a fork.

Hellboy reluctantly opens his mouth.

Mignola includes an extreme close-up frame of the letters "USA" on the army-issue fork to stretch the tension out a moment longer—before Hellboy announces his newfound love for pancakes.

The *Green Eggs and Ham* moment is not the point; in the very next frame, Mignola gives us an establishing shot of Pandemonium, the city of the fallen in hell, rendered in reds, oranges, and yellows to suggest the searing heat of the place. The inhabitants of Pandemonium are screaming, their arms lifted in anguish. The archdevil Astaroth asks Mammon what can possibly be happening.

"It is the boy," Mammon explains. "He has eaten the pancake."

Another powerful demon laments that Hellboy will never return to them now.

"Truly," Astaroth says, "this *is* our blackest hour."[15]

As we've always imagined, hell is a bad place, burning eternally; what makes it even worse? You can't get pancakes there.

The concept of purgatory has fallen somewhat out of favor (although it remains an official item of belief for Roman Catholics, who profess that those imperfect souls who die in God's grace must "undergo purification, so as to achieve the holiness necessary to enter the joy of heaven").[16] Perhaps surprisingly, however, even such a dodgy concept as purgatory offers us a multitude of cultural touchstones. When all-star baseball pitcher Roger Clemens was acquitted of charges he used steroids and lied about it, a headline opined that nonetheless, Clemens was "in baseball purgatory."[17] Alex Rodriguez, another baseball superstar accused of such violations, was said in a recent newspaper column to be on "the road to Baseball Purgatory, where you'll find faded stars who have either been banned from the game or been told, without any nuisance paperwork, that they're not welcome at the ballpark."[18] Rockstar Games, the maker of the popular Max Payne series of shooters, announced that cheaters, hackers, and "miscreants" who violated game decency would be placed "in their own little purgatory" that works a bit like the Catholic one: "If you serve your time in the cheater's corner and clean up your act, you may get a second chance to play with others. If you are a repeat offender you will result in indefinite banishment [*sic*]."[19] The U.S. stock markets, waiting anxiously in 2012 for some resolution of the Euro crisis, were said by the Associated Press to be in purgatory, although how exactly the markets might earn themselves out of that state was not explained.[20] *Grantland*, the sports and popular culture website, features a regular column, "Escape from Pop Purgatory," asking if well-known but out-of-favor musicians have at last earned their way back into the pop mainstream with their current releases. And even the stodgy old *Economist* offered the headline

"Finance in Purgatory" for a recent article on possible restrictions on international money transfers.[21]

Our appropriation of purgatory may arise more from narrative need than from theological aptness, but culture can help us crack open even a challenging religious teaching such as purgatory. One of the central fan theories about the television show *Lost*, for example, was that the strange desert island where Jack (Matthew Fox), Kate (Evangeline Lilly), John Locke (Terry O'Quinn), and the other "Lostees" had crashed was purgatory. As a Lost wiki notes, this was "the favorite theory seized upon by every viewer new to the show," that "everyone on the island is actually dead and their actions on the 'island' determine when they will leave Purgatory for heaven."[22] Certainly there seemed to be evidence in favor of this—dead people walked the island, no babies could be born there, and this gathering of people lost in every conceivable way a human being could be lost suggested to many viewers that some sort of testing or redemption was under way. All the same, the show's producers made it clear from early on that these characters were not dead and in purgatory.[23]

That early denial, however, didn't prevent *Lost* from at last employing the purgatory model of refinement and testing on the way to ultimate redemption. In the sixth and final season, *Lost* began to feature a "Sideways world," a reality in which the Lostees lived out lives as though they had never crashed on the island, interspersed with the reality of their lives on the island. It became clear that although the island itself might not be purgatory, this sideways world did function as a halfway station in which the characters were actively working toward their eventual salvation. *Entertainment Weekly's Lost* aficionado Jeff Jensen explored the connection in an interview with *Lost's* executive producers Damon Lindelof and Carlton Cuse:

EW   Season 6 gave us the Sideways world, which was ultimately revealed to be a kind of purgatory where the castaways went after they died.... Perhaps one reason that [fans] didn't guess the secret is because back in the first two seasons of the show, you pretty vociferously ruled out purgatory as a theory of the Island.

CUSE   I agree with you. Because we said the Island was not purgatory, people extrapolated that to mean that a concept that resembled it couldn't even exist within the entire show....

LINDELOF I know [fans] had lists of questions they wanted answers to. What did the numbers mean? Where were the Dharma food drops coming from? What was up with the polar bears? But the list of questions we wanted to explore included: What happens when you die? What is the nature of man—good or evil?[24]

In the Sideways world, characters were faced with decisions they had made before, and usually made badly. On the island, Benjamin Linus (Michael Emerson) sacrificed his daughter Alex (Tania Raymonde) to his ambition for power. But in the sideways world, where Linus was a high school history teacher, he faced another test when Alex, his brightest student, asked him for a recommendation to college. Alex's future became tied up in Benjamin's power play to become principal of the school, but this time he chose correctly; this time he chose love over power. In this purgatory world, the Lostees were offered the opportunity to change, and ultimately, to be transformed into people capable of moving into the light in the final moments of the series finale.

Our movies, novels, and other forms of culture often feature stories of people who are caught between one state and another and who are being changed for the better so that they can pass into whatever comes next for them. Sometimes this story of redemption clearly happens in the context of life after death, as we'll explore in movies such as *Ghost* and *The Sixth Sense*. We meet ghosts or spirits who can't move on until they accomplish something profound. But we also discover other understandings of purgatory that emerge when characters are simply stuck in their everyday lives and seem to be unable to move forward.

Take weatherman Phil Connor (Bill Murray), the sad, self-centered soul in need of redemption in *Groundhog Day*. Unaccountably, inexplicably, Phil is stuck reliving the same day over and over again. Every morning, Sonny and Cher's "I Got You, Babe" awakens him as it blares from the clock radio in his hotel room in the small town in rural Pennsylvania where he's been sent to cover Groundhog Day. Every morning, Phil goes off to do a broadcast from the groundhog site, interacts with the locals, and attempts to get out of town.

He thinks this is strange, of course, imagines that his experience is unique, doesn't dream that anyone else could understand his suffering.

"What would you do," Phil asks a stranger late one night in a bowling alley, "if you were stuck in one place and every day was exactly the same, and nothing that you did mattered?"

"That about sums it up for me," is the response. This lonely drunk—and many of the people with whom Phil interacts—are also slogging day by day through an existence that seems to be interminable and unchanging.

What is one to do in the face of such a long, gray existence? The message of *Groundhog Day*—and, as we will see, the central narrative of many of the stories depicting purgatory—is both dramatic and theological: if you don't like your life, if you don't like your identity, change. By the end of *Groundhog Day*, Phil has said goodbye to the hedonistic, sardonic boor he was in the opening scenes. He has transformed himself, through his own planning and hard work, into a person with realized talents and genuine compassion and he is dramatically rewarded with the love of the lovely Rita (Andie MacDowell), who wouldn't give the old Phil the time of day—for good reason. We'll consider in detail why the purgatory narrative remains so central in our culture, despite the fact that the Protestant mainstream of American Christianity doesn't accept the doctrine, but perhaps one reason is that it allows for a powerful story about change and growth.

In all of these snapshots of the afterlife, we are learning something about how heaven, hell, or purgatory can be used to help us understand earthly concepts like pleasure, love, joy, satisfaction, and security. We're seeing how the characters of those landscapes, whether they be lost souls or the redeemed, angels or devils, ghosts or spirits, teach us something about our own humanity. The art and culture we consume plant images and ideas in our heads about the big topics they explore in the process of entertaining us. These images of and stories about the afterlife, wherever they come from, help us to make sense of challenging concepts and along the way they offer us some peace of mind. In the *Washington Post* Hank Steuver wrote of *Lost*: "America, it's so obvious. Millions of you loved 'Lost' because you feel lost."[25] For a people who were lost and wanted to be found, for a people afraid of the future, *Lost* met many needs, some emotional, some spiritual. Its dramatization of life and the afterlife helped us make at least one version of sense out of this crazy mixed-up post-9/11 world.

Lost and other narratives can be considered as alternative wisdom traditions of a sort, helping readers and viewers to find comfort and make meaning about ethical and spiritual questions. *Star Trek*'s legions of fans could talk with you about the Prime Directive, and some could perhaps explain how it might be interpreted in our own lives. *Star Wars* fans are sometimes consciously drawn to live out the philosophy of the mythos (or to tweak the beard of census takers), but for whatever reason, "Jedi" remains a popular choice in religion censuses around the world. Although—like many churches—the Jedi "faith" has declined in recent years, its British adherents remain sufficiently numerous for it to rank only behind Christianity, Islam, Hinduism, Sikhism, Judaism, and Buddhism. Compare its 176,000 adherents in the United Kingdom's 2011 census to the 29,000 identifying as atheists.[26]

While it may be a lark for many of them, why this particular lark? Why not claim to be an adherent of Wonder Woman or Big Bird, both of whom also have an observable ethos? Something about the ideas behind *Star Wars*, about the concept of a force that binds all things together appeals in some way. Likewise viewers of *Doctor Who*, the longest-running science fiction show—and one of the most venerable television series ever—find meaning and comfort in its ongoing narrative. For its fans, as Matthew Sweet notes in his article describing the "Tao of Who" in the *Telegraph*, "*Doctor Who* has the moral and ethical influence of a religion."[27]

A study by cultural critic Clive Marsh discovered that for British filmgoers, like the audiences surveyed by Lynn Schofield Clark, "philosophy, theology, and ethics are happening as furtive, incidental activities amid enjoying a supposedly escapist culture."[28] C. S. Lewis argued that in great stories, plot is merely the net that snags what is truly important.[29] Likewise, Diane Winston notes how for television viewers, "the experience of watching, and responding to, TV characters' moral dilemmas, crises of faith, bouts of depression, and fits of exhilaration gives expression—as well as insight and resolution—to viewers' own spiritual odysseys and ethical predicaments."[30] Literature and culture deal with all manner of human concerns caught in their nets: love and hate, war and peace, life and whatever comes after life.

In literature as ancient as the early Mesopotamian *Epic of Gilgamesh*, we find human beings speculating on what might follow death, expressing their hopes and fears, trying to make sense of death and how our actions in this life may affect what follows death. Today, through the music and imagery of rock bands like U2, Iron Maiden, and AC-DC, in the storylines of TV's *Lost*, *South Park*, and *Fantasy Island*, in the implied theology of films such as *The Corpse Bride*, *Ghost*, and *Field of Dreams*, in the wildly popular populist paintings of Thomas Kinkade, who in 2004 had a gallery showing entitled "Heaven on Earth" at California State University, Fullerton, and within the supernatural landscape of ghosts, shades, and otherworldly way stations in the Harry Potter novels and films, writers, musicians, and artists of all sorts continue to investigate those hopes and fears.

Theologian Jeremy Begbie affirms that literature and the arts may be and often are "vehicles of *discovery*, not just of ourselves, but of other people and indeed of virtually anything with which we engage from day to day, from physical objects to grand ideas."[31] Art may address spiritual and religious questions obliquely rather than directly, as theology tries to do, but it has always had a role in exploring every part of the human condition.[32] So it is that the chapters to follow will explore the ways in which literature and culture have shaped our understanding of the physical settings of the afterlife, and of the grand theological ideas encompassed within them.

I have spent my life studying and writing about films, fiction, comics and graphic novels, and some forms of popular music, and I consider myself something of an expert in those areas. I will focus largely on those media. Someone who truly knows rap or performance art or sculpture would bring their own strengths, expertise, and insight; someone who spends more time playing computer and console games than I do could expand our knowledge of that burgeoning field. Until such a time as one chooses to write further on this topic, I'll perform as complete an examination as I can of this substantial but admittedly incomplete data field. I believe we have more than enough information to draw some conclusions.

We will be learning about religion, politics, culture, psychology, and virtually every area of human inquiry. It is also my hope that this journey will show us how our books, movies, music, and culture have been leading us on a search for what really matters in this life. In that respect, I expect this voyage of discovery to uncover a great deal of interesting information. But even more important, I hope it will prompt reflection, discussion, and action that might prove formative as well. Our stories of the afterlife have shaped human beings for centuries. I believe that as we enter into these stories, we too may be shaped for the better.

CHAPTER ONE

IN BETWEEN

Death and the Undead

"They're dead. They're all messed up."
SHERIFF McCLELLAND (GEORGE KOSANA),
NIGHT OF THE LIVING DEAD (1968)

"To die—to be really dead. That must be glorious!"
COUNT DRACULA (BELA LUGOSI), *DRACULA* (1931)

A few summers ago, I stood beside a man and watched him die.

Now, this is not something I do regularly. As with many people in contemporary Western culture, my observation of this death was a rarity. We tend to segregate the dying from the dead, to remove the prospect of death to hospitals and hospices where we aren't forced to face it directly. On this particular rainy afternoon, I was in the presence of death precisely because I was working as a hospital chaplain, a requirement of my seminary education.

The patient had ravaged his body with drugs and hard living and was suffering a total system failure. Nothing the medical staff could do would save him, and the family had gathered around him for a final vigil. So it was that I stood in a room filled to overflowing by this Hispanic family, who had asked me to read the Prayers for the Dying and to watch with them as their grandson, son, brother, cousin, father, and ex-husband passed from this existence into whatever it is that comes next.

His breathing was slow and shallow and scarcely visible; the only real sign of life was the slow beep of the monitors recording his heartbeat, his breath. I began reading the prayers and responses from the

Book of Common Prayer. The family bowed their heads. The mother, her hand on her son's shoulder, wept quietly. Outside, the rain fell.

I read the entire prayer and finished with these words:

> Into your hands, O merciful Savior, we commend your servant. Acknowledge, we humbly beseech you, a sheep of your own fold, a lamb of your own flock, a sinner of your own redeeming. Receive him into the arms of your mercy, into the blessed rest of everlasting peace, and into the glorious company of the saints in light. *Amen.*
>
> May his soul and the souls of all the departed, through the mercy of God, rest in peace. *Amen.*[1]

When I looked up from the prayer book, I saw that the patient too was finished. Although I had not marked the precise moment, he had stopped breathing. His heart had finished pumping blood through his veins. His brain had gone on sparking for a minute, two, three, then faded into blackness. Now all that was left was the battered shell of his body, slowly cooling to room temperature.

What had just happened? Was some part of this man still conscious someplace else, or was his consciousness now as inert as his body?

While his family and I had beliefs and opinions, none of us knew for certain what had just happened or what it meant. Death is, as Hamlet tells us, "The undiscovere'd country, from whose bourn / No traveller returns."[2] It is mysterious to us, as it must be, for few pass into that undiscovered country and return again to tell us of what they have experienced. We make best sellers of books that promise or pretend to have inside information on what comes after death. An entire cottage industry has grown up around after-death tourism, from pioneering studies of near-death experiences like *Life after Life* by Raymond Moody and Maurice S. Rawlings's *Beyond Death's Door* to contemporary best sellers like Betty J. Eadie's *Embraced by the Light* and Todd Burpo's *Heaven Is for Real: A Little Boy's Astounding Story of His Trip to Heaven and Back*. Burpo's account of how his three-year-old son Colton made a visit to the afterlife has spawned countless best-selling spin-off products and a movie directed by Randall Wallace, the director of *Braveheart*.

When someone has apparently died and returned, we hope that person might shine a light into the unknown and tell us something that might assuage our anxieties. We hope also to have our faith and belief confirmed, whatever that faith and belief might be. (As Gary Scott Smith wryly notes, if a near-death experience confirms what we believe, it is believable; if not, it is demonic.)[3] If, for example, we believe the dead will encounter a bright light, heavenly gates, or a wall of flame, we would dearly like for the nearly dead to report thusly. The southern novelist T. R. Pearson parodies these popular afterlife accounts (and the reasons for their popularity) in his novel *Gospel Hour*. Donnie Huff, a lumberjack who dies and is resuscitated, is asked leading questions by his devout mother-in-law about what she hopes he might have encountered during his time among the dead: "Had Donnie Huff dropped off in the course of his demise into pitchy darkness or could he recall some manner of illumination [?], and while she did not expressly mention the Savior…and the dramatic heavenly backlighting she did in fact fairly completely insinuate the both of them with a thoroughly beatific smile."[4] Donnie's mother-in-law—like most of us—wants her belief system affirmed empirically, and clearly she is not above nudging her way to that outcome. She just wants to hear something about what comes next. A few words from the other side are enough—hence our fascination with mediums and spiritualists, and the popularity of Mitch Albom's novel *The First Phone Call from Heaven*, in which the dead call the living to let them know that they are okay, not to cry, that heaven is even more amazing than anyone could imagine. Anything that might help settle our minds about what comes next is valuable.

It may explain why we parse the dying words of people like Steve Jobs ("Oh wow!") for inside information on what they might see across the divide at the moment of their passing. This study of famous last words has been, as Joseph Harris notes, "an enormously widespread cultural phenomenon" by which people for centuries have hoped to discover something definitive.[5] Whether it is Elizabeth Barrett Browning's hope-inducing "Beautiful," Thomas "Stonewall" Jackson's "Let us pass over the river and rest under the shade of the trees," or Oscar Wilde's irreverent and probably apocryphal last words ("Either this wallpaper goes or I do"), we pay close attention to what the dying say in hopes that it might help us map a bit more of the undiscovered country. We also hope it might suggest something of their experience at that moment, so we might prepare ourselves for it.

But famous last words are often inexplicable or personally meaningless, and even those with some sort of religious content are necessarily brief and cryptic. Since death is so far outside our understanding—and now often indeed out of our sight—we have come to rely on the imaginative accounts of writers and artists who seek to describe what happens on that final journey to us, their readers, viewers, or listeners. Hamlet is one of those characters who walk us through their movement into the undiscovered country, offering his final words in Shakespeare's characteristic iambic pentameter:

> *Oh, I die, Horatio;*
> *The potent poison quite o'er-crows my spirit:*
> *I cannot live to hear the news from England;*
> *But I do prophesy the election lights*
> *On Fortinbras: he has my dying voice;*
> *So tell him, with the occurrents, more and less,*
> *Which have solicited. The rest is silence.*[6]

WHAT IS DEATH, REALLY?

"To die will be an awfully big adventure."

J. M. BARRIE, *PETER PAN*

Our artistic views of the final transition often resemble the observer viewpoint that the family of the dying man and I possessed; as we read or watch, we too are sometimes permitted to stand as witnesses to the transition from life to death. Most of us became acquainted with dramatic death scenes in our earliest youth, whether our experience began with Bambi's mother in *Bambi*, Simba's father, Mufasa, in *The Lion King*, or Hedwig the owl in the book or film versions of *Harry Potter and the Deathly Hallows*. Then, as we grew older, most of us saw deaths on television, read about them, viewed them in films, until we became familiar with the dramatic conventions: a gangster grabs his chest and crumples; a dying archer somersaults off the wall. Failing, as most of us have these days, to be present at an actual death, we may come to mistake dramatic depictions for the actuality of dying.

In *The Return of the King*, Peter Jackson's third and final *Lord of the Rings* film, we witness the death of Theoden (Bernard Hill), the king who dies in battle in the company of his niece Eowyn (Miranda Otto). From a high angle, we observe as Eowyn approaches Theoden where he lies, pinned beneath his horse. He looks up at her, his breathing shallow, and he recognizes her: "I know your face...Eowyn.... My eyes darken." She protests, as witnesses always do, when he tells her he is dying, but his last words are stirring and undeniable; he is looking across the river into that far country: "I go to my fathers...in whose mighty company, I shall not now feel ashamed." Then, his lips lined with blood, he utters Eowyn's name one final time, his eyes lose their focus and remain open and unblinking, the elegiac horns sound, and the camera cuts away to a discreet distance. It is, all in all, a typical heroic death in Hollywood—it tells us very little about the actual experience of that death.

A slightly more revealing death scene is found in Thomas Harris's novel *The Silence of the Lambs*, source of the Academy Award–winning 1990 feature film starring Jodie Foster and Anthony Hopkins. Clarice Starling, the FBI trainee who is the story's protagonist, has tracked a serial killer, the bizarre and bizarrely named Jame Gumb, back to his lair. There, in his basement, she has gotten the drop on him, shooting him before he can do the same to her. She lies there in total darkness, listening intently, and through her close observation, we witness Gumb's passing:

What was that sound? Whistling? Like a teakettle, but interrupted. What was it? Like breathing.... It's a sucking chest wound. He's hit in the chest....

> Over the sucking in the dark, Starling heard Mr. Gumb's ghastly voice, choking: "How...does...it feel...to be...so beautiful?"
>
> And then another sound. A gurgle, a rattle and the whistling stopped.
>
> Starling knew that sound too. She'd heard it once before, at the hospital when her father died.[7]

Through Harris's description, we are made party to some of the physical processes that take place as the body fails, and we are also presented with the serial killer's final words, directed to Starling. But still we remain outside the experience itself—how it feels, what the dying man sees and imagines as he dies.

Works that attempt somehow to take us inside the minds and bodies of the dying must necessarily be more speculative—but can perhaps be more powerful. Sometimes we are presented with a mixture of objective observation and the perspective of the dying; in the final moments of *Lost* we recognize familiar external views of the dying hero, Jack (Matthew Fox), but we also experience some events from his point of view. We are invited into his consciousness as he gasps for breath in a clearing on the desert island where the great adventures of his life took place. Jack sees a dog running through the bamboo toward him. Jack will not depart on his journey alone. Then, through the bamboo and the trees, Jack sees his friends escaping the island, their plane roaring by overhead. He dies with these happy images in his mind—and the series ends as it began, with an extreme close-up of Jack's eye as he lies on the floor of the forest. This may be a traditional image of death—but we have also received some entry into the dying Jack in his final moments.

Other imaginative accounts take us deeper into the actual experience of the dying—or even of one who has died, like J. R. R. Tolkien's Gandalf. Although Gandalf was of the race of angelic beings, the Maia, in Tolkien's cosmology, he was clothed in flesh, and that flesh was mortal. When he stood against the Balrog in the Mines of Moria so that the Fellowship of the Ring could escape, he actually experienced death. The story seems to make clear that Gandalf has died, and Tolkien himself wrote to a reader that "Gandalf really 'died', and was changed: for that seems to me the only real cheating, to represent anything that can be called 'death' as making no difference."[8] To the extent that Gandalf had a human aspect, that part of him died, with all the attendant pain, suffering, fear, and transcendence.

As befits a heroic epic, death and what follows death are important subjects in the *Lord of the Rings* story, both in Tolkien's novels and Peter Jackson's films. Perhaps the culmination of that exploration comes in the film version of *The Return of the King*, when Gandalf tries to explain death to the frightened hobbit Pippin as they face probable destruction during the siege of Minas Tirith:

GANDALF and PIPPIN sit on stone steps…Both covered in sweat and grime, bone-weary from fighting, spirits and hearts bruised…

PIPPIN looks towards the WOODEN GATES at which a NUMBER of SOLDIERS continue to build a BARRICADE…

> PIPPIN
> *(quiet)*
> *I didn't think it would end this way…*

GANDALF looks at the SMALL HOBBIT a beat.

> GANDALF
> *(gently)*
> *End? No, the journey doesn't end here.*

PIPPIN looks up at GANDALF, questioningly.…

> GANDALF *(cont'd)*
> *Death is just another path, one that we all must take.*

ANGLE ON: GANDALF looks down to see PIPPIN looking up at him with fear in his eyes…

> GANDALF (cont'd)
> (remembering)
> The grey rain curtain of this world rolls
> back and all turns to silver glass...
> (to himself)
> and then you see it...
>
> ANGLE ON: GANDALF breaks off, lost in reverie...
>
> PIPPIN
> What, Gandalf? See what?
>
> GANDALF
> White shores...And beyond...A far green
> country under a swift sunrise.
>
> PIPPIN stares up at the OLD WIZARD'S FACE, softened, quiet
> and full of peace...
>
> PIPPIN
> (quiet)
> Well, that isn't so bad.
>
> GANDALF
> (gently)
> No...No, it isn't.[9]

It is a poetic and comforting vision of death to be certain—but still one from the point of view of one who knows that far country, since he had been there and returned. Just as this vision soothes Pippin, it also comforts us as we await our own journey into the unknown, and this is a great gift offered us by J. R. R. Tolkien and Peter Jackson.

Other artists have given us fictional equivalents of Colton Burpo's trip to heaven. One of the best-known contemporary examples is Leif Enger's *Peace Like a River*, in which the young narrator, Reuben Land, is shot by the villainous Jape Waltzer, "the old *morte* settled its grip," and he is pronounced dead in this life and approaches the border of the next before returning through some miracle as marvelous as Gandalf's return.[10] But to speak of death with true artistic authenticity—that is, by rendering the death of one who does not return and thus knows death fully and completely—represents an obvious difficulty, since unlike Gandalf, Reuben Land, and Colton Burpo, the dead are not normally permitted to return to report what they have experienced.

Storytellers have had to devise imaginative solutions to permit characters to narrate their own demise. In *The Lovely Bones*, protagonist Susie Salmon is able to describe her rape and murder at the hands of her neighbor because she narrates the entire book from her perch in heaven. British author Kate Atkinson's novel *Life after Life* likewise invents an intriguing answer to how the dead might relate their final experience: Atkinson kills her protagonist, Ursula Todd, and brings her back to life over and over again. This allows her to describe those repeated deaths, beginning with her first, as an infant, through the consciousness of the protagonist:

> Little lungs, like dragonfly lungs failing to inflate in the foreign atmosphere. No wind in the strangled pipe. The buzzing of a thousand bees in the tiny curled pearl of an ear.
>
> Panic. The drowning girl, the falling bird....
>
> The little heart. A helpless little heart beating wildly. Stopped suddenly like a bird dropped from the sky. A single shot.
>
> Darkness fell.[11]

So this is death: Darkness falls. A bright light shines. Bright shores beckon.

These are poetic representations of what happens during and after that biological failure we call "death." Those who die pass out of earthly existence and either into nothingness (as some believe) or into some other state of being (as many others hold). At death, the individual consciousness departs from the body, the body itself falls into decay, and the soul, if such a thing exists, moves on to whatever judgment or reward might await it.

The Judeo-Christian tradition sees this movement as universal and right. Psalm 146 advises,

> Do not put your trust in princes,
> in mortals, in whom there is no help.
> When their breath departs, they return to the earth;
> on that very day their plans perish.[12]

Psalm 90 too reminds its hearers that the lot of all who live is death:

> The days of our life are seventy years,
> or perhaps eighty, if we are strong;
> even then their span is only toil and trouble;
> they are soon gone, and we fly away.[13]

The book of Job makes this point poetically, alluding to other forms of life that experience a sort of false death before returning to full earthly life:

> A mortal, born of woman, few of days and full of trouble,
> comes up like a flower and withers,
> flees like a shadow and does not last....
> For there is hope for a tree,
> if it is cut down, that it will sprout again,
> and that its shoots will not cease.
> Though its root grows old in the earth,
> and its stump dies in the ground,
> yet at the scent of water it will bud
> and put forth branches like a young plant.
> But mortals die, and are laid low;
> humans expire, and where are they?
> As waters fail from a lake,
> and a river wastes away and dries up,
> so mortals lie down and do not rise again;
> until the heavens are no more, they will not awake
> or be roused out of their sleep.[14]

Christians too understand human life to have a definite conclusion. The Roman Catholic Catechism offers an orthodox understanding of the end of life: "Death is the end of man's earthly pilgrimage, of the time of grace and mercy which God offers him so as to work out his earthly life in keeping with the divine plan, and to decide his ultimate destiny. When 'the single course of our earthly life' is completed, we shall not return to other earthly lives: 'It is appointed for men to die once.' "[15] Thus Jews and Christians alike regard death as a transitional moment from earthly life to eternal destiny, whatever that may be, and indeed most people regard it in this way, regardless of their religious beliefs—or lack of them.

Those who seek to understand death and life after death from the standpoint of science instead of religion may likewise regard it as the transition of the soul from one state to another. Craig Minowa, the singer and songwriter of the indie rock band Cloud Cult, lost his son Kaidin to crib death in 2002. Although he doesn't speak the language of heaven, hell, or purgatory, he nonetheless considers death to be a transitional moment from earthly experience to another realm. The band's album *Love* features a haunting instrumental called "Love and the First Law of Thermodynamics," and Minowa says that he bases his belief in the continuing life of his son on that first law of thermodynamics: "Energy cannot be destroyed; it can only be transformed.... So any kind of energy that you put out there never goes away. Everything that we did together, every moment that we had together, everything that he felt and everything that I felt for him still resonates out there in the universe. And I refuse to believe anything less than the idea that I'll somehow be with my son again."[16]

Augustus Waters, a cancer survivor in the best-selling novel *The Fault in Their Stars*, also expresses some hopeful beliefs about what happens to those who die. While he does not believe in a heaven "where you ride unicorns," he argues with narrator Hazel Grace, "I believe something becomes of us." Unlike his religious parents, Augustus argues on the basis of pure logic that, while he fears earthly oblivion—that moment of physical death—"I believe humans have souls, and I believe in the conservation of souls." The body dies; the soul continues in some state, even if that state isn't a heaven populated by unicorns and filled with cloud mansions.[17]

Whether one explains the passage of the soul through the prism of religion or logic, death is an irrevocable boundary. On one side we find the living; on the other, passing on either to nothingness or another form of existence, are the dead. In many stories, it is made clear that this boundary cannot be breached without horrible consequences. The classic W. W. Jacobs short story "The Monkey's Paw" and Stephen King's *Pet Sematary* (later made into a film and a radio serial for the BBC) offer two examples from the horror genre of why death must be final, but this belief is expressed in many stories, including the world's most popular fictional narrative. Although Harry Potter lives in a world where seemingly anything is possible, death is an irrevocable threshold. As Harry's mentor Albus Dumbledore notes, magic cannot bring back the dead, and even the greatest wizards have not found a way to reunite body and soul after death takes place.[18] No magic can raise the dead, and projections of the dead in the Harry Potter story (wizarding photos, ectoplasmic projections from wands, magic mirrors, and the like) are merely pale re-creations of the dead.[19] Anything else is either a delusion—or something unholy, like the raising of dead bodies as Inferi to fight for Lord Voldemort.

Yet Western literature and culture are rife with stories of souls or bodies (or both) that continue to be bound to this world after death. In some stories—those of vampires and zombies, for example—the body remains, perhaps animated by soul or consciousness, perhaps (as in stories of ghouls and most zombie mythologies) devoid of any consciousness beyond hunger. In some stories, as with those of ghosts and shades, the spirit remains on earth following the death of the body rather than passing on to the afterlife. In some stories—as with mummies and revenants—an abiding will or a mystic spell holds soul and substance somehow together despite the death of that corporeal form. In all these narratives, the undead violate what we consider the most basic tenet of life: that eventually everything dies and departs.

This is one reason we consider the undead to be monsters: because the undead transgress all of our beliefs about orderly progression from this world to the next. As novelist Pearson dryly states of the resuscitation of the drowned Donnie Huff in *Gospel Hour*, signs of life among those we've declared deceased are "a wholly unanticipated and startling sort of display."[20] The undead in our stories are not the compliant corpses who populate our reality; they are the ones described by the sheriff in *Night of the Living Dead*: "They're dead. They're all messed up."

The undead are "messed up" because the dead are supposed to remain in their graves; they are not supposed to walk, talk, stalk, seduce, or haunt us. In Hebrew law, concerned as it often is with boundaries, the faithful were rendered unclean by contact with corpses and were commanded not to use mediums to summon spirits of the dead or to have anything to do with necromancers, who spoke with the dead.[21] Many Christians too accept these Old Testament admonitions that the boundary is not to be tampered with, yet in popular works from *Dracula* to *The Walking Dead* to *Shaun of the Dead* to *The Sixth Sense*, the dead do not have the decency to stay decently buried. As the title of the popular Twilight novel and film series suggests, the undead—ghosts, zombies, and vampires notably—defy our deeply held belief by existing in a tenuous state between life and the afterlife. We will begin our journey with ghosts, those spirits of the departed mentioned in ancient literature and the Hebrew Testament, but still haunting us today.

SPOOKED: GHOSTS AND WHY THEY HAUNT US

"Whose house are you haunting tonight?"

OK Go, "Oh Lately I'm So Tired"

It is a staple of pop songs that what we have lost comes back to haunt us. In one of the saddest songs ever written, Roy Orbison's "In Dreams," the singer falls asleep to dream of the woman who took his heart—and will never return. But as the song records, "In dreams, I walk with you. In dreams, I talk to you." In Bad English's "Ghost in Your Heart," a jilted lover asks the woman who wanted picket fences instead of a life of adventure if she thinks of him when she lies with her husband, and as the title suggests, he promises (or threatens) to be the ghost in her heart. In other songs—other stories—the departed come back to remind us what we had, and it is always a prospect both fearful and poignant.

In this, our literature and culture are simply reflecting human nature. As John Casey notes, the ancients' understanding of the afterlife had less to do with some personal hope for another realm after death than with the fear that the dead might return to this realm if not treated with care. In their burial practices and in their ceremonies, early humans were trying to slam the door on the dead so that they remained in their place rather than pouring back into the land of the living. The ancients considered the spirits of the dead to be malevolent if not appeased.[22] Judging from their burial sites and the other remains of preliterate cultures, we imagine that being haunted was a great fear of these peoples—as it remains for us. Later, as written records and stories appear, human beings set up proscriptions against inviting the dead to return, and react with fear when they do. When King Saul of Israel asks the witch of Endor to call up the spirit of the prophet Samuel to advise him, the witch herself is filled with terror at the sight of Samuel—and Saul is condemned for breaking religious law about consulting with the dead.[23]

In the Christian testament, the disciples of Jesus, seeing him walking on the waters of the Sea of Galilee, believe that Jesus must be a spirit returned from the grave (in Greek, *phantasma* or "phantom"): "And early in the morning he came walking toward them on the sea. But when the disciples saw him walking on the sea, they were terrified, saying, 'It is a ghost!' And they cried out in fear. But immediately Jesus spoke to them and said, 'Take heart, it is I; do not be afraid.'"[24] The canonical gospels' accounts of Jesus's post-Resurrection appearances also sometimes show the disciples reacting with fear and amazement, believing him to be a *pneuma* or "spirit" returned from the grave: "They were startled and terrified, and thought that they were seeing a ghost."[25] Part of their amazement about the Resurrection—now, of course, Christian dogma (as the Nicene Creed records, the church agreed in its first few centuries that "on the third day [Jesus] rose again in accordance with the Scriptures")—comes from their awareness that dead people are not supposed to rise again, or appear to those who loved and mourned them.

Like the disciples, we continue to acknowledge rationally that the dead are supposed to remain in their proper place, but the emotional and spiritual truth for many of us is that the dead are not always gone, and that we too may continue to be haunted by those who are no longer with us. We may believe that the dead have some information, some wisdom to pass on to us to assist us in our lives. Even today, the elders or the departed are sometimes considered to be present, whether in the practice of leaving a place for Elijah at Passover, the Japanese Buddhist home shrines to the ancestors, the hovering saints of the Celtic Christian tradition, or the modern medium who claims to be able to speak with the departed.

We know from our own experience that we are affected by the presence of those who have gone before, even if that presence resides purely in our own minds. When we consider the dramatic hauntings we find in literature and culture, however, we can see how we have taken that emotional and spiritual truth and made it into a tangible—and, because transgressive, often frightening—story of the dead refusing to leave us in peace. When a spectral Kenny flies around Cartman's bedroom in *South Park: Bigger, Longer, and Uncut*, it's frightening because usually when Kenny dies, he has the courtesy to stay gone—but Cartman is also overwrought because he knows that if he hadn't presented Kenny with a ridiculous dare, he wouldn't have burned alive. In the *South Park* movie, Kenny returns to warn Cartman that Satan and Saddam Hussein are planning to take over the earth. But while some of our ghosts—like Kenny—are benign or even helpful, others are filled with anger and hatred; witness the spirit that haunts Toni Morrison's *Beloved*: "124 was spiteful. Full of a baby's venom. The women in the house knew it and so did the children."[26] As the ancients feared, the living dead are malevolent if not appeased.

In the movie *Inception*, Mal Cooper (Marion Cotillard) embodies the malevolence of the haunting ghost. "Mal" (short here for "Mallorie") in many Romance languages is a word for "bad," "evil," "wrong," or "sorrow." Mal committed suicide before the film began, but she appears regularly in the dream constructs of her husband Dom (Leonardo DiCaprio), and each time she arrives, she shakes the foundations of that dreamworld to the ground. Mal is certainly malevolent, a dramatic illustration of the dead who don't know their proper place.

The ghosts that haunt our dreams need to be put to rest if we are to find peace. This explains why haunting has become the metaphor for all those things from our past we cannot forget, as Thompson Square sings in "I Can't Outrun You," from the band's 2013 album *Just Feels Good*:

> *You're in my heart, you're in my mind*
> *Everywhere ahead, everywhere behind...*
> *It's like your ghost is chasing me*
> *When I'm awake, when I'm asleep.*

Ghosts must be paid attention, since their hauntings are often at least as much of our own material as their insubstantial stuff.

For an example of this, let's revisit that most famous ghost story, *Hamlet*. It opens with the night watchmen, Marcellus and Bernardo, initiating Hamlet's friend Horatio into the dread mystery that for the past two nights they have seen something Marcellus calls "In the same figure, like the king that's dead," that is, Old Hamlet, the recently deceased king of Denmark, Prince Hamlet's father.

MARCELLUS	What, has this thing appear'd again to-night?
BERNARDO	I have seen nothing.
MARCELLUS	Horatio says 'tis but our fantasy,
	And will not let belief take hold of him
	Touching this dreaded sight, twice seen of us:
	Therefore I have entreated him along
	With us to watch the minutes of this night;
	That if again this apparition come,
	He may approve our eyes and speak to it.[27]

The three men are amazed by the appearance of King Hamlet's ghost (simply "Ghost" in the play), but no one is more directly affected by this specter than Prince Hamlet, who sees and speaks to it on the following night. Hamlet, who has been in mourning for his father (and, perhaps, for other things, since his uncle, Claudius, now sits on the throne, unseasonably married to Hamlet's mother), hears from the ghost that it has returned from a place of purifying flame (purgatory, as we shall see) to tell Hamlet of his murder at the hands of Claudius. This story weighs on the prince because the ghost's haunting so closely corresponds to his own pain—the loss of his father, the passing of the throne (and his mother) to one so inferior to his father, his uncle.

The ghost is a fearful figure—but also a necessary goad to Hamlet to deal with those elements of his own life that have gone rotten in the state of Denmark. Shakespeare scholar Catherine Belsey notes that—as when Kenny returns to speak with Cartman—spirits like Old Hamlet often return in tales to report unseen injustices that need to be put right. But they also offered the living a mirror where they were invited to see themselves and consider their futures without the handicap of reality: "Apparitions...not only make for compelling narrative but also allow intimations of mortality not easily registered within a realist frame."[28] In many ghost stories, the haunting is at least as much about the living as the dead. Our fear indeed arises partly from the transgressive nature of the dead returned to some semblance of life, but also because of our own deep-seated issues that may prompt or mirror the haunting. Old Hamlet's ghost returns each night from the place where his sins are being burned away because he cannot rest quietly while his murdering brother possesses his throne and his wife. But neither can Hamlet rest while his beloved father lies uneasy in the grave—and in Hamlet's own psyche.

Hamlet clearly is more than simply required reading for much of the English-speaking world; it is also a psychologically astute play about human experience. All of us are haunted by what has been and what may be. John Caputo and Gianni Vattimo echo Belsey, writing that hauntings (which they refer to as "events") are "provocations and promises, and they have the structure of what [Jacques] Derrida calls the unforeseeable 'to come.'...Or else they call us back, recall us to all that has flowed by into the irremissable past.... Events call and recall."[29] In this, Hamlet's Ghost is not a singularity, but a reminder to all of us of our own hauntings that tell us that something is rotten, that our time is out of joint. Harold Bloom has it right when he writes that "Elsinore's disease is anywhere's, anytime's. Something is rotten in every state, and if your sensibility is like Hamlet's, then finally you will not tolerate it."[30] Ghosts may sadden us or frighten us, but they also beckon us toward a more just future for ourselves or our clan. In stories from *The Iliad* to *Hamlet* to *The Sixth Sense*, ghosts haunt us from our past but simultaneously beckon us forward toward our future. A good haunting may be just the thing we require to achieve our best destiny, to become the people we are called to become.

This truth is most clearly illustrated by Charles Dickens's *A Christmas Carol*, that classic tale of hauntings that serve as catalysts to effect change. The word "Scrooge" has deservedly become a descriptor for avarice, and Ebenezer Scrooge is a particularly joyless miser, neither enjoying his wealth not permitting joy in his vicinity. Scrooge answers his nephew's proffered "Merry Christmas" with the desire that "every idiot who goes about with 'Merry Christmas' on his lips, should be boiled with his own pudding, and buried with a stake of holly through his heart." When good-hearted gentlemen come collecting for the needy poor, Scrooge asks why he should give, seeing that there are workhouses and prisons available (Dickens, who knew firsthand the wretched existence of those in the workhouse, damns Scrooge in this offhand comment). Finally, he responds to his employee Bob Cratchit's request for a day off to celebrate Christmas as though Cratchit is committing some mortal sin: "'A poor excuse for picking a man's pocket every twenty-fifth of December!' said Scrooge, buttoning his great-coat to the chin. 'But I suppose you must have the whole day. Be here all the earlier next morning.'"[31]

Scrooge is truly in a parlous state. To quote his nephew's short speech on why Christmas matters, Scrooge has forgotten that Christmas is "the only time I know of, in the long calendar of the year, when men and women seem by one consent to open their shut-up hearts freely, and to think of people below them as if they really were fellow-passengers to the grave, and not another race of creatures bound on other journeys."[32] His nephew's heartfelt sentiment is insufficient. If

Scrooge is to ever open his shut-up heart, rediscover some essential goodness, and share that good with others, he requires intervention, and clearly nothing in his immediate surroundings will prompt that change. No; Scrooge will require a good haunting if he is to be changed in any substantial way.

Not that Scrooge accepts this at first; he asks the ghost of his former partner, Jacob Marley, "Why do spirits walk the earth, and why do they come to me?" But the fearful apparitions who come to Scrooge on Christmas Eve haunt Scrooge for a reason. The ghost of Jacob Marley appears wearing the chains he has forged in life and warns him that there is yet a chance to escape that same fate: during the course of the night, Scrooge will be haunted by three spirits (the Ghosts of Christmas Past, Christmas Present, and Christmas Yet to Come). Although naturally Scrooge would prefer not to undergo this haunting, Marley is adamant: "'Without their visits,' said the Ghost, 'you cannot hope to shun the path I tread.'"[33] Fortunately Scrooge pays heed to the fear and wonder these ghosts induce, remembers the person he once was, and is transformed into a person who need not be tied to his past existence as Marley is. Because he has been haunted and pays heed to that visitation, Scrooge, like Hamlet, is altered. He reenters the world on Christmas morning and makes dramatic amends to his nephew, to Bob Cratchit, and to all those he has offended. In fact, the difference is apparent from his mien:

> He dressed himself "all in his best," and at last got out into the streets. The people were by this time pouring forth, as he had seen them with the Ghost of Christmas Present; and walking with his hands behind him, Scrooge regarded every one with a delighted smile. He looked so irresistibly pleasant, in a word, that three or four good-humoured fellows said, "Good morning, sir! A merry Christmas to you!" And Scrooge said often afterwards, that of all the blithe sounds he had ever heard, those were the blithest in his ears.[34]

The haunting has been a success; Scrooge's transformation is complete.

The Henry James short story "The Jolly Corner" offers another literary account of how hauntings may draw attention to the chains we tote in life and prompt reflection about our futures. The story concerns

Spencer Brydon, who returns to his family home in New York after decades abroad. He has missed much by leaving America—the Civil War, the period of unrest that followed, the time of the great robber barons, a princely caste he might have entered. The weight of the past is palpable to him, haunts him in and of itself:

> the mere sight of the walls, mere shapes of the rooms, mere sounds of the floors, mere feel, in his hand, of the old silver-plated knobs of the several mahogany doors, which suggested the palms of the dead: the seventy years of the past in fine that these things represented, the annals of nearly three generations, counting his grandfather's, the one that had ended there, and the impalpable ashes of his long-extinct youth, afloat in the very air like microscopic motes.[35]

At night, as the insomniac Brydon wanders his old family home, he begins to sense a figure just at the edge of his vision, just out of sight—a ghostly figure who is revealed to him in the story's climax as the Spencer Brydon who might have been had he remained in America. The fear in the story comes partly from the supernatural apparition, but what is even more haunting for Spencer Brydon is that this ghost confronts him with what he cannot resolve within himself: whether he has made right or wrong choices in the living of his life. It confronts him with his failure to truly live—but this confrontation gives him the courage to accept the love of Alice Staverton, and perhaps to launch a next generation of Brydons.

What is at stake in this understanding of the role of ghosts in our literary and pop culture narratives is the possibility of *metanoia*, the Greek word translated in many versions of the New Testament as "repentance," but more properly meaning both a renunciation of past missteps and a turning toward some future good. It is, as we shall see, at the heart of many of our stories, this notion that human beings can change, although each of us knows that human character changes gradually and reluctantly, if at all. Often we require a cataclysmic push for change to become possible, for the seeds that may have been planted over time to take root. Hauntings prompt radical changes in Hamlet,

Scrooge, and Spencer Brydon, and in our earlier example from the *South Park* feature film, we observe how even a human so vile as Eric Cartman—perpetually in denial about everything from his weight to his many sins—is forced by the appearance of his dead friend to finally admit complicity in something: "I killed Kenny." Perhaps, it is true—as the Mumford and Sons song "Ghosts That We Knew" suggests—that ghosts give us "such a fright," but they can also be a part of our movement toward health and wholeness, as the refrain suggests: "And the ghosts that we knew will flicker from view / And we'll live a long life."

Ghosts frighten us, but they haunt us for a reason. The same can be said of vampires. Whether we speak of the sexually charged monsters of the classic *Dracula* variety, the sparkly vampires of the Twilight novels and films, or the "zompires" of Justin Cronin's *The Passage*, *I Am Legend*, and the *Buffy the Vampire Slayer* comic, vampires seem to be everywhere in recent years, and, as with any stories of the undead, their stories reveal much about our own present-life concerns.

BEAUTIFUL BLOODSUCKERS: MEET THE VAMPIRE

"In love with all of these vampires"

My Chemical Romance, "The Sharpest Lives"

"He will haunt your soul," lectures Andrew, the über-geek in Joss Whedon's *Buffy the Vampire Slayer*, "and his very gaze holds the power to make you his slave. You must stay on guard at all times around him. For he is the Lord of Darkness." On the chalkboard behind him, Andrew has listed some of the "KNOWN POWERS" of Dracula: "Transmogrification—(Rat, Wolf, Night Panther, Fog, Bees); Piercing Hypnotic Stare; Impervious to Stakes; Romantic Undertones (technically not a power)." Later he contemplates adding motorcycle riding to the list, since Dracula's friend Xander once taught him to ride.

Although he's supposed to be teaching vampire slayers about their most dread enemy, Andrew is clearly just as attracted to the idea of

Dracula as he is alarmed by him. He is, after all, delivering his lecture in the very Dracula suit worn by George Hamilton in the movie *Love at First Bite*—and he has the certificate of authenticity to prove it.[36] Still, why shouldn't Andrew feel tugged in two directions by Dracula? Andrew is no different from any of us who love stories about vampires. Vampires have always been both dangerous and beautiful. Jonathan Harker describes the three female vampires he encounters in Bram Stoker's *Dracula* as simultaneously "thrilling and repulsive."[37] Depending on their whims, vampires could eviscerate us (witness the headless corpses strewn about the artic tundra in Steve Niles's *30 Days of Night*) or seduce us against our will (as in Stephen King's *Salem's Lot*, where the hunchbacked Dud Rogers finally gets cheerleader Ruthie Crockett to pay attention to him when he becomes a vampire). It could be horrible, to be forever cursed to walk the night, consume human blood, take human lives. Or we could look on the bright side (as in *Twilight*, *The Vampire Diaries*, or any number of contemporary vampire romances): We could be young and beautiful forever, be in love forever, love forever—

If, in fact, you can call walking death and eternal bloodlust "living."

Because they simultaneously thrill and repulse us, vampires have swarmed our cultural landscape. They've visited television in *Being Human*, *True Blood*, *Buffy the Vampire Slayer*, and many other recent shows. They've stalked movie versions of the myth including the Twilight series, *Interview with the Vampire*, *From Dusk till Dawn*, *Vampire Hunter D*, *Bram Stoker's Dracula*, *I Am Legend*, the Underworld series, and *Dark Shadows*. They represent a literary genre that will not die: *Chicago Tribune* writer Alexia Elejalde-Ruiz writes, "These days you can't throw a wooden stake without hitting a sultry vampire series on the bestsellers list."[38] The same is true in comics (*30 Days of Night*, *Hellboy*, *Buffy*, *X-Men*, *Captain Britain and MI-13*, *American Vampire*, *Blade*, *Vampirella*, and *I, Vampire*) and in computer, console, and role-playing games (*Baldur's Gate 2: Shadows of Amn*, *Bloodrayne*, *Legacy of Kain*, *Vampire: The Masquerade*, *Buffy*, and *Diablo I, II, and III*). Gamers can now actually fight against—or play as—vampires. In the 2013 role-playing game *Dark*, players awaken as newly turned vampire Eric Bane ("It all began in darkness. I awoke to a world of pain"), and use their newly developing skills as one of the undead to stay "alive," slipping past foes like fog, hypnotizing them, or lunging to deliver a deadly bite.

What accounts for such rabid devotion from fans of vampire stories, games, and movies? Well, vampires are unusually fluid as symbols, as a recent essay on the Twilight Saga suggests: "At Its Core, the 'Twilight' Saga Is a Story about _____." The essay goes on to list a number of themes scholars and readers have observed in the works, among them gender roles, sex and romance, prejudice, and the Mormon Church.[39] While in a longer work we might explore all these cultural and psychological reasons vampires have so consumed our attention, in this book we are considering how literary and popular stories of the undead help us make meaning about death and the afterlife. What do these narratives tell us about our fears and desires?

Let's begin with fears. Like all the undead, the vampire violates our notions about boundaries and what is right and fitting, but unlike most ghosts, who have to exert themselves to the utmost simply to interact with the material world (as in the classic scene in *Ghost* in which Sam [Patrick Swayze] manages to "float" a penny), vampires and zombies are physical beings, their dead but still ambulatory corpses doubly transgressive. When Lucy Westenra walks the night in *Dracula*, it is worse than a haunting; she can and does do both emotional and physical harm to those she visits.

Vampires also transgress boundaries in our faith traditions, since they live on blood, that most powerful symbol of life. Blood is taboo in Hebrew and Islamic law, and shed blood is thought to be ritually defiling. The dietary laws of both faiths dictate that blood be drained from meat before it is consumed, while in each tradition, menstruating women must separate themselves from others during their cycles.[40] Consuming blood from any creature—let alone from a human being—would be unthinkable to a faithful Jew or Muslim. Only a monster would do so; in fact, one of the early claims made against Christianity by Jews and others was that the Eucharist, in which the blood of Jesus was said to be consumed, was monstrous.

Christians, for their part, accused Jews of kidnapping their children to drain their blood for rituals such as the Passover meal or for medicinal use. This "blood libel" is one of the most pernicious slanders against the Jews, but it also illustrates the transgressive nature of blood across faith traditions. Christians too find vampirism offensive. Accustomed as many of us have become to the idea of the Eucharist it is difficult to recapture the outrage generated by Jesus's demand to remember him by eating his flesh and drinking his blood. The very thought was powerfully countercultural, a taboo in its own day. The vampire's consumption of blood is a diabolical parody of the Eucharist and makes vampires monstrous according to Christian belief. Whether or not the vampire kills human beings (vampires from *Twilight*, *True Blood*, Marvel Comics' Morbius the Living Vampire, and the 2013 Jim Jarmusch film *Only Lovers Left Alive* may choose to feed on animals, or even to drink blood from blood banks!), vampires receive eternal life not by consuming the blood of Christ, but simply by consuming blood. This perversion of Christianity's holiest sacrament marks the vampire as a creature beyond the pale, worthy of fear and loathing.

When I speak of vampires in this volume, I am primarily talking about what we might call the "Stoker vampire"; those of us in the West trace the vampire myth primarily to the novel *Dracula*, published by Bram Stoker in 1897 and made into popular film versions including *Nosferatu*, *Dracula*, and *Bram Stoker's Dracula*. The myth's literary genesis in English comes earlier (and in other languages, earlier still!). Lord Byron's personal physician, John William Polidori, wrote a novella called *The Vampyre*, which first appeared in 1819, and it achieved much of its early popularity because its authorship was originally attributed to Byron himself.[41] Polidori's story was adapted into operas and plays like the tremendously popular *Le Vampire* by Charles Nodier, which prompted a vampire craze that swept across nineteenth-century Europe, something like the Twilight boom of recent years.

Sister Clare Therese Brandon wrote her doctoral dissertation on Nodier. She told *Fordham Magazine* that Nodier's passion for the vampire story emerged from wrestling with his own religious questions: "'One thing he always had were doubts about life after death,' said

Sister Brandon. 'He had a lifelong fear of becoming nothing. Some of his interest in the vampire theme was due to his quest for certainty on the question of life after death.' "[42] The vampire myth offers us too a narrative that invites us to think about life, death, and the afterlife, and to contemplate a cocktail of the alluring, the forbidden, and the spiritual. All of these elements help explain the enduring appeal of vampires.

Despite the taboos we have noted, the everlasting life of the vampire might seem desirable, and vampires can appear as creatures of supernatural appeal. Like the three wives in Dracula's Castle, like Dracula himself after he has fed, vampires are noted for their beautiful and even sensual appearances. After Dracula has killed Lucy Westenra, many observers nonetheless remark on her beauty: the woman who prepares her body calls her "a very beautiful corpse," Dr. Seward writes in his diary, "God! How beautiful she was. Every hour seemed to be enhancing her loveliness," and upon examining her corpse a week after her death, he remarks that somehow she was "more radiantly beautiful than ever.... The lips were red, nay, redder than before; and on the cheeks was a delicate bloom."[43]

Indeed, the preternatural desirability of vampires is as central an element of the mythos as their hatred of sunlight and aversion to garlic. In Stephen King's *Salem's Lot*, the body of Mike Ryerson, freshly undead, is a thing of unearthly beauty. As protagonist Ben Mears—staunchly heterosexual—notes, "in the first delicate light, he was more than handsome; he was as beautiful as the profile of a Greek statue." Toward the end of *Salem's Lot*, when Ben is forced to stake his beloved Susan Norton, she is described as a girl who in life had missed beauty by inches, but in vampirism had achieved "dark beauty.... Death had not put its mark on her. Her face was blushed with color, and her lips, innocent of make-up, were a deep and glowing red."[44]

All vampires today seem to be hip, young, and beautiful. In the opening teaser of the pilot of the TV series *Buffy the Vampire Slayer*, a beautiful teenager, Darla (Julie Benz), reveals herself as a vampire when she buries her fangs in a boy, and throughout the series, the vampires (with the notable exception of the Master) generally appear as young and extremely desirable humans.[45] The vampires of *True Blood*, *The Vampire Diaries*, and, yes, the Twilight Saga, are likewise beautiful

beyond belief. When Edward Cullen and his vampire family are introduced at the beginning of *Twilight*, they are presented largely in terms
of their appearance: "their faces…were all devastatingly, inhumanly
beautiful. They were faces you never expected to see except perhaps
on the airbrushed pages of a fashion magazine. Or painted by an old
master as the face of an angel."[46]

This beauty satisfies our desire for an eternal life in which we will
be perfected. My deeply religious grandmother, who looks forward to
heaven with great hope, speaks often of how she cannot wait to be
eternally young, eternally strong, and in a body that will never fail her,
the "spiritual body" of which the Apostle Paul writes and into which
Christians believe they will someday be resurrected. Paul argued in 1
Corinthians that someday the souls and bodies of Christians would be
reunited, and the faithful would inhabit not imperfect earthly bodies,
but perfect spiritual bodies.[47]

So the beautiful vampire offers us an embodiment of beliefs held by
orthodox Christians and by members of the Church of Jesus Christ
of Latter Day Saints, more commonly known as the Mormons. If one
takes into account only their beauty and strength, they become a repre-
sentation of another theological concept. Christians have long spoken
of the idea of deification, of becoming like God, or even of becoming
"gods" ourselves. The second-century saint Justin Martyr interprets a
teaching in the Psalms to say that "all men are deemed worthy of becoming 'gods,' and of having power to become sons of the Highest,"
and remarks that "Christians were made like God, free from suffering
and death, provided that they kept His commandments."[48] Likewise,
Augustine of Hippo wrote that "if we have been made sons of God, we
have also been made gods: but this is the effect of Grace adopting, not
of nature generating…. The rest that are made gods, are made by His
own Grace, are not born of His Substance, that they should be the same
as He, but that by favour they should come to Him, and be fellow-heirs
with Christ."[49]

This transformation into gods comes not in the present, but in the
future, after death. As my Baylor University colleague Roger E. Olson
notes, in mainstream Christianity, after death, believers expect to dwell

in a heaven "populated by glorified human persons with resurrection bodies."[50] After death, we might thus imagine that we become something like these beautiful creatures we read about or see in vampire tales. If in life we were sad, worn down, or somehow unbeautiful, after death, a supernatural translation will occur: we will be forever young, beautiful, and vital.

In addition to our desire to live forever in perfected bodies, many of us wish we could live forever with those we deeply love. The film *Bram Stoker's Dracula* and the Twilight Saga are at least partially about the possibility of an eternal love between a man and woman. Artists of any faith consciously or unconsciously incorporate their beliefs in their work, and Stephanie Meyer clearly draws from her Mormon beliefs about exaltation and eternal marriage as she spins her yarns about sparkly vampires in the Twilight Saga.

As in orthodox Christian belief, Mormons believe in deification. According to Mormon teaching, humans once lived with God, and as the official Latter Day Saints Church teaching *Gospel Principles* says, if we live properly and faithfully apart from God, "We could become like Him, an exalted being."[51] That exaltation, however, cannot happen in isolation. In Mormon belief, one is seeking an eternal companion when one looks for a mate, and *New Moon* shows Bella coming to the realization that she and Edward are destined to be those eternal companions: "Option three: Edward loved me. The bond forged between us was not one that could be broken by absence, distance or time. And no matter how much more special or beautiful or brilliant or perfect than me he might be, he was as irreversibly altered as I was. As I would always belong to him, so would he always be mine."[52]

The love between Edward and Bella reflects a universal desire to be with the one we love for all time and reflects Mormon theology. Russell M. Nelson, an elder in the Church of Latter Day Saints, explained the concept in terms strikingly similar to the romantic compact of *Twilight*: "The noblest yearning of the human heart is for a marriage that can endure beyond death. Fidelity to a temple marriage does that. It allows families to be together forever."[53] In contrast to civil or religious marriage ceremonies, which are only "so long as you both shall live,"

Mormons believe in a teaching called celestial marriage—that a proper Mormon temple marriage prepares a husband and wife to be a married couple throughout eternity. While this teaching stands at odds with Christian orthodoxy (Jesus, when asked a test question about marriage in the afterlife, answered that "in the resurrection [people] neither marry nor are given in marriage, but are like angels in heaven"), it has been part of Mormon teachings as far back as Joseph Smith, who declared it in the *Doctrine and Covenants*.[54]

Vampire romances tap into our spiritual and emotional desires to have that which is good now—the love of our beloved—and could only be better when we are perfected spiritual beings. There is something comforting and beautiful about narratives that portray that sort of eternal love as possible, as vampire romances do—but often they do so at the expense of downplaying the transgressive and taboo elements of the vampire mythos. As beautiful or desirable as they may seem, whether Bela Lugosi in his tuxedo or Kate Beckinsale in her leather outfit in the Underworld films, at some point, vampires will break your heart—or rip out your throat. Often, their beauty is revealed as a sham, an illusion, and the brokenness and true horror of their walking death shows through.

Castle Dracula is illustrative of this illusion of vampiric beauty; when Jonathan Harker enters it in the 1931 film, he finds behind the imposing façade a disgusting ruin, filled with bats, spiderwebs, and wandering wildlife. Although Dracula himself descends the shattered stairway as the handsome Bela Lugosi, Bram Stoker's novel describes Dracula as an old man at first, and Francis Ford Coppola's film introduces him (Gary Oldman) as a wizened, white-haired, and frankly bizarre-looking ancient. Likewise, when Dracula is first introduced as a character in the Buffy season 8 comic, he is a shell of his former self—dressed in a bathrobe, white-bearded, and smelling of vomited cabbage and rubbing alcohol. Not all is sparkling eternal life in the vampire world.

The story of Dracula himself is cautionary; this former defender of the faith against the Turks becomes a monster who is repelled by the cross and sanctified water that once sustained him. Vampirism comes from different sources in various stories, but all the genesis stories are dark and diabolical, and how can something that begins so badly ever be beautiful? One story of how Dracula became undead (referred to in the film *Bram Stoker's Dracula*) tells that, after learning that his beloved had leapt to her death during a Turkish attack on his castle, he renounced his faith, cursed God, consumed blood—and became a vampire. In Elizabeth Kostova's novel *The Historian*, Dracula is said to have attained his power "through a heresy in the monastery of Saint-Matthieu-des-Pyrenees-Orientales" and is forced to visit the monastery every sixteen years to "renew the influences that have allowed him to live in death."[55] These are not, it need hardly be said, wholesome heresies or healthy influences.

The origins of the vampiric undead are equally horrifying in other tales. Vampires in the Buffy universe are the result of demonic attacks on humans. As Rupert Giles (Anthony Stewart Head) informs his teenage charges in the first season of the television series, "the last demon to leave this reality fed off a human, mixed their blood. He was a human form possessed…infected…by the demon's soul. He bit another, and another…and so they walk the Earth, feeding. Killing some, mixing their blood with others to make more of their kind."[56] Vampires in the Buffy stories are almost all soulless creatures, humans possessed by demons who exist purely to kill and destroy, and who are influenced by the lives and memories of the human host—as Darla puts it in the first-season episode of the spin-off series *Angel*, "The Prodigal," "What we once were informs all that we become"—but they are no longer that person. Hence Angel (David Boreanaz), a sympathetic and even loving character because a gypsy's curse restored both his soul and his remorse for his horrible actions, can be taken over by Angelus, one of the most fearful of destroyers, known over the centuries as "the Scourge of Europe" and "the Demon with the Face of an Angel."[57]

In the Hellboy graphic novel *Wake the Dead*, Mike Mignola, a connoisseur of supernatural folklore, provides an equally dark origin for his story's vampire, Count Guierescu. According to Guierescu's father—himself some sort of flesh-eating ghoul who has remained alive for centuries—when his son was thrown from his horse and drowned in an icy river, the servants brought his body home, and "I brought him to her [Hecate—goddess of darkness and witchcraft]. I sacrificed all the dogs, then all the servants, and after three days…she gave him back to me. Still my boy, but now also her son."[58]

Vampirism may create a good-looking corpse, but it comes at a price—generally the loss of one's soul, whether literally or metaphorically. If at its core the ghost story asks why we are haunted, the vampire story might be asking this: What are we willing to do to live and to appear beautiful forever? Would we be willing to give up a substantial degree of our humanity, to treat others as cattle, to make dark bargains with evil powers?

Vampire mythology holds that the undead are unholy—and that those who walk in the light must stand up to them for the sake of all that is good in the natural order. Buffy, Professor Van Helsing, Ben Mears—all of them are participating in a cosmic battle between good and evil, with human souls in the balance. So long as they remain undead, vampires are trapped in a cycle of unholy violence to others and to their own souls, and they cannot be free to attain their next destiny. This is a particularly awful fate for those who have not chosen vampirism but had it inflicted on them, and their souls, more than any, deserve to be set free to find their ultimate destinies. As Van Helsing says in *Dracula*, after Lucy has been staked, "She is not a grinning devil now—not any more a foul Thing for all eternity. No longer she is the devil's Un-Dead. She is God's true dead, whose soul is with Him!"[59]

For Father Callaghan, the priest in the novel *Salem's Lot*, it is a battle against evil when he takes on the vampiric forces enslaving his town, a holy quest, and if his faith is not up to the task at last, the good he represents has real power. At the house where the chief vampire has taken residence, Father Callahan is filled with a feeling of excitement, is impelled by something stronger than himself, in fact, to strike a blow for good. Invoking the name of God the Father, he raises his crucifix and commands the evil powers filling that vampire house to depart. Glowing with holy power, the crucifix blows open the locked door impeding their entry. It is a signal victory for good, even if Callahan himself later flees from the vampire, Barlow.[60]

Unlike ghosts—who frighten us but may not represent pure evil—vampires represent monsters we can and must fight. Whatever they once were, they are no longer. So too with zombies, whose hunger for human flesh makes vampires look refined. Here, though, is the interesting catch—as with all of our stories of the undead, the zombie story is as much about ourselves as it is about monsters.

ALL YOU ZOMBIES: WHY IT'S NOT THE END OF THE WORLD

"They're us, that's all!"

PETER (KEN FOREE), *DAWN OF*
THE DEAD (1978)

Maybe you wake up and everything has changed. As is true for characters at the beginning of *The Walking Dead* (graphic novel, TV series, or computer games) and *28 Days Later*, perhaps you were asleep or unconscious, and while you were out the dead started walking. Maybe you watched the plague spread, region by region, as in *World War Z* (novel or film). Maybe you watched it happen on the telly and then in your garden, as in *Shaun of the Dead*.

But anyway: something has gone badly wrong. The world has gone to hell, and people have changed as well. They want to eat you. And if they bite you, you become one of them: mindless, an eating machine, nothing left of you except the shell of your body. As Max Brooks, author of *World War Z* and the *Zombie Survival Guide* said in a *Washington Post* online chat, "zombies have no memories of their former life. You won't see the undead trying to wash windows or do your taxes. All they know how to do is swarm and feed."[61] They have that one mandate, to eat, and that wipes away all other human imperatives—love, loyalty, honor, even faith. This is reflected throughout zombie literature, as in the alpha of modern stories *Night of the Living Dead* (1968), where toward the end of the film we discover the zombie Karen (Kyra Schon) feasting on her father, Harry (Karl Hardman). When you're a zombie, it doesn't matter whom you eat next, or who you were before. This is perhaps most strongly apparent in the *Marvel Zombies* series, where in an alternate universe, even noble spirits like Captain America, Spiderman, and Thor cannot override their hunger for human flesh after a zombie virus infects them. When once-sacrificial superheroes begin to eat other people, it is clear that with zombies, we are dealing with the simplest of all operating systems: feed or die.

Like vampires, zombies are multivalent, and their recent popularity is partly a function of their ability to embody whatever we find most nerve-racking at the moment. Political scientist Daniel Drezner can write about the zombie apocalypse and interest group politics for *Foreign Policy* or give a TED talk called "Metaphor of the Living Dead" and no one bats an eye.[62] The Centers for Disease Control can release a comic telling people how to survive the coming zombie apocalypse because the skills that allow one to prepare for that disaster are of a piece with the skills needed to survive a pandemic, a nuclear attack, or any other of the real apocalypses threatening us on a daily basis.[63] Brooks suggests that the zombie apocalypse is the perfect tale for an anxious world: "I think they reflect our very real anxieties of these crazy scary times. A zombie story gives people a fictional lens to see the real problems of the world. You can deal with societal breakdown, famine, disease, chaos in the streets, but as long as the catalyst for all of them is zombies, you can still sleep."[64]

Apocalypse is a powerful and long-running storyline with both emotional and spiritual touchstones, and it has pervaded popular culture, literature, and religion for centuries. As John Gray observes, "visions of Apocalypse have haunted Western life" since Jesus and his followers created a narrative about how "sickness and death, famine and hunger, war and oppression would all cease to exist after a world-shaking battle in which the forces of evil would be utterly destroyed."[65] Even those who do not consider themselves followers of Christ or who may be proponents of a political system rather than a religious belief system (Gray's book, for example, explores the powerful apocalyptic leanings in Soviet Communism, Nazism, and the George W. Bush administration) find themselves retelling the story of Christian apocalypse and, in some sense, living it out, so that secular attempts to remake the world or prevent a feared disaster join religious attempts to predict, faithfully endure, or even prompt the end of the world.

More influential even than the apocalyptic tenor of the general Christian narrative, however, is the book of Revelation. The Revelation to John, as it is also sometimes called, or the Apocalypse, as it is in the original Greek, has pervaded fantasies, fears, and hopes about an approaching apocalypse and has become a meaning-making narrative for most of us in the West. As Jonathan Kirsch writes, "Revelation is always present, sometimes in plain sight and sometimes just beneath the surface."[66] For two thousand years the apocalyptic ideas communicated in Revelation have shaped the way we live, believe, vote, and are entertained, and perhaps that has rarely been more true than in the post-9/11 West.

Fears of the end of the world—or the end of one's way of life, or one's individual life—account for many of the expressions of dis-ease in post-9/11 American culture and life, zombie and otherwise. Even before the attacks in 2001, Daniel Wojcik had noted that "ideas and images about the end of the world permeate American popular culture," and Lee Quinby had argued that although relatively few Americans read the Bible, "the metaphors of biblical apocalypse guide perceptions of everyday events for most people in the United States."[67] American popular culture narratives frequently depict the human race facing an imminent doom, and 9/11 gave those fears a specific focus and also made end-of-the-world images and storylines more topical and perhaps more necessary. Brooks has suggested that in some ways the fear of terrorists and the success of world-threatening zombie tales go hand in hand:

> The lack of rational thought has always scared me when it came to zombies, the idea that there is no middle ground, no room for negotiation. That has always terrified me. Of course that applies to terrorists, but it can also apply to a hurricane, or flu pandemic, or the potential earthquake that I grew up with living in L.A. Any kind of mindless extremism scares me, and we're living in some pretty extreme times.[68]

But stories of the apocalypse—including the zombie apocalypse—also offer something else, catharsis, and often hope. The apocalypse threatens;

humans (often, somehow, miraculously) survive. At the end of *Dawn of the Dead*, after a darker alternative ending was considered and rejected, two survivors fly away from the zombie-overrun shopping mall in a helicopter; at the end of *28 Days Later*, survivors are spotted by an airplane, suggesting that some institutional power survives somewhere; at the end of *Shaun of the Dead*, the army rolls in on giant lorries that squash zombies beneath their wheels. These endings in which the inexorable destruction is halted offer hope that we too will survive the threats we perceive as existential. But apart from the generic story structure of the apocalypse found in zombie stories, how might zombies offer insight into our hopes and fears about life and death?

Unlike ghost stories, which give us hope that existence continues after death, and vampires, which offer at least, in some mythos, the possibility of eternal and intelligent life, zombies suggest the opposite. Whatever we were before, our souls, our memories, those things that make us human, vanish—but our bodies, our disgusting, dead, decaying bodies, will go on consuming long after our souls have departed them. This is perhaps the ultimate theological horror story—we may fear zombies because they represent everything we fear about our existence and what follows it. Perhaps we are just biological creatures whose wiring compels us to move and eat and little else; perhaps when those bodies ultimately are destroyed or decay to nothing, all memory of us is lost.

Our sacred stories are full of the dead being raised, but there are fundamental differences that explain why, as comedian Sam Kinison used to say in one of his best-known routines, "Jesus is the only guy who came back from the dead who didn't scare the f—— out of everybody!"[69] In the Hebrew Bible, both Elijah and Elisha raised from the dead sons of women who depended on them. Jesus raised several people from the dead, most notably Lazarus (who perhaps comes closest to our undead archetype, since he emerges from the grave trailing his burial clothes), and Peter and Paul are each credited with raising someone from the dead. Jesus himself, of course, rises from the dead on Easter morning, inspiring the Christian religion, Kinison's comedy routine, and the "Zombie Jesus" meme. But Jesus, Lazarus, and these others are not zombies; somehow, their souls and bodies are reunited. Just as in the near-death experiences we looked at earlier, in these real-death experiences, spiritual and physical forms are brought back together. In Elijah's miraculous raising of the widow's son in 1 Kings, he requests exactly this thing, as the narrative records: "'Yahweh my God, may the soul of this child, I beg you, come into him again!' Yahweh heard Elijah's prayer and the child's soul came back into his body and he revived."[70]

In these miracles from sacred story, we see the clear progress of death—the departure of the soul, the bodily decay—arrested. In zombie literature, miraculous in its own way, the soul apparently departs, but the body remains—and decays. Because of this, the zombie mythos raises provocative questions about when we are truly dead. In *The Walking Dead*, the governor (played in the TV series by David Morrissey) keeps his undead daughter, Penny (Kylie Szymanski), nearby and feeds her parts of those who displease him. In *Shaun of the Dead*, Shaun (Simon Pegg) is distraught at the thought that anyone might want to shoot his mother after she is killed by zombies ("Don't point that gun at my mum!"). Later, after the military rescue, he keeps his undead best friend Ed (Nick Frost) in the shed and continues to play video games with him. *Shaun of the Dead* is a comedy (a "romzom-com," to be precise), and one of its humorous conceits is that there is little difference between the living and the undead.

The movie begins and ends with Shaun making his slow torturous way across a room and letting out an inarticulate howl—before revealing that this is just his normal slow waking up to a new day. Ed is fairly subhuman even as a living being, making it possible to play his final fate as something less horrifying than that of Penny, the governor's daughter. Other stories too play on the similarity between the living and the living dead for humor; *Day of the Dead*'s satire relies on the idea that humans and zombies are both drawn to the shopping mall; in *Pride and Prejudice and Zombies* (2009), the Rev. Mr. Collins, a dim bulb in any telling of his story, does not seem to notice the slow transformation of his wife, Charlotte, into one of the undead, and so is shocked by her death, "beheading, and burning."[71]

If zombie stories play on our inability to directly mark the moment when death occurs—if like Shaun, we cannot mark the precise moment when our loved ones are no longer themselves, when the dying become the dead (or the undead), when our loved ones are no longer our loved ones—then we have come full circle. What is death? What, precisely, follows death? And where can we place the boundary? In her study of George Romero's zombie films, Kim Paffenroth marks out this territory as particularly difficult. "Zombie movies imagine a scenario far worse than nuclear war or a cabal of vampires taking over the world," she says. "They present us with a world in which humans and monsters become very hard to distinguish, and therefore the moral rules that guide our dealings with other humans…are discarded as irrelevant and unfeasible."[72] These are ultimately more than theological and ethical questions—they are potentially legal questions too. Law professor Adam Chodorow actually wrote an article for the *Iowa Law Review* about zombies and property law, his tongue only slightly in cheek, because he argued that zombies offer us a great deal of insight into when we consider someone legally dead:

> It seems a stretch to conclude that those who transform seamlessly into zombies should be considered dead. They never lose heart or brain function, though they function quite differently than they did before their transformation. While it might be tempting to declare them dead, significant line-drawing problems would arise as one tried to distinguish between zombies and those who have suffered some mental or physical breakdown. Put differently, categorizing such zombies as dead simply because they suffered a personality change, physical disability, or decreased brain function would open the door to declaring dead a wide range of people we currently consider to be alive.[73]

In this age of controversies over precisely when life ends and end-of-life care, how exactly do we decide when someone is dead? Zombie stories give us the chance to wrestle with this question and to come up with some answers for ourselves. If we're the governor in *The Walking*

Dead, so long as something looks like a daughter, it is still a daughter; if we're Shaun in *Shaun of the Dead*, the moment our mother sits up with red eyes and teeth bared and tries to take a bite out of us, she stops being our mother. And if we ourselves come to the point where we begin to resemble the walking dead, it is probably time to stop and reassess our lives.

We've seen how stories of the undead simultaneously frighten and comfort us, how they help us understand ourselves and make sense of where we might fit into the grand scheme of things. So too do tales about the other denizens of the afterlife, angels and devils, who populate the heavens, hells, and sometimes our own earth. Let's turn our attention to these characters now and consider how they operate in stories of life and what comes next.

CHAPTER TWO

DENIZENS OF THE AFTERLIFE

Angels, Demons, and the Devil

"Every time you hear a bell ring, it means that some angel's just got his wings."
CLARENCE ODBODY (HENRY TRAVERS),
IT'S A WONDERFUL LIFE

"Angel and devil.... One is but a shade of the other."
DANIELLE TRUSSONI, *ANGELOLOGY*

Perhaps you grew up with one of those ubiquitous and just slightly tacky prints in the hallway or in your bedroom: a guardian angel holding the hand of a feckless child who insists on walking next to the crevasse, or watching over a brother and sister as they cross a rickety bridge. (My favorite: the 1950s guardian angel bundling up a brother, sister, and dog as an oblivious commuting dad starts to back his obnoxiously large chrome and finned vehicle down the driveway toward them.) Perhaps you have angels on your shelf—or on your refrigerator—or on your table, dispensing salt and pepper. You may pray to an angel—whatever your religious persuasion—or talk about "your angels." You may listen to CDs, tapes, or podcasts explaining how to be more in tune with your angels. You may read best sellers like Doreen Virtue's *How to Hear Your Angels* or Lorna Byrne's *Angels in My Hair*, which in its first two years of print has (at this writing) sold more than half a million copies and been translated into twenty-six languages.[1]

Maybe you've watched the lovely and life-affirming ministrations of angels Tess (Della Reese) and Monica (Roma Downey) on *Touched by an Angel*, or cheered for the *Angels in the Outfield* who help a hapless baseball team win the pennant, or cried every Christmas when Clarence saves a life and finally gets his wings in *It's a Wonderful Life*. You may have watched as the archangel Michael (John Travolta) brings a beloved dog back to life in *Michael*. You may enjoy *The Bishop's Wife*, with angel Cary Grant sent to help David Niven and Loretta Young remember what really matters—or its contemporary remake *The Preacher's Wife* with Denzel Washington and Whitney Houston. These stories are everywhere: as far back as *The Bishop's Wife* in 1947, the *New York Times* recognized the ubiquity of these sorts of stories in the entertainment world: "Emissaries from heaven are not conspicuously exceptional on the screen, the movies having coyly incarnated any number of these supernatural types, ordained by their fanciful creators to right the wrongs of this world (not to mention the bookkeeping errors that seem to occur up above)."[2] They are not "conspicuously exceptional" in current movies, either.

The same is true in music. Whatever your age or musical preference, you are almost certain to know the words to a song with "angel" in the title—"Teen Angel," by Mark Dinning, "Johnny Angel" by Shelly Fabares, "Heaven Must Be Missing an Angel" by Tavares, "If God Will Send His Angels" by U2, "Angels" by Diddy, or some version of "Angel of the Morning" (which has charted in the United States, United Kingdom, and other countries over the past forty years). You probably have one of the dozens of songs called simply "Angel" on your iTunes or in your music collection, since they have been recorded by every conceivable type of artist: Elvis Presley ("Angel, with those angel eyes / Come and take this earth boy / Up to paradise"); Anita Baker ("You're my angel"); Madonna ("You're an angel in disguise"); Aerosmith ("Baby, you're my angel / Come and save me tonight"); Sarah MacLachlan ("In the arms of the angels"); and even heavy-metal band Judas Priest ("Angel— put sad wings around me now / Protect me from this world of sin").

Angels throng around us in Western culture, visible and invisible, but however much we may love or revere them, it is inevitable that we see them through our human filter, and that our angels have been domesticated and brought down to earth, a metaphor largely stripped of true heavenly glory. We compare ourselves or our loved ones to angels, use the word as a term of endearment, or appropriate angels so that they function as our servants instead of our guardians. As Richard Woods writes, today "the mighty beings of scripture and tradition [have become] little more than decorations."[3] The supernatural creatures of heaven have become all too natural, too familiar from overexposure—which is perhaps as it must be. Who could abide to be in the awesome presence of the angel of the Lord? Much easier to be in the presence of a collection of pastel-colored Precious Moments angel figurines—or to visit the Precious Moments Chapel in Missouri, "inspired by Michelangelo's Sistine Chapel in Rome," and decorated with paintings of blank-eyed child-angels acting out scenes like the creation and the second coming.[4]

The same may be true of demons and devils, which have become names and metaphors largely divorced from their diabolical origin. Although devils are less omnipresent than angels in our culture, they too surround us as metaphor and product. Maybe you scarf down deviled eggs or enjoy devil's food cake. Maybe you've ridden the Demon, a roller coaster at the Six Flags Great America parks in Illinois and California. Maybe you run across an image of the devil in horns and a tail, carrying a pitchfork. My senior class adopted the Harvey Comics character Hot Stuff—a pint-sized devil with horns, pitchfork, and an asbestos diaper—as our class mascot ("Mustang Seniors: Hot Stuff!"), and my favorite taco shack in Austin, Torchy's, uses its own version of the little devil on its logo.

Maybe you read or watch a cartoon, TV show, or movie in which a character's guardian angel and competing devil perch on opposite shoulders and argue about what he or she should do next. Maybe you root for (or against) the NHL's New Jersey Devils, whose logo is a red "NJ" formed so that it has horns and a pointed tail. Maybe you have seen Ann Coulter's book *Demonic: How the Liberal Mob Is Endangering America* or encountered some other book, radio broadcast, or TV show in which the speaker's foes are referred to as "satanic" or "diabolical." Maybe you have enjoyed the Fleetwood Mac song "My Little Demon" ("My little demon is coming after me"). And while our material culture isn't as awash with devils as with angels, maybe you have even bought My Little Demon (a takeoff on My Little Pony) stickers or plush toys for yourself or the kids in your life because you found them cute or funny.

Again, the point is clear: it used to mean something to call something or someone "demonic" or "diabolical," but perhaps those days too are over. As with angels and heaven, though rationally we understand demons and devils to be purest evil, the supernatural denizens of hell, they are largely employed these days as metaphors that rob them of most of their power. Instead of being creatures we fear so much that we pray to our guardian angels to protect us from them, now they may be no more menacing than plush toys themselves.

In both of these cases—if our sacred stories are to be given any weight—we have moved far from the awe-inspiring reality of angels and devils. By domesticating these denizens of the next world and remaking them in our own image, we may have brought them down to earth, but the unworldly angels and fallen angels introduced in the Bible and the Qur'an and depicted by Dante, John Milton, and other writers and artists refuse to be caged or diminished. In our sacred tales, angels were created by God to be God's agents throughout the universe. They are a race given power, beauty, and the ability to speak and act for God in the world. Fallen angels (demons or devils) and the children of angels (like the Nephilim we find in *Diablo III*, the Angelology novels, and many other science fiction, fantasy, and horror stories) likewise wield great power and possess great glory, although their wills may be turned toward evil.

The pervasiveness of stories featuring angels and demons offers us ample opportunity for reflection. Gabriel Fackre explained the problem thusly in a special "angels and devils" issue of *Theology Today*: "On the one hand, a subject too long ignored in mainline pulpits and classrooms is now breakfast talk. On the other hand, angels who fix flat tires and run errands in the snow do not sound much like "Isaiah's awesome six winged seraphim circling the throne of God." At the very least, media angelology and demonology can make this a moment for theological distinctions."[5] This chapter is our opportunity for theological distinction, but also represents our moment to consider the mythology of angels and devils. The premise throughout this book is that myth is a primary way that humans make sense of this world and the next. Myth is not simply a made-up story or stories, as some would have it; it is a human attempt to say something true about existence on the deepest level.

As we've seen, contemporary myths of zombies, say, or of heaven, may or may not be objectively and quantifiably true, but they nonetheless offer deep insights about who we are and what we need to believe. Joseph Campbell argued that myth has four functions: it permits us to understand life, our cosmos, our societies, and ourselves.[6] At its heart, the myth of angels centers on how (or whether) we believe there is some force of ultimate creativity and good at work in the universe and in our lives. At its heart, the myth of fallen angels wrestles with whether the clear power of destruction and evil in the universe comes from a source outside ourselves or is somehow part and parcel of existence. Whether or not we believe in angels and devils as a matter of faith, our consumption or awareness of these stories and images offers us a way of making some meaning of these ultimate questions. Without them, we are left awash, shipwrecked sailors on a raging sea; with them—even if our reflection is limited to those domesticated angels on our shelves and at our bedsides—we hold some understanding of who we are and where we fit in the cosmos. So in this chapter we will explore some of the varied depictions of angels and demons in literature and culture and consider what we gain by recognizing them as creatures with great power and authority in the world as well as in their respective realms of heaven and hell.

ANGELS FROM THE REALMS OF GLORY

"I can walk like a man. But I'm not one."
ANGEL, *BUFFY THE VAMPIRE SLAYER*

Artists of the Victorian era saw angels everywhere—or so it seems, to judge by the incredible panoply of images, both sentimental and sacred, in paintings and postcards, on wallpaper, tapestries, and stained glass windows, as gravestones and on funerary monuments. As in our own era, in the nineteenth century one could consume angels by the cart-load, usually beautiful women with wings or cute cherubs who more resembled Cupid than "Isaiah's awesome six winged seraphim circling the throne of God." But Victorian artists also produced serious and beautiful representations of angels that pushed back against sentimentality (consider Dante Gabriel Rossetti's *Ecce Ancilla Domini!/The Annunciation* [1849–50] in which the angel Gabriel brings the word of God to a very frightened Mary). One Victorian artist created so many glorious and dignified angels that he has helped elevate the image of angels for the faithful and the faithless alike for the past 150 years.

Edward Burne-Jones, a painter who also designed tapestries and stained glass with designer and craftsman William Morris, has quite possibly shaped your own views on angels—even if you aren't aware that you've ever seen his work. Across a span of decades and those several different artistic media, Burne-Jones went to battle with his time's (and our) images of sentimentalized or domesticated cherubs. His angels, mysterious, beautiful, and powerful, were based on medieval and Renaissance art, and became an embodiment of Victorian piety: dignified, stately, powerful, useful. Although he was not himself a Christian, Burne-Jones created sacred art for many worshippers and reminded all his audiences of the many roles that angels are said to play.

Art historian Fiona MacCarthy assesses the artist's contribution in this way:

> Christmas would not be Christmas without a Burne-Jones angel. Archangels. Guardian angels. Ministering angels, feeding the hungry, clothing the naked, leading the blind. Annunciation angels with blush-pink wings. Joyful angelic cheerleaders, the Angeli Laudantes: angels playing trumpets, angels swinging censers, angels striking bells. Even in a multi-faith, multicultural society, Christmas comes in with a rush of angel wings.[7]

Burne-Jones and Morris collaborated on thousands of stained glass windows, which they sold to great cathedrals as well as tiny parish churches. An Annunciation designed originally for a college chapel in Cambridge was also bought in quick succession by ten other churches across Britain—as well as in the United States. Churches in the United Kingdom proudly advertise their nineteenth-century Burne-Jones windows online, and tourists continue to visit them, but his legacy is not limited to the Victorian Age. Following World War I, his nineteenth-century designs of angels received a second life in memorial windows commemorating the Great War. Since then, they have been granted a third life, as his windows and sacred tapestries have also been widely reproduced in other forms, most particularly the modern Christmas card.

By the time he designed his final angels for an 1898 memorial to William Gladstone in the parish church in Hawarden, Wales—just next door to Gladstone's Library, where I wrote much of this book—Burne-Jones had had enough of angels. "I must by now have designed enough to fill Europe," he said.[8] Indeed, he had painted and drawn enough angels to fill the entire world, but in the process, he had retold a story we apparently needed to remember: true angels are something more than just winged babies who flutter around making us feel good. In paintings, tapestries, stained glass, and all the many ways his angels have been reproduced, Burne-Jones gave us an image more Miltonic than moronic; he gave us angels who could protect, correct, and communicate with us, but who were clearly something other than and in some ways above the human race.

When angels in art and literature are taken seriously as characters—or cosmic forces—they are often treated with the sort of Miltonic gravity Burne-Jones illustrated. They become powerful supernatural creatures who may assist human beings, but who are servants to a greater power than angels or humans. An example of exalted angelology in contemporary popular culture is Tyrael, the archangel of justice in the Diablo series, one of the most popular role-playing games of all time. Tyrael hails from the High Heavens, is a servant of the Light, and even imprisoned, as players first encounter him in *Diablo II*, he is clearly a figure of power and glory. Like those of other archangels, his powers include flight, control over the elements, and superhuman strength, and in the everlasting battle between the High Heavens and the Burning Hells, he has ever been one of the Light's most feared servants.

Like that of all the angels we encounter in the Diablo mythos, Tyrael's appearance is imposing: he is encased in golden armor, his wings are glowing tendrils of energy, and his power is so far beyond human experience as to seem godlike. The cutscenes and sound design associated with Tyrael and the other archangels in the Diablo mythos reflect their nature as supernaturally powerful creatures who are at the forefront of cosmic conflict. In *Diablo II* and *Diablo III*, Tyrael is a central plot figure who aids human heroes as they encounter purest evil, and who guides them toward a successful completion of their quests.

The Diablo cosmology is similar to but not the same as the one familiar to us from scripture. While the Diablo heaven does not center around Yahweh/God/Allah (though there was a Godlike cosmic entity known as Anu who has left the Diablo reality for a higher plane), it boasts a heaven and a hell, and its reality is as flush with angels and demons as many believe our own to be. The American evangelist Billy Graham is one of those who have argued for the multitude of the heavenly host. In his best seller *Angels: God's Secret Agents* (1976), he said, "I am convinced that these heavenly beings exist and that they provide unseen aid on our behalf.... Millions of angels are at God's command and at our service."[9] Graham concluded this not because he had ever seen an angel, but because the Bible is filled with accounts of angels, and to disregard those accounts is to set aside a significant part of the scriptural record. In this belief, he is in line with the beliefs of the ancients, with Jews, with all sorts of other Christians, and with Muslims, all of whom have believed that angels exist and are somehow involved in the everyday lives of human beings.

The scriptural record and millennia of mythmaking help us understand why angels have been seen as worthy characters for movies, music, and story, from Milton to Madonna: they are actors. What are angels? At the most basic level, they are messengers of God—God's secret agents, if you will. They do things: they protect and guide human beings, they carry word and prophecy from God to humankind, they act as agents and sometimes enforcers of God's policies, they are agents of judgment, and they are warriors in the battle against cosmic evil who will help bring about God's intended good.

The Hebrew and Greek words we find translated as "angel"—
mal'akh and *angelos,* respectively—mean, simply, "messenger." When
I was part of the team writing *The Voice* Bible translation (2004–12),
we made a conscious decision *not* to translate these words as the familiar word "angel," given the associations so many people now have.
As I explained in the *Huffington Post,* "Pop culture and bad theology
have turned angels into big-eyed guardian babysitters who were human
in their previous life, rather than awe-inspiring messengers from the
Most High God who are most definitely another form of creation."[10]
For *The Voice,* we chose to translate the Hebrew and Greek terms as
"heavenly messenger," a phrase more in keeping with the actual function of angels.

Angels are what they do; they are verbs, not nouns. Although the biblical and theological references we will examine establish some of the
things we think angels are, the defining element of angels is that they
are God's agents in the universe, always acting. The Catholic Catechism
quotes Augustine of Hippo on this matter: "The name angel refers to
their office, not their nature. You ask the name of their nature; it is
spirit. You ask their office; it is that of an angel, that is, a messenger."[11]
When angels are given their due and treated as something more than
ornaments and decoration, the scriptures, literature, and culture agree:
angels are actors. They protect and interact with humans, and they
participate in the eternal struggle of good versus evil. We can see this in
depictions of divine messengers or spiritual guardians going back into
antiquity.

The ancient Sumerians, around 3000 BC, believed in both divine messengers and guardian angels; they called them "anu naki," "creatures
from the sky." Twenty-five hundred years ago in ancient Persia, the
angel Vohu-Manah carried God's message to the mystic Zoroaster—
who founded Zoroastrianism, an ancient monotheistic faith. The British
Museum displays monumental statues of bull-bodied winged guardians from Assyria and winged men and eagle-headed guardians from
ancient Nimrud that offer other early evidence of supernatural guardians. Leo Oppenheim reports that the faithful in ancient Mesopotamia believed they were "surrounded and protected by one or more

supernatural beings charged with that specific function," and that these beings were akin to angels.[12] Clearly stories about powerful agents sent from God—or the gods—are embedded deep in human history and emerge in multiple cultures. Malcolm Godwin goes so far as to argue that these common images of angels are almost a part of our genetic makeup, archetypes drawn from the collective unconscious.[13] If angels didn't exist, we would have had to make them up.

We find these agents operating in consistent ways, whatever the faith tradition might be. The angels depicted in the Hebrew Bible serve three primary roles. They protect humans, represent and act for God, and pass on essential knowledge. In the Psalms, angels are described in their role as guardians of the faithful. We hear that "the angel of the LORD encamps around those who fear him, and delivers them" and that "he will command his angels concerning you to guard you in all your ways."[14] In the story of Moses and the Exodus, we see angels function repeatedly as God's agents: angels appear to Moses out of the fiery bush, accompany the escaping Israelites as a pillar of cloud, and precede them into the Promised Land.[15] Like the warrior angels we sometimes find on monumental statuary or monuments such as the Arc de Triomphe in Paris, they can even function as God's enforcers. A story recounted in 2 Kings and 2 Chronicles tells how the angel of the Lord cuts down the invading Assyrian army, an event that leads to the downfall of their king, Sennacherib:

> That very night the angel of the LORD set out and struck down one hundred eighty-five thousand in the camp of the Assyrians; when morning dawned, they were all dead bodies. Then King Sennacherib of Assyria left, went home, and lived at Nineveh. As he was worshiping in the house of his god Nisroch, his sons Adrammelech and Sharezer killed him with the sword, and they escaped into the land of Ararat. His son Esar-haddon succeeded him.[16]

Finally, angels in the Hebrew Testament convey vital information from God to humans: they inform Abraham and Sarah that they are going to have a child despite their advanced age, and they come to Lot and warn him to abandon the city of Sodom, for God is going to destroy it and all its inhabitants.[17] To be a messenger of God, then, seems to be to serve by speaking God's words, carrying out God's commands, and accompanying God's faithful.

Angels perform the same functions in the New Testament: protecting the faithful, doing God's will, and communicating God's directions. When Jesus goes into the wilderness following his temptation, he is surrounded by angels who "wait on him"; angels save Peter from jail in the book of Acts, causing him to exclaim that "the Lord has sent his angel and rescued me from the hands of Herod"; earlier in Acts, angels free the Jerusalem followers of Christ from jail and encourage them to return and preach the gospel of Jesus in the temple.[18] Angels perform powerful actions on behalf of God. An angel strikes down King Herod (just as the Assyrian army was devastated), and angels are perceived to carry cosmic power against evil in the prophecies of the book of Revelation, where John sees them carrying plagues from God that they will pour out on the earth and envisions them taking up arms as warriors against Satan and the fallen angels.[19]

Finally, the angels in the Christian scriptures are messengers from God to humanity. It is angels who first communicate the great good news of the New Testament. Gabriel tells Zechariah that he and his wife Elizabeth will conceive a child, John, who will be a mighty predecessor of the Messiah. Gabriel later tells Mary that although she has not known a man, she will conceive a child who will be the Son of the Most High God. An angel tells Mary's betrothed, Joseph, that although Mary is pregnant, she has not been unfaithful to him, and instructs him not to put her away, but to help her raise the child, who is to be called Jesus "because he will save his people from their sins."[20] It is also angels who send the birth announcement:

> In that region there were shepherds living in the fields, keeping watch over their flock by night. Then an angel of the Lord stood before them, and the glory of the Lord shone around them, and they were terrified. But the angel said to them, "Do not be afraid; for see—I am bringing you good news of great joy for all the people: to you is born this day in the

city of David a Savior, who is the Messiah, the Lord. This will be a sign for you: you will find a child wrapped in bands of cloth and lying in a manger." And suddenly there was with the angel a multitude of the heavenly host, praising God and saying, "Glory to God in the highest heaven, and on earth peace among those whom he favors!"[21]

After Jesus completes his mission, angels continue as messengers to the early Christian church: an angel speaks to Philip and encourages him to have a conversation with a passing eunuch that results in the eunuch's conversion, and an angel appears to Paul and communicates that he and all the men aboard ship with him will survive the terrible storm endangering them. In the book of Revelation, as is often true of apocalyptic literature, the very prophecy that forms the book is delivered by angels: "The revelation of Jesus Christ, which God gave him to show his servants what must soon take place; he made it known by sending his angel to his servant John, who testified to the word of God and to the testimony of Jesus Christ, even to all that he saw."[22]

Within the Muslim traditions, angels serve these familiar functions, but they occupy an even more central doctrinal position than in Judaism or Christianity. In many Islamic credal statements we find that faith (*iman*) can be said to consist of belief in God, in his messengers, in his books, in his angels, and in the final days. The Verse of Righteousness asserts that the righteous person "believes in Allah and the Last Day, in the angels and the divine books and the prophets."[23] The Qur'an retells some of the Hebrew and Christian appearances of angels (to Abraham, Lot, and Mary, for example), and angels are also a vital part of the story of Muhammad and the faith he founds. Gabriel (Jibreel) is a central figure in Islam; he is said to have appeared to Muhammad on several occasions, including in the Hadith of Gabriel, where he questions Muhammad on faith, and Gabriel is the source of God's revelation to the Prophet: "Say, O Muhammad, to humankind: Who is an enemy to Gabriel? For he has revealed this Scripture to your heart by Allah's will, confirming what was revealed before it, and a guidance and glad tidings to believers."[24]

Finally, Gabriel is at the heart of one of Islam's foundational stories, the Night Journey (*Isra*). The subject of oblique references in the

Qur'an, the Night Journey was a mystical vision—or a supernatural journey—of Muhammad while in Mecca. As told by later writers, Gabriel visited Muhammad, lifted him up onto a heavenly steed, and together they flew through the night to Jerusalem, where they landed on the Temple Mount. They were greeted there by Abraham, Moses, Jesus, and the other great prophets. Muhammad and Gabriel ascended a ladder and passed into the heavens—the part of the journey Muslims know as the *Mi'raj*. Finally, Gabriel ushered him into the presence of God. There Muhammad received instruction, including how many times a day his followers should pray. Karen Armstrong notes that this angel-guided journey is a movement away from all that Muhammad had known and believed before—and thus the ultimate illustrative act of Islam, surrender to the will of God.[25] And Gabriel was instrumental in all of this, the journey and the revelation.

So in Islam we find angels as agents of revelation, but Muslims also believe in guardian angels, often based on Qur'an 86:4 ("There is no soul that does not have over it a protector"). Angels also carry out important functions for God. Two angels interrogate the newly dead in the grave; the angel Michael is in charge of the rains; the angel of death and his assistants have the vital task of separating souls and bodies: "Say: the Angel of Death, put in charge of you, will take your souls, then you shall be brought back to your Lord."[26] Angels punish, protect, record the good and evil deeds of believers, will blow the horn to announce the day of judgment—clearly they make up an integral part of the Islamic universe, just as in other faith traditions.

Thus the foundational texts and traditions of all three of the Abrahamic faiths indicate a belief in powerful beings who serve God. But although Islam contains some speculation on the nature of angels, very little doctrine about angels is actually to be found in the Bible. The Hebrew Testament contains no information about the creation of angels, or about fallen angels, and the Bible as a whole contains only oblique references to particular angels, their functions, and their respective spheres.[27] Michael seems to be mentioned in the late Hebrew Testament book of Daniel as a prince assisting the Most High God. Only one angel (Raphael) is referenced in the intertestamental literature (he appears in the book of Tobit, a wellspring of angelic lore), and only two angels (Michael and Gabriel) are named in the Christian Testament (unless you count, as some do, Apollyon, the destroyer, who is referenced in Revelation).

How did we get from scant mention of angels and occasional stories about the work of angels to the detailed angel literature we now possess? How did we develop the mythology held by many in the West: good angels, fallen angels, many of them known by name, and all of them involved in an eternal war between good and evil? Well, largely it came from the imaginative work of theologians, artists, and writers.

A great interest in angels grew in the early years of the Christian Church. Novelist Danielle Trussoni's angelologists may be fictional, but one of them speaks the truth when she reflects that "once angelology was the center of attention in religious circles, one of the most revered branches of theology."[28] Many of the church fathers chose angels as a particular subject of interest. In the East, Cyril and John Chrysostom pioneered a theology of angels. Among the Western fathers, Ambrose and his protege Augustine of Hippo advanced the vanguard of angelology. Augustine in fact wrote extensively about angels—and the fallen angels—in works as central to Christian thought as *The City of God*.

Later writers considered the topic of angels as well. Thomas Aquinas references them almost 3,000 times in his *Summa Theologica*, including a substantial "Treatise on the Angels." Some commentators believe that Aquinas's focus on angels actually threatens to become a distraction from his writing about God! The reformer John Calvin speaks less about angels in his magnum opus, *The Institutes of the Christian Religion*, but given his reticence to discuss other supernatural elements of the faith, we can see that the topic is of some importance to him: Calvin's 263 references to angels are fewer than the 447 he makes to heaven, but substantially more than the 44 times he speaks of hell. While many of today's theologians and Christian apologists (setting aside Billy Graham for the moment) do not seem to entertain thoughts of angels, one twentieth-century giant, Karl Barth, contributed what Densil Morgan describes as the most extensive treatment of angelology since Aquinas.[29] "To deny the angels," Barth concluded, "is to deny God himself."[30]

All these angelologists across the ages owe a debt to one ancient predecessor, the anonymous Syrian monk we know today as Dionysius or, more usually, "Pseudo-Dionysius the Areopagite." This fifth- or sixth-century writer thought deeply about angels and how the Judeo-Christian tradition had spoken of them, and he gathered his thinking in *On the Celestial Hierarchy,* a book that proved to be immensely influential on Aquinas, and remains so for writers and artists to this day. It is Dionysius who systematized the Apostle Paul's comments about heavenly powers in Ephesians 1:21 and Colossians 1:16 ("all things in heaven and on earth were created, things visible and invisible, whether thrones or dominions or rulers or powers" [NRSV]) to imagine the ranks and spheres of the angelic hosts. In the first sphere, devoted to heavenly praise and counsel, he places the seraphim, cherubim, and thrones. In the second, devoted to the administration of the cosmos, are dominions, virtues, and powers. In the third sphere, we find those angels who are active in the relationship between God and humanity, principalities, archangels, and angels.

The strict hierarchy of angels reflected the strict hierarchies to be observed in the secular state and within the church. Everything fit in its proper place, some beings were higher than others, and God ruled them all. While later scholars proposed variations on this scheme of Dionysius, his became the most widely known organization of the angels. Thomas Aquinas accepted and expounded upon *On the Celestial Hierarchy*, and Dante employed it in his *Paradiso*.[31] One of Gustave Dore's most famous illustrations, *Dante and Beatrice and the Heavenly Host of Angels*, shows this celestial arrangement, circle after circle of the angelic hosts, and the ineffable light that is God at their center.

In Trussoni's novel *Angelology*, Dionysius's hierarchy dictates the design of the fabulous (if fictional) Maria Angelorum Church of the Franciscan Sisters of the Perpetual Adoration in Milton, New York. (The "real" Sisters of Perpetual Adoration and their Maria Angelorum Church may be found in La Crosse, Wisconsin, and their chapel too is awash with angels in windows, in paintings, and over the altar.) What *Angelology* and its sequel *Angelopolis* suggest is that the reality of angels (and of their offspring!) affects not only architecture, but all of human culture and history. As reviewer Helene Wecker said of *Ange-lopolis*, the books tell us that "angels do in fact walk among us, and they are not at all to be trifled with," that whether we know it or not, angels shape our lives in ways large and small.[32]

A theological understanding of angels and our popular culture representations of them come together just here: both seem to agree that angels enter into our human world, and that they have missions to fulfill among us. In some cases that mission is guidance or protection, some sort of ministry among and to human beings; in others, their mission is to project God's power against the powers of darkness. Angels may even be seen as some sort of subgods with whom we may relate, and who may intercede on our behalf—witness the popularity of "praying to your angels." But in all cases, angels are at work in the world, and answering that mythological question ("Is some force of order and goodness at work in the universe and in our lives?") with a resounding yes.

ANGELS IN ACTION

"And when all hope is gone, I'm here...
I am your angel."
CELINE DION AND R. KELLY, "I'M YOUR ANGEL"

Angelology suggests that heavenly messengers fulfill a number of roles. In addition to those whose job is to offer praise and adoration at the throne of God, angels rocket around the universe serving as God's diplomats, God's cleanup service, and sometimes as God's police force. Of all these understandings, it is as guardians that angels are most prominently represented in our culture. As Roger Ebert noted, "Angels are big right now in pop entertainment, no doubt because everybody gets one."[33] Angels made the cover of *Time* magazine in 1993; writer Nancy Gibbs marked the surge in interest in angels among religious and nonreligious people, and the flourishing trade in products and ideas featuring angels, and decided, "What idea is more beguiling than the notion of lightsome spirits, free of time and space and human weakness, hovering between us and all harm? To believe in angels is to allow the universe to be at once mysterious and benign. Even people who refuse to believe in them may long to be proved wrong."[34] Surely the profusion of angels in material and popular culture is evidence of this.

That 1990s boom did not mark the end of angelmania; far from it. My colleagues working on Baylor University's ongoing Survey of Religion found the popularity and prevalence of belief in angels to be holding steady in 2008. Their U.S. survey revealed that a majority of respondents actually believed they had been protected by guardian angels. As Christopher Bader, the sociologist who directed the study, notes, this is of real significance: "If you ask whether people *believe* in guardian angels, a lot of people will say, 'sure.' But this is different. It's experiential. It means that lots of Americans are having these lived supernatural experiences."[35] The result, as *Time*'s headline announcing the survey results suggests, is a pervasive belief: "Guardian Angels Are Here, Say Most Americans."

That belief in guardian angels is reflected in various ways—in what we say, believe, and pray, and in what we buy and consume. Amazon—which, by the way, actually employs the book category "Angelology"—lists twenty thousand books dealing with guardian angels, many of them published in the past ten years, their treatments varying from scholarly to popular, Christian to New Age and witchcraft. If we look just at material culture—things we can hold and use—we find guardian angel products everywhere. Besides books, CDs, and movies on the topic of angels, we find such a flood of other guardian angel products—shrines, key rings, refrigerator magnets, bookends, T-shirts, charms for people and pets, crystals, baby bracelets and crib ornaments, yard sculptures and wind chimes, even iPhone cases—that one wonders if one of the tasks of guardian angels is to keep the world economy afloat.

But in addition to finding ourselves surrounded with guardian angel merchandise, we also find ourselves immersed in stories about angels. John Milton's *Paradise Lost* is one of the most formative of our literary texts on angels. The devils, particularly Satan, may engage our dramatic interest, but angels still serve important roles. On many occasions in *Paradise Lost*, angels are bid to watch over and comfort Adam and Eve, and indeed, the narrator notes the passage of angels to earth "to guard by special grace" even before the human race has been introduced.[36] The archangel Gabriel, on learning of Satan's approach to the garden, instructs Uzziel to divide the angelic forces and guard the perimeter, and he chooses "two strong and subtle spirits," Ithuriel and Zephon, to watch over the humans.[37] Although God knows in advance that Adam and Eve will fall for Lucifer's wiles, he nonetheless sends the archangel Raphael to warn and offer counsel to Adam.

In Milton's summary of the action of book 10 we read that "Man's transgression known, the guardian angels forsake Paradise," but this is not the end of angelic protection and guidance.[38] In book 11, although the archangel Michael and a band of cherubim are sent to drive Adam and Eve from the garden and out into the world, he does not leave the humans without comfort. Adam despairs at the arrival of death and their loss of paradise, but Michael responds

> *Yet doubt not but in valley and in plain*
> *God is, as here, and will be found alike*
> *Present, and of his presence many a sign*
> *Still following thee, still compassing thee round*
> *With goodness and paternal love, his face*
> *Express, and of his steps the track divine.*
> *Which that thou mayest believe, and be confirmed*
> *Ere thou from hence depart, know I am sent*
> *To show thee what shall come in future days*
> *To thee and to thy offspring; good with bad*
> *Expect to hear, supernal grace contending*
> *With sinfulness of men.*[39]

Grieved as Adam may be by the loss of immortality and of the garden of Eden, all hope is not lost. Michael unfolds history to him (in particular, what Jews or Christians might think of as salvation history: the covenant with Abraham, the life of Moses, and the life, death, and resurrection of Jesus). Adam, comforted by Michael's words, remarks on the mercy and glory of God in bringing ultimate good out of evil and he resolves to leave the garden: "Greatly instructed I shall hence depart/ Greatly in peace of thought."[40]

But even this is not the end; Adam and Eve are not driven out of the garden like cattle or directed to walk out alone, as if their sin has rendered them unloved and unprotected. In a scene that actually does resemble our most sentimental artistic depictions of guardian angels, the archangel Michael takes Adam and Eve each by the hand and leads them out of the garden. They are accompanied into their new world by an angel—and, many of us believe, we have been accompanied by angels ever since.

It's true that few of us read *Paradise Lost* any more, although its theology and mythology are pervasive. But a truly popular version of the guardian angel does appear in *It's a Wonderful Life*. This Christmas perennial, named by the American Film Institute as the most inspirational film of all time, concerns George Bailey (Jimmy Stewart), a small town businessman who faces disaster on Christmas Eve. He is actually contemplating suicide until his guardian angel, Clarence (Henry Travers), shows him what a difference he has made in the lives of others and to his small town. It is a surprisingly dark and heartbreaking film—is there a sadder feeling than wondering if your life has mattered?—redeemed in its final act thanks to the angelic intervention of Clarence, and by George's own growing awareness that, as Clarence says, "Each man's life touches so many other lives. When he isn't around he leaves an awful hole, doesn't he?"

This story perpetuates a familiar theological misunderstanding— that at least some angels are humans who have gone to heaven and gotten promoted—but despite this error, we can observe an interesting and elaborate angel protection network in *It's a Wonderful Life*. As prayers rise up from George's friends and family for his safety, they are being registered as if at some heavenly switchboard as 911 calls, and angelic help in the form of Clarence Odbody is dispatched to the human in desperate need. Clarence isn't much to look at as a guardian angel—he is only an angel second class, and has been seeking his wings for two hundred years—but while one of his supervisors says he has the intellect of a rabbit, another counters that he has the faith of a child, and that simple faith in God and in humanity is what matters in this story. George Bailey does not need to be reasoned out of his depression or awed by some glorious angelic figure; he needs to be accompanied as he journeys toward understanding. By story's end, George has realized that no man who has friends is ever a failure. And Clarence, for his part, has earned his wings.

In *Michael*, John Travolta plays the titular archangel taking the last of his earthly "vacations" as an outsized human. In the mythology of this film, the archangel is able to partake of and enjoy food, drink, and other earthly pleasures, but he does have a mission beyond simply drinking, burping, and dancing, even if it may be a guardian mission that is only appropriate for a romantic comedy: he is trying to unite a man and woman who ought to be together. This movie reflects a very low angelology; unlike *It's a Wonderful Life*, where humans become angels, *Michael* seems to make angels human. In fact, the film depicts heaven's most powerful warrior and one of God's most-favored servants as generally inferior to most human beings. In a reversal of roles, they actually seem to be watching over him through most of the movie. Still, the film does reflect a deeply held belief that angels are involved in all of our trials, romantic and otherwise, and in its depiction of John Travolta's character dancing and flirting with women who lust after him at least partly because he exudes the odor of cookies we approach a story of angels that is familiar to us: the angel as lover not just of humanity but of individual humans.

Angel, the vampire who loves Buffy Summers in the *Buffy the Vampire Slayer* mythos, functions very much like his namesake. In the first episode, "Welcome to the Hellmouth," he follows Buffy through dark streets, and when confronted, offers her a cryptic warning—and a cross for protection from evil creatures. Later in the first season, he watches Buffy from on high, steps in when she requires aid, delivers more cryptic warnings, and disappears. It's a bit disconcerting for Buffy, who wonders if their relationship is going to consist largely of exchanges like "Hi honey, you're in grave danger, see you next month."[41] However, while Angel goes through many changes, the crux of his character is always that he looks out for and watches over Buffy. Even though

Angel proves to be the Big Bad in the Buffy season 8 comic, the villain who has harassed Buffy and all of her followers to the ends of the earth, he is actually trying to help Buffy move to the next step of her evolution—and to find joy, for once. It doesn't hurt that her joy will come with him, at last.

In the vampire series Twilight, it is likewise possible to read the male lead, Edward, as guardian angel. Throughout the series—certainly until he and Bella consummate their love and she becomes a vampire herself— he watches over her and continually comes to her rescue. But in his first appearance as a supernatural being in the first novel, *Twilight*, he comes to Bella's aid in typical guardian angel fashion, saving her from an onrushing van:

> Just before I heard the shattering crunch of the van folding around the truck bed, something hit me, hard, but not from the direction I was expecting. My head cracked against the icy blacktop, and I felt something solid and cold pinning me to the ground. I was lying on the pavement behind the tan car I'd parked next to. But I didn't have a chance to notice anything else, because the van was still coming. It had curled gratingly around the end of the truck and, still spinning and sliding, was about to collide with me *again*.
>
> A low oath made me aware that someone was with me, and the voice was impossible not to recognize. Two long, white hands shot out protectively in front of me, and the van shuddered to a stop a foot from my face, the large hands fitting providentially into a deep dent in the side of the van's body.[42]

It is a heroic thing Edward does to save Bella—a superheroic thing, given his strength and the amazing speed with which he interposes himself—and contemporary culture is filled with other supernatural and superheroic figures who function as angelic guardians, from Spider-Man to Wonder Woman. In the Superman mythos, while the title character is sometimes treated as a Christ figure, he might more profitably be considered as a guardian angel; in fact, the first arc of the Smallville season 11 comic, which continued the story begun in the TV series, was called "Guardian."

Malcolm Godwin remarks that Superman is America's "benevolent guardian angel."[43] Like those of the archangels Raphael and Gabriel, Superman's given name "Kal-El" is a Hebrew name conveying relationship with God (Kal-El means "All that is God"). An iconic scene from the movie *Superman* and the *Superman: Secret Origin* comic (now DC Comics' official origin story for Superman) might be instructive in his role as guardian: Superman catches Lois Lane as she falls from a building. Like Angel, like Edward, Superman is always watching over those he protects, and he has carried out similar protective acts in the tens of thousands during seventy-five years of service to Lois and humankind in comics and graphic novels, television, movies, radio serials, games, and other media.

Superman and other superheroes (most obviously including Marvel Comics character Angel, a winged X-Man who in recent years actually believed he was an angel of God, and the DC guardian angel Zauriel, who was a longtime member of the Justice League of America) combine the angelic tasks of watching over humanity and performing powerful deeds against evil and chaos. The closeness of observation and the job of protection given to angels may sometimes lead to admiration of humanity. Zauriel falls for a human woman (as for that matter does Superman), and the attraction supernatural beings feel toward human beings is reflected in stories at least as far back as *Paradise Lost*, where Gabriel sends Ithuriel and Zephon to watch over "those two fair creatures," Adam and Eve.[44] In other stories, angels grow to love the humans under their charge in ways that seem, well, less than angelic. As admirable as angels may be in the scriptural record, they rarely get starring roles in our culture merely for watching over or rescuing people. Roger Ebert wrote that "Hollywood is interested in priests and nuns only when they break the vow of chastity, and with angels only when they get the hots for humans."[45] The possibility of love—even sexual passion—with a heavenly creature is titillating to audiences, because it is forbidden, and emotionally powerful, because it crosses barriers that human lovers cannot even imagine.

The idea of romantic love between human and angel does have possible scriptural precedent in scripture and apocryphal literature.

Although Jesus spoke of the angels as sexless, neither marrying or being given in marriage, some commentators have read the story of the Sons of God taking human wives in Genesis 6 as representing a sexual union between angels and human beings.[46] "The Book of the Watchers"— part of the intertestamental first book of Enoch—relates how a certain set of angels felt lustful feelings for human women, took them as their own, and fathered the Nephilim—giants who devoured all that humans produced and then humans themselves.

The watchers brought evil into the world on an epic scale, and this tale is attractive not only because it offers the possibility of supernatural beings who can't keep their hands off human beings. It also provides an alternative (or additional) theory of the origin of evil: because the angels fell, the present fallen world is at least partly a result of events outside our control. As Veronika Bachmann notes, "By explaining the negative turn of history with the narrative about the Watcher angels, the [Book of the Watchers] combines this overall picture with the priestly idea that the decline of history started at a very early stage in human history, in the time of the earliest forefathers of humankind."[47] It may be at least metaphorically true that humans fell from grace—but angels also were capable of falling, of turning from serving God to serving themselves, and some of our secular narratives mirror these tantalizing hints we find in the scriptures and other holy writings.

Wim Wenders's classic film *Wings of Desire* features Peter Falk as a former angel and Bruno Ganz as Damiel, an angel who falls in love with a trapeze artist and so also desires to renounce his angelic citizenship. Critic Rita Kempley located the core of the conflict in her original review of the film: "Angeling is lofty but lonely work. It is a thankless occupation—a billion years of sleepless nights, filled with human whining and existential dread. They can comfort souls, but they can't feel the wind on their wings or wiggle their toes. It's no wonder, then, that every once in a while, an angel defects."[48] Damiel has been observing humans and trying to bring them hope since the beginning of time, since before recorded history, in fact. Now he wants to feel.

So too does Seth (Nicholas Cage), the angel who comes to care for Maggie (Meg Ryan), a doctor who has lost a patient at the opening of

City of Angels. (*City of Angels* is a loose remake of *Wings of Desire.*)
Seth becomes obsessed with Maggie—and with the possibility of feeling,
the sensory experience that in both of these movies human beings have
and angels do not. As he and his friend Cassiel (Andre Braugher) say,
there is much of human life they wish they could experience: the smell
of the air, the taste of water; to read a paper, lie through their teeth, feed
a dog, touch a woman's hair.

The allure of interspecies romance is also one of the driving narrative
forces behind *The Bishop's Wife*, a romantic comedy that reinforces
the theme of forbidden love through the power of Hollywood casting.
Originally, the producers had picked David Niven to play the angel
Dudley, but when Cary Grant came on board, he preferred to play the
angel, and Niven was left with the titular—and less interesting—role
of stiff and overworked Episcopal bishop Henry Brougham. Although
the story, constrained as it is by the Hollywood Production Code,
could never have permitted any sort of extramarital affair—let alone
one across species—who could ever believe that Julia (Loretta Young)
could prefer her stuffy husband, Henry, to Cary Grant? (This romantic
subplot—and the corresponding star power thrown into the role of
Dudley—are also present in the 1996 remake *The Preacher's Wife* with
Denzel Washington, Whitney Houston, and Courtney B. Vance.)

When Dudley takes Julia ice skating in Central Park, it is the kind of
scene endemic to romantic comedies, and Dudley seems to come dan-
gerously close to forgetting that he is an angel who is supposed to be
helping out the bishop. In fact, although *The Bishop's Wife* never goes
as far as to consummate the possible relationship between Dudley and
Julia, some contemporary reviewers were nonetheless offended; *Time*'s
notice said that *The Bishop's Wife* was a big and glossy production,
and "the only thing it lacks is taste."[49]

In its implications—acted on in other stories—that angels and human
beings might find each other mutually attractive, *The Bishop's Wife*
and *The Preacher's Wife* reflect some of the fears—and desires—of any
narrative about radically different lovers, whether from different races,
planets, or species, particularly when one holds more power than the
other. Can love flourish between human and supernatural creatures?

Isn't the status of the respective parties dramatically unequal? What sort of life might such lovers have together?

The best-selling novels *Angelology* and *Angelopolis* also consider these questions. Certainly there is attraction between angels and humans. In *Angelology*, we glimpse a young woman, Gabriella, taking a Nephilim as a lover in the 1940s; decades later, that Nephilim, Percival Grigori, effortlessly seduces a woman because at first she reminds him of the young Gabriella. As he walks her out of a restaurant, he can feel "the pure sexual attraction between them—since the beginning it had been thus, human women falling prey to angelic charm."[50] What is good for the gander is also, apparently, good for the goose. In *Angelopolis* we encounter Mara angels, "the darkly beautiful prostitutes who were such a temptation to humans," and read about a male angel hunter's obsession with a killer angel.[51] Even though she is dangerous beyond belief, when she is near, it is "as if he had stepped into a field of electricity, one that made all rational thought impossible," a product of the "dark and persistent sexual allure, a phenomenon of sheer lust" that drives him toward her.[52] However, relationships between the two species tend to go badly—even tragically. Ultimately humans and angels want different things. *Angelopolis* revolves around its viewpoint character's love for a Nephilim, and it is at the same time genuine—and impossible. "Holding her," he realizes, "was like trying to embrace a shadow."[53]

Love stories are not the only narratives in which angels come to identify so closely with humans that they wish to renounce their wings. In *Diablo III*, Tyrael gives up his status as one of the most powerful of angels and is cast out of heaven, falling to earth like Lucifer, although he does so for justice, not lust, which is a refreshing change. The first act of *Diablo III* revolves around rescuing Tyrael and restoring his memory; afterward, he accompanies the game player–hero as he or she attempts to defeat the prime evils in their bid to overrun the world—and heaven. Tyrael is the archangel of justice, and he casts his lot with humans because he recognizes in them some powerful potential for good. His attraction to humans is chaste, and he sides with them against his fellow angels because he finds them a stronger force for good. But this archangel fell, too, because of humans.

The attraction between angels and humans characterized by the story of the watchers—who ushered cosmic evil into the world, and in a different part of their story taught humans to forge metal so that men could create weapons of warfare and women begin to lust for fine jewelry—does offer us a powerful narrative about why the world is as it is. Just as the fallen angels in *Angelology* and *Angelopolis* are the villains in their stories, so are the fallen angels who became Satan and his devils in ours. They are the ultimate authors of evil—both their own and human evil. Because these stories have become formative myths for us, they have tremendous power. A failure to take ourselves and our own evil seriously may be one of the implications of populating our sacred and secular stories with demons and devils; rather than force ourselves to be complicit in our own deeds, the first fall, that of the dark angels, can become our excuse to shirk full responsibility. Our stories of the demonic can also—however—affirm the importance of choice, and the ultimate power of good in the world. Let's turn now to consider how Satan, demons, and devils have been presented in our cultural artifacts.

ANGELS GONE BAD

"A brush with the devil will clear your mind
And strengthen your spine."
"WHISPERS IN THE DARK," MUMFORD AND SONS

Al Pacino is John Milton. Not John Milton the writer of *Paradise Lost*, although that is the obvious in-joke of the movie *The Devil's Advocate*. No, this John Milton is a partner at the law firm Milton, Chadwick & Waters and—in what might be another obvious in-joke—this highly successful lawyer is also Satan, the prince of darkness. As John Milton, he hires the fine young defense attorney Kevin Lomax (Keanu Reeves), and offers him an escalating set of heinous—and high-profile—cases to try, a set of ever-growing temptations, if you will. As Satan, he slowly drives Kevin's wife, Mary Ann (Charlize Theron), insane, at last assaulting her and provoking her to commit suicide, all to enlist Kevin in his ultimate plan to bring the Antichrist into the world.

Near the end of the film, the poet John Milton's Satan is actually quoted, when Kevin asks,

> "'Better to reign in Hell than serve in Heaven,' is that it?" John replies, "Why not? I'm here on the ground with my nose in it since the whole thing began. I've nurtured every sensation man's been inspired to have. I cared about what he wanted and I never judged him. Why? Because I never rejected him. In spite of all his imperfections, I'm a fan of man! I'm a humanist. Maybe the last humanist."

Satan claims to have been on humanity's side since the beginning. But Satan is the father of lies. Humankind has always been just his medium for revenge against God, and the lesser devils and demons are his messengers and emissaries in carrying out that revenge. In *The Devil's Advocate*, Kevin foils Satan's current plan, although the ending suggests that his victory over temptation may be temporary. But judging by the omnipresence of the devil in our stories and in our belief systems, he has a multitude of other plans—he is always scheming, never content, tireless, and—of course—immortal.

The poet Rainer Maria Rilke repeats in the *Duino Elegies* that every angel is terrifying.[54] We sometimes forget that our devils were angels first, that the Satan some believe orchestrates the world's evil was once responsible for carrying out God's will in heaven. There are few more potent stories of the power of evil than those where angels go bad. Evil angels make chilling villains in *Angelology*, *Angelopolis*, and a flood of other novels for adults and young adults. They serve as effective antagonists in the five films of the Prophecy series (1995–2005), in which angels and fallen angels played by Christopher Walken, Viggo Mortenson, and Eric Stoltz contest for the fate of heaven, hell, and humankind. The tag line for the first movie, *The Prophecy*, summarizes the action concisely: "An evil born in Heaven is about to be unleashed on earth."

Not all the characters who function as angels in imaginative literature are supernatural creatures originally hailing from heaven. Angelic evil appears, to great effect, in tales of the Weeping Angels, some of the most frightening villains from the *Doctor Who* series. While not actually God's heavenly messengers, the Weeping Angels are creatures of great antiquity; The Doctor (David Tennant) says that, like the angels, they are as old as the universe, or almost so. They are a race of aliens who appear as carved stone angels, such as you might find appearing as gravestones or on memorials, beautiful and serene until you look away. In the episode introducing the Weeping Angels, "Blink" (which won a 2008 Hugo Award), The Doctor explains that "in the sight of any living thing, they literally turn into stone. And you can't kill a stone. Of course, a stone can't kill you either, but then you turn your head away. Then you blink. Then, oh yes, it can." Neil Gaiman and other critics have said that the Weeping Angels are among the most frightening monsters in modern popular culture.[55] Perhaps the Weeping Angels scare us so much because they tap into archetypal fears: things that go bump in the night, things that move when we aren't watching them. However, just as important, the Weeping Angels also tap into an existential fear: things that appear to be good and beautiful can instead be creatures of deadly malice. If angels are not operating as agents of good, then what can we depend on?

Angels are also used as villains in *Doctor Who* in the 2007 Christmas special "Voyage of the Damned." There, after The Doctor and his companion (Kylie Minogue) board a spacefaring version of the *Titanic*, they are menaced not just by crashing meteorites that have incapacitated the ship but by the *Titanic*'s malfunctioning angelic service robots, gold-skinned, haloed, and winged machines called the Host, or the Heavenly Host. The Host pursue their prey by flight, and throw their haloes as deadly weapons—either funny or frightening, depending perhaps on whether one is an observer or a target.

A similar twinge comes from the movie *Constantine* when the archangel Gabriel (Tilda Swinton) reveals that he (she?) is the villain behind the movie's master plan to impose hell on earth. Swinton's short hair and slender frame are employed to unsettling effect in this traditional depiction of an androgynous angel (despite the gender of the actress, for simplicity's sake I will refer to Gabriel as male). *Time* critic Richard

Corliss describes her performance as Swinton "at her most immaculately decadent," and Gabriel becomes more and more chilling as the movie moves toward its climax.[56] The filmmakers clearly meant to problematize this angelic being by giving him a logical motivation for his rebellion. Gabriel's resentment against humanity for being God's favorites causes him to ally himself with Mammon, the son of Satan, in order to bring a holocaust on the whole world. Like any good fallen angel, he can defend his choice with convincing eloquence: "Like the animals you are, you never learn unless sufficiently prodded. Pleasure has no lasting effect. But subject you to pain, unpleasantness—suffering—and you will take notice, you will fight to overcome, to earn your redemption. That is when you're at your best." As the story ends—as Satan gets wind of Gabriel's plan but good triumphs despite both of their best efforts—Gabriel becomes as debased as that Satan we observe naked and frozen in place in Dante's hell. His beautiful wings are burned away, and he becomes personally acquainted with pain, unpleasantness, and suffering. Perhaps it will make of him a better creature, but in any case, the story's revelation that an angel sought to bring great evil upon the world is a riveting plot point.

Tales of fallen or evil angels chill us. The most famous of these, which we have looked at in some of its many cultural manifestations, is the fall of Satan. Satan (also called Lucifer) led a rebellion against God, and he and his followers were defeated and cast into a place or dimension called hell. These sacred narratives have offered inspiration for our own tales of the fallen angels wreaking havoc on the universe. In *The Prophecy*, Simon (Eric Stoltz) describes that conflict and its results: "I remember the First War, the way the sky burned, the faces of angels destroyed. I saw a third of Heaven's legion banished and the creation of Hell. I stood with my brothers and watched Lucifer Fall."

The *Doctor Who* episode "The Satan Pit" retells the story of the fall from a slightly different angle. The Doctor (again, David Tennant) encounters a powerful tempter imprisoned deep within a planet. The Beast (voiced by Gabriel Woolf) tells The Doctor that he comes from a time "before time and light and space and matter. Before the cataclysm. Before this universe was created." In this time before creation,

The Beast was defeated in battle by Good and thrown into the pit, and his origin clearly matches that of the Satan whose legend he is said to have inspired: "The Disciples of the Light rose up against me and chained me in the pit for all eternity."

The opening scene of *Paradise Lost* describes Satan waking, bound, to discover himself lying in the lake of fire with his brothers, fallen "headlong flaming from the ethereal sky" to this place, "A dungeon horrible.... No light, but rather darkness visible."[57] While we'll explore that dungeon—hell—and such depictions of it in a later chapter, it is important to mark the idea that evil has a home base. In sacred story, and in literature and culture, devils are connected to hell and its ruler, just as angels are emissaries from heaven and its ruler. Despite their rebellion, Satan and the devils still serve the same roles, if sometimes darkly perverted, as their angelic brethren, and, in some tellings of the story, Satan and his lieutenants may in fact still be serving God, despite their rebellion.

We must acknowledge as we explore stories about Satan, demons, and hell that for some the very notions are problematic. Many contemporary theologians and contemporary Christians pooh-pooh the notion of cosmic evil embodied in a fallen angel. Bible scholars too argue that the Satan figure is at least as much a figure of human imagination as of biblical revelation. For N. T. Wright, Satan is "important but not that important," and should be regarded as "a nonhuman and nondivine quasi-personal force."[58] Bible scholar Elaine Pagels invites us in words that echo this book's mythological thesis "to consider Satan as a reflection of how we perceive ourselves and those we call 'others.' "[59]

Jeffrey Burton Russell's mammoth four-volume study of Satan ("the most comprehensive history of the devil ever written," according to reviewer Leszek Kolakowski) is about much more than how people have conceived of Satan. As Kolakowski notes in reviewing the final volume (*Mephistopheles: The Devil in the Modern World*), Russell's scholarship traces "the history of European man trying to cope with the terrifying riddle of radical evil, which seemed to him to be rooted not only in contingent human depravities but also in the very spiritual construction of the universe."[60] For generations, some have thought Satan a figment of our own imaginations, but the myth of Satan and the fallen angels does, as we noted, offer an explanation for the riddle of radical evil, even if we do not profess a religious belief in Satan and his minions.

Nonetheless, many people do believe. Satan remains a historic and significant figure in church teaching. His evil works are discussed in the good works of Augustine and Aquinas, are central to the opening confessions of the Fourth Lateran Council (1215; "For the devil and the other demons were created naturally good by God, but it is they who by their own action made themselves evil. As for man, he sinned at the instigation of the devil"), and are remembered in Vatican 2 and the contemporary Catholic Catechism ("Evil is not an abstraction, but refers to a person, Satan, the Evil One, the angel who opposes God. The devil [dia-bolos] is the one who 'throws himself across' God's plan and His work of salvation accomplished in Christ").[61] Evangelical and charismatic Christians join Roman Catholics in affirming the role of Satan as leader of the dark forces in the spiritual battle between good and evil.

Devils and demons are a part of our theological understanding, just like angels, even though the scriptures offer even less information on the fallen angels than on those who remained faithful, and some of the stories we might assume to be about the devil simply aren't. As Adrian Hastings points out, there is no textual reason to imagine that the serpent who tempted Eve in the garden of Eden was Satan: "It was simply a snake."[62] The original Hebrew word *nachash* used in the story indicates nothing more than a normal snake. Nor is the "Satan" named in the Hebrew testament a devil; the word is used for both angelic and human adversaries or accusers, and the Satan who appears in the book of Job is a servant of God who suspects Job of self-interested piety and requests permission to test him. Who wouldn't be faithful, he asks, logically, if he had been blessed like Job?

> Then Satan answered the LORD, "Does Job fear God for nothing?
>
> "Have you not put a fence around him and his house and all that he has, on every side? You have blessed the work of his hands, and his possessions have increased in the land.
>
> "But stretch out your hand now, and touch all that he has, and he will curse you to your face."[63]

The development of Satan into a fallen angel who rebelled against God and represents cosmic evil awaits the intertestamental literature crammed with angelology and the New Testament Gospels, in which Satan begins to appear as a figure prompting Jews to reject Jesus and his followers. That characterization allowed the early Christian communities for whom those gospels were normative to paint their own adversaries as satanic and explain their rejection of the message they brought. The author of the Gospel of John clearly imagines himself telling a story about the battle between darkness and light:

> *In the beginning was the Word, and the Word was with God, and the Word was God. He was in the beginning with God. All things came into being through him, and without him not one thing came into being. What has come into being in him was life, and the life was the light of all people. The light shines in the darkness, and the darkness did not overcome it.*
>
> *There was a man sent from God, whose name was John. He came as a witness to testify to the light, so that all might believe through him. He himself was not the light, but he came to testify to the light. The true light, which enlightens everyone, was coming into the world.*[64]

This conflict between divine light and darkness, between Jesus and Satan is played out in all the gospels, but in John it assumes a cosmic dimension. In the synoptic Gospels, Satan never seems to have such power, but readers of John have been left to infer a dualistic cosmology: light and dark, good and evil, love and hate, God and Satan.

Satan is also present in some of our most formative liturgy. In the 1662 Book of Common Prayer, one of the most influential books in (and on) the English language, the litany asks God to deliver believers "from all evil and mischief; from sin, from the crafts and assaults of the devil…and from all the deceits of the world, the flesh, and the devil."[65] Satan takes prime position in the baptismal liturgy at the opening of the baptismal covenant. Before any other covenants are entered into, the godparents are asked and respond: "Dost thou, in the name of this Child, renounce the devil and all his works, the vain pomp and glory of the world, with all covetous desires of the same, and the carnal desires of the flesh, so that thou wilt not follow them or be led by them? *Answer.* I renounce them all."[66] As movie fans remember, at the christening scene that is the climax of *The Godfather* Michael Corleone (Al Pacino) renounces Satan and all his works on behalf of his godson at the precise moment that his lieutenants are unleashing a satanic spree of murder and terror.

Given the religiosity of Americans, it comes as no surprise that so many of us believe in hell, demons, and Satan. A Gallup Poll from 2004 found that fully 70 percent of Americans believed in hell and the devil, a number that seems to be slowly climbing. A more recent poll from my colleagues at Baylor found that 75 percent of Americans believe that Satan "absolutely" or "probably" exists (with almost 60 percent saying "absolutely"!), and that, again, 70 percent of Americans believe in hell. Almost the same percentage believe that demons are active in the world.[67]

While intellectuals may laugh at the gullible who believe in personified evil, and some progressive Christians find Satan too ridiculous to contemplate, the majority of Americans go right on believing. The question, of course, is which Satan do they understand to be real? And where are they getting their information? Again, despite a widespread reverence for the Bible, most American Christians at the very least have supplemented what they believe they know about the diabolical from the Bible with a healthy dose of culture.

Over the course of millennia, the stories on Satan, devils, and hell have piled up in our stores of cultural memory. Plays, music, fiction, and more have fleshed out the scant references to the devil in the scriptures. We find the devil personified in medieval mystery plays and William Langland's *Piers Plowman* (ca. 1367), and described in horrifying— and heartbreaking—detail in Dante's *Inferno*: "If he was fair as he is hideous now, / and raised his brow in scorn of his creator, / he is fit to be the source of every sorrow."[68] We find the devil represented in the art of Gustave Dore and William Blake. In our time, we find the devil as Lucifer represented graphically in the critically acclaimed comic *The Sandman* and as the star of his own Vertigo comic, *Lucifer*, and we discover an alternative devil presented as "the First of the Fallen" in *Hellblazer*. We even see him prowling through the crowds for the entirety of Mel Gibson's *The Passion of the Christ*. The devil, like him or not, is the greatest villain of all time; who else stands for every quality and condition that we claim to despise?

That reflexive opposition helps explain the popularity of the master narrative of satanic intervention we find across the centuries, a common legend of demonic temptation in the world and of humans inspired to sell their souls because of it. That legend has inspiring retellings as diverse as Christopher Marlowe's *Doctor Faustus*, Goethe's *Faust*, Robert Johnson's "Crossroads Blues" (later recorded by Eric Clapton and Cream among many others), Stephen Vincent Benét's "The Devil and Daniel Webster" (both short story and film), the musical *Damn Yankees* (again, play and film), two versions of *Bedazzled*, "The Devil and Peter Tork" episode of *The Monkees*, *Constantine*, the second and third films of the Pirates of the Caribbean series (*Dead Man's Chest* and *At World's End*), Snoop Dog's "Eyez Closed," and of course *The Devil's Advocate*.

Just as we can with imaginative renderings of angels, we can also discern the Devil in other characters who represent supernatural or preternatural evil; if writers and artists can be said to create "Christ figures," then it makes sense that they might also create "Satan figures." Some representative Satan figures would include Professor Weston in C. S. Lewis's Perelandra space trilogy, Sauron in the *Lord of the Rings* trilogy of books and films, Darkseid, the ruler of the hellish planet Apokolips in DC Comics, Ridley Scott's Alien, Thomas Harris's Hannibal Lecter (first appearance in print in *Red Dragon*), and Lord Voldemort, the dark lord of the Harry Potter mythos (first appearance in *Harry Potter and the Philosopher's Stone*). Such characters—dark, scheming, and because of their tremendous capacity for evil, all but all-powerful—may tell us as much about Satan as our stories of Satan do. In fact, Mads Mikkelsen, who plays Lecter in the television series *Hannibal*, makes that comparison explicit:

I believe that Hannibal Lecter is as close as you can come to the devil, to Satan. He's the fallen angel. His motives are not banal reasons, like childhood abuse or junkie parents. It's in his genes. He finds life is most beautiful on the threshold to death, and that is something that is much closer to the fallen angel than it is to a psychopath. He's much more than a psychopath, and there is a fascination for us.[69]

British scholars Christopher Partridge and Eric Christianson would second that we in the West have a "phenomenal popular fascination with the demonic, iconic, other" that we explore through the art, stories, and music we consume about devils and demons.[70] After all, Satan and his demonic servants populate everything from our horror films (too many to mention, but including *Rosemary's Baby*, *The Exorcist*, *Constantine*, and *The Conjuring*) to our comedy (Flip Wilson's "the devil made me do it," *Futurama*'s Robot Devil Beelzebot, who reigns in Robot hell, and *South Park*'s Satan, who sings campy musical numbers, is unlucky in love, and decides to throw himself the best Halloween costume party ever under the intoxicating spell of the MTV reality show *My Super Sweet Sixteen*). Clearly we are trying to work out what—if anything—the devil stands for.

It may be that we don't all believe that Satan—an actual fallen angel who rules this world and contends with God—exists in real life. But most of us have come to accept that Satan is a logical and emotionally satisfying explanation for all that goes wrong in real life. The stories in which Satan chills us prove this beyond doubt. What could be more frightening than Al Pacino's devil laying waste to the life of our hero (Keanu Reeves) in *The Devil's Advocate*, his every plan only moments away from coming to fruition? What could be more menacing than Lucifer (Peter Stormare) in *Constantine*, coming to earth, black goo dripping from his feet as he descends in some horrible parody of his former angelic grace to collect the soul of our hero (Reeves again)?

Evil is real and has real power. We see it in the daily headlines and history books, in our own lives, and even in ourselves. To find out where that evil comes from—to understand why human beings do things that are so clearly wrong—perhaps we need to consider the fallen angels, to reckon with the possibility of Satan. But to be convinced of the power of good, we also need to hear stories of fallen angels who choose not to fall, of devils who align themselves against evil, for just as little could be more chilling than when angels are villains, what could be more hopeful than seeing the fallen rise?

Among the imaginative depictions of heroic demonic figures, none is more mainstream than Batman, created in 1939, and the star of movies, movie serials, television, cartoons, comics, comic strips, popular games, and every form of material culture we can imagine, from toothbrushes to Underoos. Bruce Wayne—who lost his parents to random violence—chooses to operate in the hellish Gotham City as a dark angel. He is often depicted looking down on the city, brooding like the angels of *Wings of Desire* as they follow the lives of the humans they are tasked to protect. In the bestselling Arkham games, Batman is actually given a special mode of attack in which he drops from high above onto his adversaries.

That the character considers himself an avenging angel, a dark knight, is clear in almost every manifestation of the Batman story. In the *Batman: The Animated Series* episode "Nothing to Fear," we find this representative quotation: "I am vengeance. I am the night. I. Am. Batman!" In his earliest appearances in comics, Batman showed no reluctance to injure—or even to kill—evil men, and even after DC Comics' publisher decreed that the character could no longer kill with impunity, Batman's willingness to do physical and psychic damage to evildoers remains a core part of his character. We see this in the combat system in the Arkham games, where Batman terrorizes, intimidates, and brutally beats his foes. This dark angel born of violence uses violence to protect others and argues for its efficacy against the angelic Superman, who exerts a bare minimum of force against most evildoers. Batman's visual look—the black cape that resembles black bat wings—also stands as a contrast to the white or multicolored wings of centuries of illustrations of angels. But the simple fact that Batman—who could have gone so wrong, who could have used his great resources and his skill in inflicting pain on others to become a true devil—fights on the side of light is a powerful counterweight to the myth of fallen angels.

This story of a creature capable of great evil turning to good offers us all hope when we experience it through films, TV programs, games, comics, and consumer goods.

Like Batman, Daredevil too is an avenging devil who is constantly tempted to fall, but who chooses justice. In a seminal run of the comic in the late 1970s and early 1980s, Frank Miller transformed Daredevil from a wisecracking variant on Spider-Man to an almost supernaturally powerful guardian of the people of Hell's Kitchen who lurked in shadows borrowed from film noir and German Expressionism. In 1998, independent filmmaker Kevin Smith took his first comics assignment, relaunching Daredevil in the Frank Miller mode in a storyline called "Guardian Devil." The later feature film starring Ben Affleck takes inspiration from both Miller's and Smith's runs, and now that rights to the character have reverted to Marvel, it will be interesting to see if the company continues to explore the darker side of its hero on-screen.

Perhaps the most powerful example of a demonic creature drawn to darkness but fighting for the light is Hellboy. His appearances in comics have won multiple Eisner Awards, and he has appeared in two feature films directed by Guillermo del Toro, *Hellboy* and *Hellboy II: The Golden Army*, as well as cartoons, video and role-playing games, and novels. Hellboy (whose true name is Anung Un Rama) was born in hell, the son of a demon prince and a human witch, and was summoned to earth in 1944. The soldiers who first found him reacted with fear and disgust—he is a creature of hell and looks like traditional depictions of the devil with his red skin, tail, and horns—but Hellboy was raised by a human father, Professor Trevor Bruttenholm (John Hurt in the film version), who taught him right from wrong and encouraged him to use his skills to protect the weak and to fight against supernatural evil.

Hellboy was born to become the beast of the Apocalypse and to release the dragons of chaos into the world. His rocky red right hand, "The Right Hand of Doom," is the key that will unleash the foretold holocaust: "And I looked...and beheld an angel. And in his right hand, the key to the bottomless pit." This prophecy (roughly equivalent to Revelation 9:1–2) is believed in the Hellboy universe to refer to Hellboy himself. The goddess Hecate provides a precis in *Wake the Devil*:[71]

"Anung un Rama, loose the dragon for this is the ending of days. You were born into the world for this purpose only. Deliver the world back into chaos. Wake your devil heart. Set upon your brow that crown of fire. Your coming of age is the death knell of man." But in both the climactic action of the movie *Hellboy* (and on several occasions in the comics), although Hellboy is brought to the brink of fulfilling that role as beast of the Apocalypse, he steps back. His human nurture militates against his destroying the world or those he loves, and with great and painful effort, he overcomes his demonic nature. As he tells a demon who accuses him, in *Box Full of Evil*, of having become too human after years of living among humans, "Well, that makes me a lot better than you."[72] In this story—as before—he snaps off the horns that have grown on his head and uses them as a weapon. Two awestruck observers, the king of the fairies and the sorcerer and mystic scholar Sir Edward Grey, summarize Hellboy's epic journey in this way: "Born of human woman in Hell, reborn of human design on Earth.... And now, finally...he gives birth to himself."[73]

It's a moment worth noting, even for these observers of all things supernatural: a creature capable of great evil instead chooses great good. Though actually born in hell, this fallen angel chooses order, justice, and compassion. It is an inspiration for all of us. Whatever our lot in life, we are not limited to one way of being; however powerful evil may be, however bad the situation into which we find ourselves born, we do not have to simply accept it as our destiny.

If the angels, fallen and heavenly, teach us anything, it is that whatever the universe may be, we are endowed with choice. Like Satan, whose great sin of pride would not permit him to be anything less than lord of his own life, we can choose rebellion, deceit, and selfishness. Like John Milton's Gabriel, we can choose to be trusted and trustworthy. Like *Constantine*'s Gabriel, we can turn our back on all we have been and on all that mattered to us and seek personal satisfaction. Like Hellboy, we can overcome our bad upbringing and our ruinous family of origin and become a hero. These stories suggest that it really is up to us.

We choose how we will live our lives. And—if our stories of an afterlife have any truth to them—we have at least some responsibility for choosing where we will live our afterlives. Let us turn our attention to those realms of the afterlife and to the stories that help us understand heaven, hell, and purgatory. Who goes where? Why? And what do we imagine those places to be like? We'll begin with the heavenly realms, everyone's preferred destination, and see what those stories have to teach us.

HE. SOON AS THERE I STOOD AT THE TOMB'S FOOT,
EYED ME A SPACE, THEN IN DISDAINFUL MOOD
ADDRESS'D ME: "SAY WHAT ANCESTORS WERE THINE."

Figure 1. Dante with his guide Virgil addressing a ghost in sixth circle of hell, canto 10 of *Inferno, Divine Comedy*, 1860 edition, by Dante Alighieri, 1265–1321. © The Art Archive at Art Resource, NY. Reprinted with permission.

Figure 2. Marley's ghost appearing to Scrooge, hand-colored engraving from *A Christmas Carol* by Charles Dickens, 1843. © The Art Archive at Art Resource, NY. Reprinted with permission.

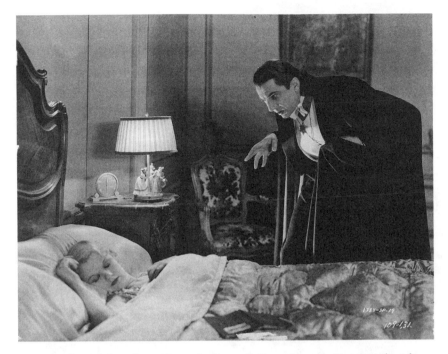

Figure 3. Screenshot from *Dracula*, 1931. © Getty Images. Reprinted with permission.

Figure 4. "Don't Be a Zombie" public health awareness poster, Centers for Disease Control, 2011.

Figure 5. "Heiliger Schutzengel" ("Guardian Angel"). Hans Zatzka, 1859–1945.

Figure 6. Gladstone Memorial, St. Deiniol's Church, Hawarden, Wales, Sir William Richman, 1906. Photo by the author.

Figure 7. The White Rose and Sacred Army. From Dante, *Paradiso*, *Divine Comedy*, canto 31. Engraving. © Album / Art Resource, NY. Reprinted with permission.

Figure 8. Heaven, screen shot, *Diablo III*.

Figure 9. The Abyss, screen shot, *Diablo III*.

Figure 10. Hellboy in Hell™ © 2014 Mike Mignola. Reprinted with permission.

Figure 11. Gotham City as hell, screen shot, *Arkham City*.

Figure 12. Jack and Kate in the forest. *Lost.* © ABC via Getty Images. Reprinted with permission.

CHAPTER THREE

HEAVEN

The Pearly Gates

"I have come home at last! This is my real country! I belong here. This is the land I have been looking for all my life, though I never knew it till now."
THE UNICORN, C. S. LEWIS, *THE LAST BATTLE*

"Dude! We're in Heaven! And we just mugged three people!"
TED (KEANU REEVES), *BILL AND TED'S BOGUS JOURNEY*

Zion is a destination, a place we go to after the lives we have lived. Everything that was false and artificial about that old life falls away, and we are surrounded by others who have sought the truth, who have chosen to live authentically instead of allowing themselves to be anesthetized by the false pleasures of the world. Maybe it doesn't look exactly like we'd imagined—if we'd imagined it—but there is no question that this is home at the end of our journey, surrounded by the faithful, and in the presence of our savior: Neo, played, again, by Keanu Reeves.

In the Matrix films, the underground city of Zion is the refuge to which human beings repair after they escape their lives in the Matrix, the computer program that looks (to most of us viewing) exactly like our everyday lives. In Zion, after their escape from the Matrix, people live simply, are surrounded by the similarly elevated, have the opportunity to regularly pay homage to their savior, Neo, and if the rave scene in *The Matrix Reloaded* is any indication, to sing, dance, and express their joy at their liberation from their previous existence on earth.

Zion, a word that appears nearly two hundred times in almost thirty books of the Bible and Apocrypha, is an ancient name for the city of God, Jerusalem, but it is also a metaphor for something larger, something nobler than any earthly dwelling place. Jews—particularly those known as Zionists—often think of Palestine as their holy refuge, set aside for them by God. Christians may have a similar understanding of what Zion might be. The author of the Letter to the Hebrews understood Zion to be a heavenly city, superior in all ways to the earthly one:

> But you have come to Mount Zion and to the city of the living God, the heavenly Jerusalem, and to innumerable angels in festal gathering, and to the assembly of the firstborn who are enrolled in heaven, and to God the judge of all, and to the spirits of the righteous made perfect, and to Jesus, the mediator of a new covenant, and to the sprinkled blood that speaks a better word than the blood of Abel.[1]

These biblical understandings of Zion as a place of heavenly refuge are carried over into the larger culture. It isn't just Jews who want to arrive in—or return to—Zion. Rastafarians, for example, seek a return to Zion (for them, Ethiopia) and set this heavenly city up as a stark contrast to Babylon, the earthly city. We find the linking of Zion and the heavenly realm in a wide range of cultural references besides the Matrix films. Popular Christian hymns and secular songs suggest a theology of Zion: the first great English hymnist, Isaac Watts, writes of our trek through this earthly life—and beyond ("We're marching upward to Zion, the beautiful City of God"). We find "Let Zion in Her Beauty Rise" in the first Church of the Latter Day Saints hymnal (1835): "Dear Lord, prepare my heart / To stand with thee on Zion's mount / And nevermore to part." "Zion's Hill," a bluegrass standard popularized by the Stanley Brothers in the mid-twentieth century, sings of a day when "The wheels of mortal life shall all stand still / And I shall go to dwell on Zion's hill." And Lauryn Hill recorded "To Zion," a song about her son Zion David on her Grammy-winning album *The Miseducation of Lauryn Hill*. "To Zion" repeats the refrain "Now the joy of my world is in Zion," and concludes by actually quoting Watts's "Marching to Zion."

Clearly Hill's own joy in her son is linked to her understanding of heavenly bliss, and the construction of the song argues that there is no other way to understand her feeling without making that comparison explicit.

Paradise is another word that we often find used to express our notions of heaven—especially a pastoral garden where problems and cares can't enter. Whatever paradise might be on earth—whether it's California, a Carnival cruise ship, a cocktail, or a casino—it's someplace better than we are at the moment. *Paradise* has become synonymous for any place that is a corrective for everyday life, a place where we can go to lose our blues. Paradise has its roots in the biblical narrative. The garden of Eden is described as an earthly paradise where pain and toil are unknown. When the children of Israel are going to their promised land, they send spies in to learn the secrets of that country; the honest spies describe it as a land of milk and honey and bring back great bunches of grapes, an exotic symbol of plenty. In the Christian Testament, Jesus, dying on the cross, tells a dying but repentant criminal next to him, "Truly I tell you, today you will be with me in Paradise."[2] The biblical markers are sufficient, but pop culture continually reinforces our calling to a beautiful place of peace and joy whenever we hear talk about a "tropical paradise" or find "paradise" linked directly to notions of happiness.

The editors of the *Sports Illustrated* swimsuit issue, for example, always seem to be finding paradise—and populating it with their own bikinied angels. On several occasions, "Paradise Found" has been used as title copy (including the iconic 1986 Elle McPherson cover and the 2011 issue). In 2013's swimsuit issue, *Sports Illustrated* featured superstar model Anne V (Anne Sergeyevna Vyalitsyna) posed in an idyllic setting with a waterfall (dressed only in a tiny green bikini bottom and a strategically placed arm), while the copy has Anne rhapsodizing about the location: "The waterfall was the most serene and beautiful place I have ever seen. It was like a little piece of heaven."[3]

In a slightly more literary reference, John Steinbeck sets up California as an earthly paradise in the minds of his battered Okies, the Joad family. They have seen a handbill advertising for hired hands to pick fruit in California and have formed their own idea of it as a promised land, a land of milk and honey. Grampa expresses what they all hope: that they are escaping the Dust Bowl devastation of Oklahoma to go to an earthly paradise. "Jus' let me get out to California where I can pick me an orange when I want it," he says. "Or grapes. There's a thing I ain't never had enough of. Gonna get me a whole big bunch a grapes off a bush or whatever, an' I'm gonna squash 'em on my face an' let 'em run offen my chin."[4]

Nine films simply called *Paradise* have been made since 1926, most of them featuring a character or characters seeking beauty, serenity, and a new life. Representative is *Paradise*, a 1982 knockoff of *Blue Lagoon* (an earlier movie about discovering paradise). It stars Phoebe Cates and Willie Aames as teenagers who find themselves alone in a place of natural beauty—and experiencing the ultimate joy together. A great many other movies have the word *Paradise* in the title, or are set in some place referred to as a paradise, and countless others use the metaphor. Take the film *Big Night*, set in a failing restaurant called Paradise; it thinks of paradise as a place to which one should aspire, and the epic meal referred to in the title is ambrosial, heavenly, out of this world.

In music, Ann Wilson of Heart and Mike Reno can see forever in each other's eyes in "Almost Paradise," their Top Ten hit from the *Footloose* soundtrack ("Almost paradise / We're knocking on heaven's door"). Van Morrison sings about "A Town Called Paradise," where the singer and his beloved can leave the world behind for a place where they can "be free," "drink that wine," and "jump for joy." Seal's "Future Love Paradise" records how cries of why and why not will fall away in the quest to find paradise ("I will drown all your sorrows / In a future love paradise"). LL Cool J's "Paradise" also intertwines sex and joy. The rapper wants to rock his woman's world, promises her pleasure and love, and tells her in the refrain, "The rest of your life, I'll take you to paradise." Whatever and wherever paradise is, it sounds like a good place to be.

We can see our cultural appropriation of paradise as a joyful refuge from this life clearly in the way the lyrics of Coldplay's Grammy-nominated "Paradise" juxtapose dreams of paradise against the heaviness of life and the image of a wheel breaking a butterfly (a phrase drawn from Alexander Pope's *Epistle to Dr. Arbuthnot* about a world that grinds the beautiful underfoot).[5] The lyrics however, can take us only part of the way to paradise. At several points, the song offers only "ooos" and soaring "Ohs," since no words can properly capture the ineffable reality of the world beyond. The video for the song presents the idea of moving from an unsatisfactory reality to—or back to—a place of beauty and joy. The narrative in the video is bizarre but serviceable: an "elephant" (lead singer Chris Martin wearing an elephant costume) escapes from a dingy cell-like zoo cage (filmed, interestingly, at Paradise Wildlife Park, north of London) and makes his way to South Africa via bike, Tube, plane, and unicycle. At last, he meets up with the other members of Coldplay—also in elephant suits—and together they play the chorus and "ohs" against the beautiful backdrop of the setting African sun, until the scene suddenly shifts to the band onstage—still wearing their elephant heads. The brightly colored stage set continues the motif and ties the idea of paradise now to the band's performance and the audience's enjoyment of it. They have all entered—or returned to—some place where the cares of this world can be set aside, if only for the length of a song.

Heaven is not simply for moderns, of course; the Greeks spoke of a land called Elysium or the Elysian Fields in which the heroic, the faithful, and those related to the gods would live after death, enjoying the good life—or an even better one. In *The Odyssey*, book 4, the god-prophet Proteus tells Menelaus, king of Sparta, about his ultimate fate:

> ...*It's not for you to die*
> *and meet your fate in the stallion-land of Argos,*
> *no, the deathless ones will sweep you off to the world's end,*
> *the Elysian Fields, where gold-haired Rhadamanthys waits,*
> *here life glides on in immortal ease for mortal man;*
> *no snow, no winter onslaught, never a downpour there*
> *but night and day the Ocean River sends up breezes,*
> *singing winds of the West refreshing all mankind.*
> *All this because you are Helen's husband now—*
> *The gods count* you *the son-in-law of Zeus.*[6]

Other classical references to this blessed realm appear in Hesiod, Plutarch, Pindar, and Virgil. Among later authors, Dante named Elysium in *The Divine Comedy* as a place for the blessed in the lower world, and Shakespeare referred to Elysium in *Twelfth Night*. In Mozart's *The Magic Flute*, the character Papageno repeatedly sings (in his best-known aria, "Ein Mädchen Oder Weibchen") how if he had a woman of his own, he would feel like he was in Elysium. Finally, in J. R. R. Tolkien's mythos, Valinor (also called the Undying Lands and the Blessed Realm) lies in the West, the destination of ships carrying elves, Bilbo Baggins, and Frodo Baggins to their final destinations at the end of the Ring trilogy. Only those few who know how to reach it may pass into those realms. Annie Lennox sings of the Undying Lands in the Oscar- and Grammy-winning "Into the West," which plays during the closing credits of *The Lord of the Rings: The Return of the King*: "The ships have come to carry you home.... White shores are calling." Tolkien's Blessed Realm is an Elysian Fields for the inhabitants of Middle-Earth.

Elysium lies all around on our own earth too, if we pay attention. American baseball fans know that Elysian Fields in Hoboken, New Jersey, was the site of the first baseball game, itself a little claim to heaven—or the original garden. While I was writing this book, I went to Paris for a speaking engagement and had the chance to walk the glittering streets of the Avenue des Champs-Élysées (Elysian Fields), high-rent home to Vuitton, Cartier, and other elite shopping names. Walker Percy's National Book Award–winning novel *The Moviegoer* is set in New Orleans, and its protagonist, Binx Bolling, resides on the Crescent City's Elysian Fields Avenue, a five-mile-long street connecting Lake Pontchartrain to the Mississippi River. Bolling's search for the meaning of life operates out of the room he rents along Elysian Fields, and seems to find its climax there on Ash Wednesday, when he observes a black man emerging from a Catholic Church offering the imposition of ashes: "It is impossible to say why he is here. Is it part and parcel of the complex business of coming up in the world? Or is it because he believes that God himself is present here at the corner of Elysian Fields and Bons Enfants? Or is he here for both reasons: through some dim dazzling trick of grace, coming for the one and receiving the other as God's own importunate bonus?"[7] In Percy's imagination, the sacramental somehow functions as it is supposed to, bringing together heaven and earth there on Elysian Fields.

The Elysian Fields myth also figures in recent films. In Ridley Scott's *Gladiator,* the general Maximus (Russell Crowe) offers a speech to his soldiers who are about to fight and concludes, "If you find yourself alone, riding in the green fields with the sun on your face, do not be troubled. For you are in Elysium, and you're already dead!" Interposed throughout the film are golden scenes of Maximus himself walking through fields of grain—the heaven for which he longs. More recently, the 2013 Matt Damon science fiction film *Elysium* depicts the heavenly realms as a space colony whose inhabitants enjoy lives free from sickness, poverty, and want—in sharp contrast to the dirty, overcrowded, and pain-filled lives of those left behind on earth.

The concept of a heaven is not limited to the Western sensibility. *Shangri-La,* the 1933 novel by James Hilton, depicted a valley in China full of happy immortals separated from the outside world. The name has since been taken by hotels and nightclubs—and appropriated by the Chinese themselves. In 2001, a county in the mountainous Yunnan Province was officially renamed "Shangri-La" and came to the attention of many in the West in 2013, when an earthquake struck "scenic Shangri-La" and thousands had to be evacuated.[8] Nirvana, meanwhile, is the name for the realm of "ultimate cessation of ego and desire" in Buddhist belief.[9] But it is also the name of the most influential rock band of the 1990s, and, sadly, represents a desire for peace and rest from struggle that its lead singer, Kurt Cobain, never attained in this life.

Something about the idea of a heavenly realm—call it Zion, call it paradise, call it Elysium, call it Shangri-La, call it nirvana, call it what you will—meets a deep-seated need of human beings to hope for something more after this life. As Gary Scott Smith has noted in his book about American understandings of the heavenly realm, the concept has been around for millennia, whether created and debated by Babylonian, Egyptians, Greeks, and Romans or the indigenous peoples of Australia, Polynesia, Peru, Mexico, or America.[10] Whether because it fits our sense of justice that the good should be rewarded or because it appeals to our ingrained hope that this sometimes difficult existence isn't all that we will experience, the idea of heaven has helped to dry the tears of the suffering and offered the possibility of some greater meaning in our earthly lives.

In our faith and in our stories, we seek heaven or some version of it. Truly, this existence is difficult, and sometimes this world seems alien to us. It may even feel as though, in the words of the old gospel hymn, "I can't feel at home in this world anymore." Albert Brumley, the writer of gospel songs like "I'll Fly Away" and that hymn, "This World Is Not My Home," captured the transience of this life and our desire for some-thing—some place—different, better, more beautiful, where we will live eternally without pain or loss. More recently, the rock-Tejano band Los Lonely Boys sang in their song "Heaven" (which hit number 1 on the Billboard Adult Contemporary Chart in 2004) about having "been locked up way too long / In this crazy world" and wondering in the repeated refrain, "How far is heaven?"

The vast majority of Americans believe that heaven exists. The Baylor Survey of Religion has determined that over 80 percent of us are sure or probable that there is a heaven (and, not surprisingly, the survey indi-cates that most of us are pretty sure that we and our friends and family are going there).[11] But, to use the words of Los Lonely Boys, how far is heaven? Where is it? What is it? What may be even more important is to recognize that our conceptions of what heaven is like fuel our under-standings of how we are supposed to live and what is supposed to matter.

SEEKING HEAVEN

*"They say in heaven love comes first
We'll make heaven a place on earth."*
BELINDA CARLISLE, "HEAVEN IS A
PLACE ON EARTH"

Heaven is, for us, as much a concept as an actual place, even if we be-lieve in the actual place. Our conceptions of heaven (and our willingness to pull heaven down into this life in our literature and popular culture) grow out of our need for respite from the ills of this life and our desire for more than we experience now. As the Victorian poet Robert Browning's narrator says in "Andrea del Sarto," "Ah, but a man's reach should exceed his grasp, / Or what's a heaven for?"[12] Our imaginative literature and culture constantly offer us the future hope of heaven— and ways in which our daily life on earth might be leavened by the idea of the heavenly. My friend the Rev. Dr. Roger Paynter argues that human beings have "a deep longing for home, for completion, for connection, and Heaven represents that place of deepest security, that sense of 'knowing and being known,' that perfection (with all its definitions) we strive so hard to fulfill in this life."[13]

Literature and culture serve a vital role in helping us to imagine what heaven might be. Dante and Milton certainly have shaped our conceptions of a realm beyond human speech and reckoning where someday we will know and be known. In canto 30 of the *Paradiso*, Dante offers us a vision of light and joy, of the blessed arranged as a rose with the Virgin Mary at its center, even as he speaks at length about his inability to speak of what he has seen. Milton too shows us God enthroned, and in glorious language supplies the dignity and beauty a human description of heaven would again necessarily leave lacking:

> *Now had the Almighty Father from above,*
> *From the pure Empyrean where he sits*
> *High Thron'd above all highth, bent down his eye,*
> *His own works and their works at once to view:*
> *About him all the Sanctities of Heaven*
> *Stood thick as Stars, and from his sight receiv'd*
> *Beatitude past utterance; on his right*
> *The radiant image of his Glory sat,*
> *His onely Son.*[14]

This sort of imaginative view of heaven is much needed because, as we have seen, there is very little teaching in the Bible, whether in the Hebrew or Christian testaments, about heaven as a place for the departed faithful. According to N. T. Wright, most Christians assume that when the Bible speaks of heaven it means the place where Christians go after death: for that reason they misread Jesus's teachings about the kingdom of God or the kingdom of heaven. Believing that Jesus "is indeed talking about how to go to heaven when you die" may make us feel better but, says Wright, it "is certainly not what Jesus or Matthew had in mind."[15] Barring those mentions in Jesus's cryptic kingdom teachings (in what way, precisely, would a place called heaven be like a mustard seed, or like a merchant who finds a pearl of great value?), we are left with some references to a heavenly realm in apocalyptic writings like Daniel and Revelation, and some few sayings of Jesus. (Little in the Hebrew Testament can be taken to refer to heaven; the paradise of Islam is mentioned considerably more often in the Qur'an and in the hadiths and other teachings.)

Many Christians have focused on one of Jesus's teachings in the Gospel of John to form their understanding of heaven. Jesus says: "In my Father's house there are many dwelling places. If it were not so, would I have told you that I go to prepare a place for you? And if I go and prepare a place for you, I will come again and will take you to myself, so that where I am, there you may be also."[16] This teaching has entered into our thinking from the King James Version, where "dwelling place" is more familiarly translated as "mansions," and prompted many to think of heaven as a place where believers will have their own mansions, although the Greek *monai* has no such denotative or connotative meaning. It simply means "a place where one may remain or live."

But don't tell my grandmother—and all of those Christians like her—who have taken those mansions, shaken them with the book of Revelation's streets of gold, and served up a heavenly gated community where every occupant has a holy-water Jacuzzi with diamond faucets. If, like them, your image of heaven is of a place where you will walk streets of gold and pluck a harp while holding forth with the saints, then you are certainly not in the minority. Jon Meacham notes in the recent *Time* magazine cover story that this version of heaven appears across Christian history and is tied up in "culture, politics, economics, class, and psychology."[17] Because belief in a possible heaven, or heavenly realms, has also shaped the thinking of Jews and Muslims, of Buddhists and Hindus, of Taoists and Zoroastrians, we should assume that those beliefs are tied up with their respective cultures, politics, economics, class issues, and psychology as well.

My argument throughout the book has been that while we may find some meaning in our sacred texts and traditions about the afterlife (or what we imagine to be in our sacred texts and traditions) we also find meanings about life, death, and what follows depicted in dramatic and narrative ways, offering us a foretaste of some future happiness, or some insight into where we might expect to find ourselves if any of the tales of our faiths are true. Sometimes our stories attempt to describe heaven; sometimes they co-opt elements of how we imagine heaven to be in order to help us understand our earthly setting. All of them, though, offer us a chance to think about what heaven might be, and how we might experience it, and they all reflect a deep need for something other. As theologian Frederick Buechner writes in *The Magnificent Defeat*, "Like Adam, we have all lost Paradise; and yet we carry Paradise around inside of us in the form of a longing for, almost a memory of, a blessedness that is no more, or the dream of a blessedness that may someday be again."[18] All the great religions share this insight in one form or another and embed it in different myths.

Heaven may be a haven, an eternal dwelling place where we are reunited with our loved ones and reconciled with all. Heaven may be a paradise, a garden, a place filled with every good thing and every delight. And Heaven may be Zion, a sanctuary, a fortress, a refuge from a difficult life, a safe place removed from pain and suffering, a heavenly city, although our human attempts to imagine—or enact—such a sanctuary on earth sometimes have hellish consequences. We'll discuss those failed utopias—dystopias, as they're properly known—as we move toward our next chapter discussing hell and its uses.

For my Grandma Irene, ninety-three years old as I write this, heaven is not just about being with the Jesus she loves, or seeing the God she loves. It is not just about having a mansion and a crown and walking streets of gold, although after a long life in which there was never enough money, she longs for these things. But within a few minutes of talking to her, she expresses her deepest desire for heaven—to be reunited with my Grampa Orval, to see her mother and father, to once again be with those she has loved in this life. Some of her favorite gospel songs—"Coming Home" and "When the Roll Is Called Up Yonder"—express and strengthen her longings. If heaven is that place where dreams come true, then this is one of those fervent human wishes—for a haven, a dwelling place, a home where we can be reunited with those we have loved and thought we had lost.

"Get Back Home" or "Find Home" is one of the fundamental story archetypes; as we will see, it informs stories from *The Odyssey* and all its varied adaptations to *O Brother, Where Art Thou* to *The Stand* to *The Walking Dead*. It accounts for the wondrous reunions in *Les Miserables* and *Titanic*, and is one of the central themes of the Harry Potter novels. In these and many other stories, characters seek to return to—or to find—a haven or home where they can be reconciled with loved ones and be part of a community. Wily Odysseus/Ulysses, waylaid by the gods on his way home from Troy, wants only to return to his homeland and to his wife and child. Wily Ulysses Everett McGill (George Clooney) in *O, Brother* breaks out of prison with two confederates who believe his yarn about buried money, although his true desire is to get back home to *his* wife and children.

The characters in Stephen King's *The Stand* are drawn from across the pandemic-devastated United States to one of two places: Las Vegas, where the Dark Man, Randall Flagg, rules, or Boulder, Colorado, to be with Mother Abigail, who pulls together all those souls more good than evil to band together with her. A pandemic is also the background for the comic and television series *The Walking Dead*. In that narrative, Rick Grimes (played by Andrew Lincoln) wants only to find his wife and son, and sets off for Atlanta in hopes of encountering them. Outside Atlanta, he finds his family in a camp of survivors, but their reunion is interrupted by a zombie attack. He seeks another haven for them—first a gated subdivision, then a farm, and later, a prison complex. The desire for safety and security is a powerful human impulse, but what drives Rick initially is simply his desire to be reunited with his family. Had that first rough camp proven safe enough, that would have been heaven for him.

The television series *Resurrection* also offers this vision of heavenly reunion with those we love; one of the shiver-inducing elements of the series has been the idea that we could somehow be reunited with those we lost in this life, not the next. The show's trailer featured the song "Coming Home" by Diddy's group Dirty Money with Skylar Gray, with lyrics expertly matching the show's theme of reconciliation and reunion: "I'm back where I belong.... Tell the world I'm coming home.... I know my kingdom awaits and they've forgiven my mistakes." But who is coming home? The dead returned to life? Or the living, offered the chance to be with those they loved and lost?

Many great stories feature beloved characters who are returned to us—and finally reconciled with each other—something we seek in this life but can't always attain. Before the curtain of the musical *Les Miserables* (and at the end of the film version), Jean Valjean (Hugh Jackman, in the film) is escorted to heaven by the spirits of Fantine (Anne Hathaway) and Eponine (Samantha Banks). There, on the barricade, we see all those who have lost their lives in the course of the story reunited and singing together—gloriously—a reprise of "Do You Hear the People Sing?" It is a joyous reunion for them—and for the audience, who have endured sadness as well as joy in the course of the long narrative. *Les Miserables'* heaven, however, does not seem to have room for the story's prime villain, the relentless Javert (Russell Crowe); he is doubtless in the other place following his suicide.

We find a similar scene at the conclusion of James Cameron's *Titanic*, once the top-grossing film of all time. Old Rose (Gloria Stuart) lies in bed after having dropped the priceless Heart of the Ocean diamond into the sea over the resting place of the *Titanic*. In dreams—or in death—she passes through the flooded halls of the wreck, and then, as the scene shifts, into the lighted and restored *Titanic* itself. There, on and around the grand staircase, stand those who died in the disaster: passengers, crew, the ship's designer, Thomas Andrews (Victor Garber), and Jack (Leonardo DiCaprio), Rose's great love and the man who saved her life by giving her his place on floating wreckage when the ship went down. He takes her hand—and we see that in this vision (or version) of heaven—she is young Rose again, played by Kate Winslet. Although the staircase was the first-class entrance on the ship, those gathered there now and applauding as Jack and Rose embrace are a cross-section of the society on board, from the rich and powerful (like Andrews) to the penniless (like Jack and his friend Fabrizio [Danny Nucci]). In this place, many are reconciled, and Rose is reunited with those she lost. And again, the bad guys—Rose's evil fiancé and her mother, who did not die on the ship, and his bodyguard, who did—are nowhere to be found. Dramatic mercy extends only so far in some stories, and there is no room in heaven for those who made our lives hell.

In these popular representations, heaven seems to be a gated enclave holding only the people we want to see there, and certainly that would be our preference. Why spend eternity with people you didn't want to spend a few years with here on earth? Marc Cohn's song "Saving the Best for Last" sums up this idea. The song's narrator, an Asian cab driver who talks about heaven "like it was real," expresses his hope for an afterlife where he will "walk around on streets of gold all day / And you never have to listen / To what these customers say." But Flannery O'Connor's short story "Revelation" suggests that as powerful as this human desire to segregate our heaven might be, the guest list isn't ultimately made out by us, and God may in fact be far more tolerant than we are. Mrs. Turpin, the central character in the story, is a respectable white southern Christian woman, happy to be just who she is. The question she poses herself—if Jesus asked her if she'd rather be black, be white trash, or be ugly, what would she choose?—reveals how superior she feels to those she is thankful not to be. So do her words and her actions. But at the end of the story, upset by being attacked by a girl who literally throws the book at her, she has a vision of the line to heaven, and it isn't an assembly of nice, middle-class white people like herself: "There were whole companies of white trash, clean for the first time in their lives, and bands of black niggers in white robes, and battalions of freaks and lunatics shouting and clapping."[19] In her usual sardonic fashion, O'Connor is reminding us that this place of refuge we think of as heaven isn't going to be our own private country club.

Like *Titanic* and *Les Miserables*, Robert Benson's film *Places in the Heart* also offers a powerful final scene reuniting the dramatis personae, but it offers us perhaps the most grace-filled and expansive depiction of heaven as a gathering place we have yet seen. Set in the small-town church many of the film's characters attend, the pews are filled with worshippers; it might be any Sunday morning. A reading is offered from the thirteenth chapter of the First Letter to the Corinthians, the so-called Love Chapter:

> If I speak in the tongues of mortals and of angels, but do not have love, I am a noisy gong or a clanging cymbal. And if I have prophetic powers, and understand all mysteries and all knowledge, and if I have all faith, so as to remove mountains, but do not have love, I am nothing. If I give away all my possessions, and if I hand over my body so that I may boast, but do not have love, I gain nothing.
>
> Love is patient; love is kind; love is not envious or boastful or arrogant or rude. It does not insist on its own way; it is not irritable or resentful; it does not rejoice in wrongdoing, but rejoices in the truth.[20]

This message permeates the entire final scene. As the scripture is read, a betrayed wife (Lindsay Crouse) reaches over in forgiveness and takes the hand of her repentant husband (Ed Harris). This first little miracle could be a reconciliation that happens in this life, but as the camera slowly pans through the congregation as members pass the communion plate, it becomes clear that this service isn't possible anywhere on earth. Characters who don't deserve to be here nonetheless take communion and pass the peace of God. At last, we see the late sheriff Royce (Ray Baker) receiving communion from his wife (Sally Field), see Wylie (De'voreaux White), the African-American boy who was killed by a lynch mob after he accidentally shot the sheriff, receive communion from him, and the movie concludes with Wylie's answering "Peace of God."

Sometimes love does conquer all. A similar heavenly miracle takes place in Terrence Malick's Palme d'Or–winning film *Tree of Life*. The movie is at once a cosmic and a family drama. Sometimes those twin impulses seem mismatched; Sean Penn, who played Jack, son to Brad Pitt's pitiless Mr. O'Brien, told a French newspaper that he thought the film was a muddled mess: "Frankly, I'm still trying to figure out what I'm doing there."[21] However, at the end, those two threads—daily life and the meaning of life—are woven together in a sandy heaven where family members dead and living, loved and reviled, are able to come together in a place of peace and love. Mr. O'Brien greets Jack joyfully; both of them greet Jack's deceased brother R. L. In each of these last two stories, we find a vision of heaven as a place of reunion and reconciliation, of a place where suffering is past, and the peace of God is possible for all.

Finally, in the Harry Potter books and films, we see the desire for home and family reflected in a number of supernatural events by which Harry is reunited with those he loves. We see it first in *Harry Potter and the Philosopher's Stone*, when he sits for hours looking into the Mirror of Erised, a magical device that shows the viewer what he or she most desires. For Harry, that is a picture of his family: father James, mother Lily, and Harry, together and well. Dumbledore cautions Harry against the mirror, for "it shows us nothing more or less than the deepest, most desperate desire of our hearts. You, who have never known your family, see them standing around you....It does not do to dwell on dreams and forget to live, remember that."[22] Still, if heaven is where dreams come true, than this mirror of desire ("Erised" backward, of course), represents heaven to Harry. Dumbledore knows something of this desire; J. K. Rowling says that when Dumbledore looked in the mirror, he too would have seen "his family, alive and whole and reconciled."[23]

Harry's desire for reunion with the family seems to find occasional reward during his adventures. In *Harry Potter and the Prisoner of Azkaban*, he firmly believes that he and his godfather, Sirius Black, have been saved from the soul-destroying dementors by a patronus charm somehow cast by his late father, and he almost stakes both their lives on this mistake. Harry later discovers that it was he himself, traveling back in time, who cast that spell. In *Harry Potter and the Half-Blood Prince*, Harry imagines for a while that the marvelous potion maker who had possessed his potions text before him and filled it with recipes and wisdom was actually his father, although that too proves to be a mistaken assumption.

Harry has other moments of connection—or attempted connection—with his parents. When he magically enters the memories of Dumbledore and Severus Snape, Harry is able to see his parents both as children and as Hogwarts students; in the collision of his wand with Voldemort's wand in battle in *Harry Potter and the Goblet of Fire*, Harry's parents return to a sort of life and actually offer him guidance and protection that help him escape; in *Harry Potter and the Philosopher's Stone*, Hagrid gives Harry an album full of wizard photographs of his parents that shows them in motion, like film clips. A more painful connection emerges in *Harry Potter and the Prisoner of Azkaban*. Whenever the dementors are near, their dark power to induce fear and despair causes Harry to hear the long-ago deaths of his parents as they protected him from Voldemort, memories that, painful as they are, he is nonetheless reluctant to lose.

All of these moments of reconnection with his family culminate with a scene toward the end of *Harry Potter and the Deathly Hallows*. As Harry prepares to give up his own life to his nemesis, Lord Voldemort, he uses the resurrection stone to call up his parents, Sirius Black, and Remus Lupin, all those parental figures who loved Harry and died for him. The stone brings them back to a half-life, "neither ghost nor truly flesh": "Less substantial than living bodies, but much more than ghosts, they moved toward him, and on each face, there was the same loving smile."[24] They are young and beautiful, and so happy to see Harry. It tames his fear of death, and together they pass into the forest where he is to meet his fate: "Beside him, making scarcely a sound, walked James, Sirius, Lupin, and Lily, and their presence was his courage, and the reason he was able to keep putting one foot in front of the other."[25]

Some critics have quibbled with the inclusion of the epilogue at the close of this final book (and in the film), but it makes perfect sense, given Harry's love of and desire for family. The epilogue, in a very real sense, is heaven: here, Harry joins his family and friends (Jenny, Ron, Hermione) in a setting he has always associated with home (Platform

9 ¾ and the Hogwarts Express). And with them—in spirit and name—are those he has lost. There is Teddy Lupin, son of the deceased Remus and Tonks; there are Harry's and Jenny's children James and Lily, namesakes of his parents. And there, also, is their youngest son, off to Hogwarts for the first time. That son, Albus Severus, is named for two late headmasters of Hogwarts, one beloved by Harry, one "probably the bravest man I ever knew."[26] Harry's dream has come true; he is reunited with those he loved, dead and living. And it is a heaven with room even for those who were not favorites in life—as witness the presence of the once-villainous Draco Malfoy and his family there on Platform 9 ¾.

Rowling has said that although she is a person of faith, she wrestles with the reality of an afterlife: "On any given moment if you asked me [if] I believe in life after death, I think if you polled me regularly through the week, I think I would come down on the side of yes—that I do believe in life after death. [But] it's something that I wrestle with a lot. It preoccupies me a lot, and I think that's very obvious within the books."[27] Although in the final scene Rowling offers us a version of an afterlife in a spectral King's Cross Station, Harry's heaven is, at last, firmly grounded in this life and in the familiar. This often seems to be true of our stories about heaven. We want our happy endings here and now, not after some future judgment. The forty-one hundred pages telling Harry's story end in this life with that much-desired state: "All was well."[28]

Sometimes, as in these stories of final meeting, we cannot help but present the afterlife in earthly settings that are familiar to us. So it is that in *Heaven Can Wait* Joe Pendleton (Warren Beatty) finds himself waiting to board a heavenly Concorde airliner after his overeager guardian angel (Buck Henry) mistakenly plucks him out of his earthly life. So it is in the startlingly racist "Going to Heaven on a Mule," a number in the 1930s Warner Brothers musical *Wonder Bar*, in which Al Jolson, in blackface on some godforsaken soundstage done up as a fluffy-cloud black heaven, gets measured for wings and a halo and sings of going where "the pork chops are a'growin' on the trees," presumably what white writers thought African-Americans hoped to find in paradise. So it is in *Defending Your Life* (mistakenly identified by some reviewers as taking place in heaven—the film belongs more accurately in the chapter on purgatory), where in Judgment City characters ride on buses, appear in hearings that resemble traffic court, and eat all they want at buffets without gaining weight. A heavenly heaven is a difficult setting to sell; even John Milton couldn't describe heaven convincingly.

Still, we know we need to try to portray heaven as a place beyond, a place better, higher, and more intensely real than our own reality. My friend the Rev. Anthony MacWhinnie tells of visiting a parishioner in her nineties whose grasp on reality is simultaneously "less and more firm than our own." This woman told Anthony about a visit she made to heaven, in the company, she suspected, of the archangel Michael: "Upon arrival, she noticed that everything had a pink hue to it. Absolutely everything looked pink. So, she matter of factly asked the angel, 'Why is everything pink here?' To which the angel responded, 'That's just how it is here, you know? That's just how it is.' "[29]

VISIONS OF HEAVEN

"I could have sworn this was heaven."
JOHN KINSELLA, *FIELD OF DREAMS*

Given the dearth of information about the heavenly realms in scripture, it's not surprising we can only imagine heaven as something more, something better than we know on earth. In classical Christian theology, heaven is sometimes described as a sort of Platonic ideal from which earthly realities flow. For the church fathers, who believed that Beauty and Truth were heavenly absolutes, beauty and truth on earth are reflections of and indicators back toward those heavenly goods and God. The fourth-century bishop Basil the Great spoke of "the unspeakable beauty of the archetype," and it might well be capitalized: Archetype.[30] First Source. Beginning. For many theologians heaven, God's realm, is a source of all beauties, joys, and virtues. As Augustine put it, "If beauty delight you, what is more beautiful than the Maker? If usefulness be praised, what more useful than He who made all things? If excellence be praised, what more excellent than He by whom all things were made?"[31] The earthly versions are just shadows, diminished remnants, of the Source.

This religious teaching—that heaven is the source of all beautiful, useful, and excellent things—is found in imaginative forms as well. In the video game *Diablo III*, archangels in heaven represent concepts such as justice, hope, wisdom, and valor. In the final act of the game, players actually ascend to heaven, where they defend the heavenly city against demonic attack and aid the archangels as they attempt to live out those qualities. The Light, which represents all that is good, has its source in this heaven as well—it passes out into the universe, but if the powers of darkness succeed in their attacks, they will snuff out the light here and everywhere.

This idea that heaven is hypersaturated with qualities found in the material world reverberates in dramatic depictions of otherworldly realms. From the outset of *The Lion, the Witch, and the Wardrobe*, C. S. Lewis's Tales of Narnia point to a deeper, bigger reality than the one we experience. The Pevensie children go into an ordinary wardrobe full of clothes in rural England and emerge in Narnia, a land that, in Rowan Williams's words, "is bigger than the one we have left behind."[32] In *The Last Battle*, this Platonic notion is made explicit. The heroes of Narnia enter into a realm that is Narnia, but "more," as Lucy says. Diggory concurs: "More like the real thing."[33] It is, as Williams writes, "not a journey away from the world we know, but one into its heart."[34] Likewise the heaven travelers encounter in Lewis's *The Great Divorce* is the most beautiful—and the most solid—reality they have ever known. The more they move into this new reality, the more real it becomes.

Leif Enger's best-selling novel *Peace Like a River* takes the reader across the river and into God's realm, a place where language is inadequate to describe the deeper reality encountered. As narrator Reuben Land says, "I laughed in place of language" and "there is no adequate simile."[35] The river he crosses is like, yet unlike, earthly rivers. It is broad, more a lake or even a sea, if not for its current, and its color is intense and varying: "Near the shore the water appeared gold as on your favorite river at sunup, but further out it turned to sky and cobalt and finally a kind of night in which the opposite shore lay hidden."[36] Indeed, in its beauty and in its exaggeration of earthly traits, Enger's heavenly realm is an imaginative second of Augustine and C. S. Lewis. Reuben in fact asks: "Is it fair to say that country is more real than ours? That its stone is harder, its water more drenching?"[37] These are archetypes of stone and water that become more real as we draw closer to the Creator of stone and water.

In the 1998 film *What Dreams May Come*, which won an Oscar for special effects, production designer Eugenio Zanetti and art director Jim Dultz create a heaven that is an over-the-top impressionist painting, an afterlife that critic Leah Rozen describes as "a paradise filled with lush, gaudily colored flora and fauna."[38] This heaven is hyperreal, a beautiful and oversaturated material reality to represent that heavenly reality that Basil says we can't describe in human words.

We might even imagine heaven through the brightly colored production design of Tim Burton's *Charlie and the Chocolate Factory*. As Charlie (Freddie Highmore) and his fellow contest winners enter into a paradise of pleasure—Willy Wonka's Chocolate Factory—they are surrounded by otherworldly sights, sounds, tastes, and smells, by colors that are too bright to be real. Similarly, toward the conclusion of *Buffy the Vampire Slayer*, season 8, we find Buffy and her sometime beloved, the vampire known as Angel, entering into—or creating—a heavenly new reality called Twilight. It is a dimension devoted to Buffy's happiness, and it comes into being, interestingly enough, through pleasure. The visuals for Twilight are phantasmagorical: it is a vampire-slayer Magical Mystery Tour. It is also, like these others, one of the heavenly archetypes: paradise.

Our desire to create a paradise isn't limited to fantasy and science fiction; it's a component of every human life, this desire to have a place filled with joy, beauty, and love. This might explain the popularity of Gene Austin's 1920s hit song "My Blue Heaven," one of the topselling singles of all time and often rerecorded by artists in every era (from Frank Sinatra to Fats Domino to Norah Jones to the Smashing Pumpkins): "Just Molly and me / And baby makes three / We're happy in my blue heaven." Almost everyone seeks the equivalent of a cozy nest where we find the simple pleasures of a smiling face, a fireplace, and loved ones. Like the "blissful bower" where Milton's Adam and Eve take their pleasure in *Paradise Lost*, every human being since Adam and Eve has sought a place of contentment and peace, of joy and pleasure.[39]

Whether we imagine it to be literal or metaphorical, our archetypal story is that we were expelled from paradise, and often we spend our lives trying to get back there, or to find a place that reminds us of that race memory. Musician Tricia Mitchell puts it simply: we strive for this place "because a part of us remembers."[40] This is reflected in all those songs about paradise. The refrain of Joni Mitchell's song "Woodstock" could not be clearer: "We are stardust, we are golden, we are billion year old carbon / And we got to get ourselves back to the garden." In almost every life, save perhaps those of ascetics who renounce the pleasures of the world as their path to ultimate meaning, we are trying to return to paradise—or to find it anew.

Eat, Pray, Love, a memoir that spent two hundred weeks on the *New York Times* Best Seller List, was twice featured on *Oprah*, then turned big-budget feature film starring Julia Roberts, may summarize our drive to find heaven on earth better than any recent work. The book, subtitled "One Woman's Search for Everything across Italy, India, and Indonesia," chronicles author Elizabeth Gilbert's escape from a loveless marriage and her conscious quest to find beauty, pleasure, and, yes, love in those three exotic—maybe even paradisiacal—locales. The film's production design and cinematography emphasize the beauty of Rome and Naples, of Delhi and Pataudi, of Bali; even negative reviews often rhapsodized about the landscape. The *Rotten Tomatoes* aggregate review for the film version concludes that "the scenery is nice to look at, and Julia Roberts is as luminous as ever," before going on to downgrade the rest of the film.[41]

Critic Barbara Fisher called author Gilbert "the epic poet of ecstasy," and the book and the film both testify to the impulse to seek pleasure and find joy, to re-create paradise, or travel until we find it.[42] Gilbert herself makes this human drive seem right and necessary and not the least frivolous, the common complaint of critics who disliked or dismissed her story. In the book, she wrote that

> to devote yourself to the creation and enjoyment of beauty, then, can be a serious business—not always a means of escaping reality, but sometimes a means of holding on to the real.... When you sense a faint potentiality for happiness after such dark times, you must grab onto the ankles of that happiness and not let it go until it drags you face-first out of the dirt—this is not selfishness, but obligation. You were given life; it is your duty (and also your entitlement as a human being) to find something beautiful within life, no matter how slight.[43]

Human beings long for the beauty manifested in paradise, but we also seek safety and security, another iteration of heaven that appears in this longing. We live in a world in which airplanes can be crashed into skyscrapers and tsunamis can kill thousands, a world where a deranged man can walk into a school or a movie theater and open fire, or an explosion in a fertilizer plant can level a town. In such a world, not even faith may make us feel safe. The desires to keep and bear arms, to hoard possessions, to keep ourselves and those we love from harm are expressions of our desire for sanctuary, and are as strong as our desires to eat, pray, and love. How else to explain the cultural relevance of bunkers and survival preparation other than that some of us fear the chaos around us and are tangibly seeking a Zion, a sanctuary, a New Jerusalem—maybe in the form of a six-bedroom underground bunker with exercise and media rooms?

In the Gospel of Matthew, Jesus makes a rare statement about heaven as a time and place of ultimate security: "Do not store up for yourselves treasures on earth, where moth and rust consume and where thieves break in and steal; but store up for yourselves treasures in heaven, where neither moth nor rust consumes and where thieves do not break in and steal. For where your treasure is, there your heart will be also."[44] This promise is of a sanctuary, but also of a place where our priorities will be perfectly aligned with God's. Those of us who try, despite this admonition, to not only store up for ourselves treasures on earth but to protect them prove the truth of Jesus's closing statement. By trying to re-create heavenly sanctuary on earth, we may simply prove the impossibility of it—although having enough money for weapons, a "bugout location," or that fifteen-thousand-square-foot underground bunker may supply the illusion of Zion (and will certainly certify, through the expenditure of massive amounts of our treasure, where our hearts are).

Not all of us can afford this level of sanctuary, of course; as the *New York Times* points out, the disproportionately white and uniformly well-off characters who appear on National Geographic's *Doomsday Preppers* and the Discovery Channel's *Doomsday Bunkers* are displaying "absurd excess."[45] But there are other stories in which less affluent—and less monochromatic—characters illustrate this drive for a place of safety and security against an uncertain world. In the Matrix films, the inhabitants of Zion represent all the colors of the rainbow. The starving and impoverished district dwellers in the Hunger Games stories look on the vanished District 13 as a possible place of refuge from the power-hungry madmen of the Capitol.

In the Oscar-winning movie *Crash*, we first see Daniel (Michael Peña), a Latino locksmith, changing the locks on a Brentwood mansion. Daniel's profession as a person who bolts doors against the outer world is deeply symbolic of a desire, expressed throughout the movie, for safety in a world where people crash into each other. Jean (Sandra Bullock) wants new locks on her doors. An Iranian shopkeeper (Shaun Toub) purchases a gun to defend his store and his family. Daniel himself has moved his family to a safer neighborhood, where bullets don't fly through his daughter's window.

All the same, when he returns home, he finds that his daughter Lara (Ashlyn Sanchez) has built her own sanctuary under her bed and is there with her pillow and blankets. She says she heard something— something like a shot—and even though Daniel tells her that they're in a good neighborhood now, she clearly still needs shielding from the violent world. It's then that Daniel remembers. When he was a little kid, he tells her, a fairy gave him an impenetrable magic cloak that kept him safe all the time he was growing up in the barrio. And he was supposed to give it to his daughter when she turned six, only he just now remembered that part. He ties the invisible cloak on her; she lies back down on the bed and he covers her up. Before he closes her door he tells her, "Leave it on all the time. 'Till you grow up and have a daughter, and she turns six.'" And he leaves her in this magical sanctuary, as secure as he can make her with his own hands and imagination.

Many of our attempts to create a heaven grow out of our desire for a safe place, a haven against chaos, a place where, so to speak, "neither moth nor rust consumes and where thieves do not break in and steal." Often these sanctuaries grow out of natural human desires for sanity in a world that frankly feels out of control. I have advanced the working definition that heaven is the place or state where dreams come true, but that means we have to ask: What if those dreams are unworthy? Is heaven supposed to be merely a haven?

I have used the language of desire throughout this chapter, and it is here that Augustine's discussion of misdirected desires helps to explain our heavens gone bad. It is not desire itself that is wrong, as Augustine notes in *The Confessions*; it is misdirected desire. When we love something temporal more than the eternal God who grants it, our lives become disordered.[46] A heaven built on those sorts of dreams and desires may begin from good (or seemingly good) motives, but it will soon deteriorate into something fallen. Security is an understandable human desire. But is it a good one? Perhaps all of this comes down to the question C. S. Lewis poses in *The Great Divorce*: Will we say to God, "Thy will be done?" Or will we choose our will instead?[47] Will we pursue our own safety and pleasure? Or is there something more important than our own small needs? Is heaven perhaps not simply built for us alone?

In *Quiver*, the story arc written by filmmaker (and devout Catholic) Kevin Smith, the DC Comics character Green Arrow appears back on earth after dying heroically. How did he get here? It turns out there is also a Green Arrow in heaven, behind those monumental stained glass gates, who spends his days firing arrows at a target in a beautiful green meadow. Green Arrow—Oliver Queen—has been split in two by supernatural means. There is a soulless body fighting crime again on earth, and a soul in heaven who has finally found peace, his greatest desire. But while peace is a great good, this division could cause great problems on earth; this is a dangerous desire (does the God or some other authority in this heaven not realize it?). The soul-less Arrow—a hollow—can be inhabited by any demon who comes along, potentially sparking an apocalypse, but the Arrow in heaven refuses to be joined to him. For him, heaven is a refuge against the pain of human life, against his "tumultuous" life, against the bad decisions and painful mistakes he had made before he died.[48] By allowing himself to be split into two, the heavenly Arrow could bring some comfort to those on earth who lost him, "without having to go through it all again myself."[49] The soul-Arrow even tries at first to stay in his heavenly refuge when things go pear-shaped on earth for his other half and for the world itself. At last, though, he allows his two halves to be rejoined and leaves behind his sanctuary to rejoin his friends and family and the hard work of earthly existence.[50]

The failure of human heavens built on safety and security is drawn in black and white in the movie *Elysium*. The Elysium space station is a sanctuary for the very rich. Earth is a ruin filled with sickness, despair, violence, and poverty. Los Angeles resembles a bombed-out Middle Eastern city and citizens are policed by robotic law enforcement. Elysium is a refuge against this chaos. No poverty, no war, no sickness. When the rich feel peaked, they simply slide into their med-bays for instant healing. They lounge by pools, under palm trees, in mansions that seem to be hung with old masters. The space station Elysium was shot on location in the Mexican resort village of Punta Mita; "earth" was filmed in Mexico City, in the world's second-largest garbage dump, and the actors ended each day literally covered in feces.[51]

Some critics and social commentators decried the not-very-subtle attack on the so-called 1 percent; Rush Limbaugh denounced the film as socialist and incendiary. But imbedded in the film is an understandable message that all of us can embrace, even though we might not agree on how it's put into practice: we seek a place of safety and security. And perhaps we'll do whatever's necessary to attain it for ourselves and not worry so much about those outside the walls who don't have it. If we believe in the idea of a Zion, then there are insiders and there are outsiders, and as long as we are the ones who are benefiting, really, what's the harm? *Elysium*'s effect, however, depends on our identifying with those outside the walls, with Matt Damon, the male lead, who forces us as privileged audiences to wrestle with the idea of gated communities, both secular and sacred. It is normally easy for us to say that bandits and criminals must be kept outside the walls. But when Matt Damon is one of the transgressors, we have to pause, consider the possibility that we might be wrong, and if the story captivates us, perhaps reconsider the cost of our desire for sanctuary against the world.

Most of our man-made heavens begin as utopias, or at least pretend to. Rapture, the setting of the BioShock games, was created in the 1940s as an Ayn Randian city of laissez faire competition and commerce, an art deco sanctuary under the sea, but it fell apart in a bloody internal conflict. Players of BioShock experience it as a ruined city, flooding with leaked seawater and filled with murderous mutations or people barricaded and struggling to survive. The city of Metropolis in DC Comics has also been depicted since 1939—in the comics, at least—as an art deco heaven, a sunlit city where everything works (Rapture, Metropolis, and the heaven gamers explore in *Diablo III* all seem to have a common architect and city planner; art deco is clearly God's favorite style).

In contrast to Gotham City, a contemporary vision of hell, Metropolis is clean, the city of tomorrow, markedly different, Bruce Wayne says, from his own Gotham.[52] It's the sort of city where an arriving visitor—say, a new reporter named Clark Kent—might find his vision drawn upward to the heights. Metropolis is a city that works, a city of beauty, but all the same it is a city over which Lex Luthor presides. In the graphic novel *Superman for All Seasons*, Luthor tells Superman, "Long before you arrived on the scene, I was here. I built Metropolis up from an ordinary 'town' to the most powerful city in the world. Enjoy the public's little infatuation…while you can."[53] As beautiful as the city of tomorrow might appear, it is still marked by greed, evil, and pride, from Luthor's penthouse down to the sewers below the city.

So-called utopias are often merely dystopias where the powerful have the naming rights; so long as they remain on top, why wouldn't it be a perfect world? In the Hunger Games mythos, the authorities punish a long-ago rebellion with the public ritualized annual slaughter of young people from every rebellious district. Only they don't package it that way; the Hunger Games are presented (and perhaps by many, even understood) instead as an overture toward a continuing peace. In the film version of *The Hunger Games*, this is made clear by the Capitol's propaganda film shown just before the selection of contestants for the games. Over visuals of a pile of skulls and an atomic mushroom cloud, President Snow (Donald Sutherland) intones: "War. Terrible War. Widows, orphans, a motherless child. This was the uprising that rocked our land." Following this civil insurrection, however, came peace, "Hard fought, sorely won." To keep the peace, each year each of the rebellious districts offers up one young man and woman to fight in "a pageant of honor, courage, and sacrifice." In the competition, all but one will fall, but that winner and his district are showered in wealth, a reminder of the Capitol's forgiveness and generosity. "This is how we remember our past; this is how we safeguard our future."

War is a terrible thing, and anything that prevents further conflict can be seen as admirable. But President Snow is a man who smells of roses and blood, and the so-called peace is imposed by armed peacekeepers who have the power of life or death over those in the districts. In truth, the Capitol is not a haven, paradise, or sanctuary except for the rich and powerful in the capital city itself, who enjoy delicacies while the people in the districts starve, who are spectators to the Hunger Games in which the people of the districts lose sons, daughters, husbands, wives for their entertainment.

In *Catching Fire*, the second novel in the series, Katniss Everdeen (played in the films by Jennifer Lawrence) describes what awaits her if she decides to stand up against the lie and against the Capitol: "Fighting the Capitol assures their swift retaliation. I must accept that at any moment I can be arrested. There will be a knock on the door, like the one last night, a band of Peacekeepers to haul me away. There might be torture. Mutilation. A bullet through my skull in the town square. The Capitol has no end of creative ways to kill people."[54] It's true: the Capitol's efficiency is startling. Perhaps the devil truly is in the details.

Katniss assumes that a blizzard will keep her district safe from further Capitol interference for at least a few days, but just pages after her realization that she is in real danger, she and her friends discover that despite the snow, their village has been transformed:

> A huge banner with the seal of Panem hangs off the roof of the Justice Building. Peacekeepers, in pristine white uniforms, march on the cleanly swept cobblestones. Along the rooftops, more of them occupy nets of machine guns. Most unnerving is a line of new constructions—an official whipping post, several stockades, and a gallows—set up in the center of the square.[55]

The Capitol bills itself as a refuge and a place where the peace is preserved, but it is simply another fascist state imposing its will on those outside its walls. Its antagonists, making their own plans for utopia, are little better. The sanctuary of District 13 in the Hunger Games mythos smacks of the practices of the Capitol when we get a closer look at it. These freedom fighters too are willing to do whatever it takes to preserve themselves. To exploit Katniss Everdeen, the "leader" of the rebellion nuances the truth by editing together propaganda clips and exhibits no regard for human dignity. In *Mockingjay*, the final book of the Hunger Games series, Katniss discovers her three beauticians, who have been kidnapped from the Capitol and chained in a veritable dungeon for "stealing" bread from the highly regulated District 13 dining room: "The stink of unwashed bodies, stale urine, and infection breaks through the cloud of antiseptic. The three figures are only just recognizable by their most striking fashion choices."[56] These three pampered children of the Capitol have been chained up for an offense out of *Les Miserables*—for stealing a mouthful of bread.

If there's a difference between the Capitol and District 13, it's a difference of intent, not of outcome. People are still suffering, are still in literal or metaphorical chains, but in the Capitol it would be a result of malice; in District 13, these three are restrained because they violated the rules of the bureaucracy. While both institutions claim to be the hope of humanity and a refuge against chaos and war, human beings ultimately don't seem to matter much to either.

Perhaps it is simply the nature of human utopias that they are or become dystopias. Because we are fallen and imperfect beings, our institutions necessarily partake of our flaws. We may build things in pursuit of what we imagine heaven to be: a paradise for the senses, a haven where we can live in peace with those we love, or a sanctuary where the unkindness of the cosmos can be kept at bay. But these utopias decay and devolve into communities that more resemble hell. If heaven is where dreams come true, then maybe hell is where our bad dreams, or our unworthy dreams, come true. Maybe it is where our dreams go to die. Maybe it is a place where it is dangerous to dream at all. We'll explore those questions next.

CHAPTER FOUR

HELL

The Fiery Inferno

"I don't believe in hell. I believe in unemployment, but not hell."
MICHAEL DORSEY (DUSTIN HOFFMAN), *TOOTSIE*

"I had a dream my life would be
So different from this hell I'm living."

"I Dreamed a Dream," Les Miserables

I first visited hell as a child, growing up in a Christian denomination fond of the place. In Sunday School and from the pulpit, we were told that hell was a real place where those who didn't love God and their fellow men were sure to wind up, a place of everlasting torment, of fire that burns but does not consume. Like James Joyce, who wrote of his own Catholic introduction to hell in *Portrait of the Artist as a Young Man*, I was scared straight. Who would want to abide the horror of demons, the stench, and above all, the fire? Who wouldn't choose to love and serve God rather than visit such a place, let alone remain there for all eternity?

Joyce's retreat preacher in *Portrait* outlines the terror awaiting the soul burning in hellfire to a room full of Catholic boys shaking in their boots:

> The torment of fire is the greatest torment to which the tyrant has ever subjected his fellow creatures. Place your finger for a moment in the flame of a candle and you will feel the pain of fire. But our earthly fire was created by God for the benefit of man...whereas the fire of Hell is

of another quality and was created by God to torture and punish the unrepentant sinner.... The sulphurous brimstone which burns in hell is a substance designed to burn forever and ever with unspeakable fury.[1]

In Joyce's novel, in the paintings of Hieronymous Bosch, in the writings of Dante and Milton, hell comes alive before our eyes. And yet today, despite centuries of religious teaching by Christians, Jews, Muslims, and other faithful, despite these potent cultural depictions, despite my formative experiences and those of millions like me, hell seems to be on its way out. It is omitted from or irrelevant to the theology of many contemporary Christians, no longer a destination one needs to fear. A cover story in the *Economist* suggests that the idea of hell is a medieval relic. Even the Catholic Church that petrified Joyce and his character Stephen Daedalus with its talk of eternal punishment has downgraded hell from everlasting flames to exile from the love of God, horrible enough, but certainly not viscerally frightening.

And yet, whatever may be happening in contemporary theology, the *Economist* admits that the idea of hell continues to absorb us: "Religion thrives on fear as well as hope; without fear, bad behavior has no sanction."[2] Moreover, just as we need heaven as a source of supernatural good, of beauty, joy, love, compassion, and peace, we also seem to need a source of all that is bad—ugliness, unhappiness, hatred, selfishness, and violence. We need hell, whether or not we actually believe in it. We need it to help us understand those things that seem to us too appalling, too inhuman to be real. We need hell to assert some sense of justice in a world where the unjust seem to prosper. Finally, dramatically speaking, we need hell for the possibility it offers of human struggle against unbelievable odds, for survival, and paradoxically, for redemption.

Maybe many of us no longer believe in hell, but don't for a moment suppose that hell is unnecessary. As with the angels and devils, even if hell didn't exist, we would have to invent it.

It would be lovely if that were untrue, but the truth is that the long sweep of human history is full of acts and places so horrible that our ordinary explanations struggle to make sense of them. When we contemplate the Holocaust and other genocides, war, torture, squalor, despair, we cannot find figurative language to express the unspeakable evil without resorting to comparison: "It was hell." General William Tecumseh Sherman is credited with coining the phrase "war is hell," but repetition of the metaphor in our literature and culture suggests that "hell" certainly doesn't stop with armed conflict. In "The Cry of the Children," one of the best-known poems of Victorian poet Elizabeth Barrett Browning, we find that "child labor is hell." In "Hell Is for Children," a song by 1980s rocker Pat Benatar, we are assured that "child abuse is hell." In *Schindler's List*, the novel by Thomas Keneally (and the film by Steven Spielberg), the fact that the Jewish toddler in the red coat witnesses and is ultimately consumed by "the horrors of Krakusa Street" convinces us that "the Holocaust is hell."[3] In Alan Moore and Eddie Campbell's graphic novel about Jack the Ripper, *From Hell* (later made into a film starring Johnny Depp), we learn that "the modern world is hell." In P. D. James's novel *Children of Men* and the Alfonso Cuaron film adapted from it we discover that "a world without children is hell." Jean-Paul Sartre's play about hell, *No Exit*, says that "other people are hell." Clint Eastwood's Will Munny opines in *Unforgiven* that "killing a man is hell." The TV show *Supernatural* even once suggests that "standing in line is hell." (I personally wonder if that's not actually more like purgatory.)

I could go on, but a general rule emerges: in regard to every real-life spectacle that appalls or irritates—racial cleansing, chemical warfare, children kidnapped and held as sexual slaves, stop-and-go traffic—hell offers itself as a partial explanation, and as a powerful metaphor that helps to explain, at least to some extent, the existence of such cruelty and suffering.

Hell is reflected in our literature and culture, which sometimes depict acts of such unspeakable evil or suffering that they strain human explanation. When Clarice Starling enters the lair of serial murderer Jame Gumb at the end of *The Silence of the Lambs*, she discovers a place of unnatural menace made more horrible by the anguished screams of his victim in the pit. In the basement bathroom, she finds a bathtub "filled with red-purple plaster. A hand and wrist stuck up from the plaster, the hand turned dark and shriveled, the fingernails painted pink."[4] Jonathan Demme's film version offers this and other indelible images of horror that are difficult to reconcile with what we want to believe we understand about this world.

Other cultural hells abound. In *Pulp Fiction*, Marcellus Wallace (Ving Rhames) and Butch (Bruce Willis) are kidnapped by hillbillies who take them to a dungeon beneath their pawn shop where they rape and kill random victims. It is inhumanity that seems inexplicable, unless we think of it as entering an anteroom of hell. Cormac McCarthy's *The Road* offers a vision of a blasted earth, of people chained up as living livestock to be carved up joint by joint, of an orchard filled with horror: "Shapes of dried blood in the stubble grass and gray coils of viscera where the slain had been field-dressed and hauled away. The wall beyond held a frieze of human heads, all faced alike, dried and caved with their taut grins and shrunken eyes."[5] Suzanne Collins's Hunger Games series also offers scenes difficult for her heroine, Katniss, or for us, to accept in any world we care to recognize: contestants seemingly transformed into ravenous mutts, insects turned into murder weapons, killer monkeys, acid fog. While it might be easy for us to push these and other inhumanities off as horrible imaginings, Collins looks our inhumanity squarely in the face, and in *Mockingjay* actually questions whether our species deserves to survive.

The evocation of hell may sometimes seem to offer us an out, a chance to duck our responsibility at the same time as it permits us some explanation of what we do not care to own as ours. But hell has other uses for us than explaining the unexplainable; hell also offers the hope of justice in a world that doesn't always demonstrate it, and it permits the prospect of victory over insuperable odds that makes for great stories.

"I'LL SEE YOU IN HELL, WILL MUNNY": HELL AS PUNISHMENT FOR THE WICKED

"Yea, I'll get even with you
You'll get what's coming to you."
FOREIGNER, "I'LL GET EVEN WITH YOU"

Clint Eastwood's revisionist Western *Unforgiven* is a challenging work about human nature, violence, substance abuse, and justice. Eastwood's Will Munny is a former gunfighter turned pig farmer who takes on one last violent deed, to claim a bounty placed by a group of prostitutes on the cowboy who defaced one of them for laughing at his small endowment. On the one hand, a person's deeds don't seem to be rewarded proportionately in *Unforgiven*. People like the young cowboy Davey die who perhaps don't deserve to (although Will tells Sheriff Little Bill Daggitt [Gene Hackman] that "deserve's got nothing to do with it"), but at the same time, a judgment is assumed to be coming at some point.

When Will is sick and thinks he is dying, he sees the angel of death, and he tells his partner, Ned (Morgan Freeman), "Oh Ned, I'm scared, I'm dying. Don't tell nobody, don't tell my kids, none of the things I done, hear me?" He knows the evil he has done and is fearful because he knows there will be consequences. That may be why Will agrees with Little Bill when in the moment before Will shoots him, Little Bill looks him in the eyes and says, "I'll see you in hell, Will Munny." In fact, Will already seems to be in hell, judging from the movie's end, where he promises to rain down judgment on sinners as open flames flicker behind him and Ned's body appears grotesquely on display on the front porch of the saloon: "You better bury Ned right!...Better not cut up, nor otherwise harm no whores...or I'll come back and kill every one of you sons of bitches."

This idea of hell as place of punishment is embedded in our religious teachings. The Hebrew scriptures contain little mention of what we understand as hell. Jewish thought about life after death developed, however, so that Sheol, the place of the dead, was no longer thought of as simply a place of residence after life. As Richard Bauckham writes for the *Anchor Bible Dictionary*, it transmutes into a place of judgment: "The notion of resurrection was connected with that of the judgment of the dead. At the day of judgment, the righteous will receive the reward of eternal life and the wicked the judgment of eternal destruction or eternal torment."[6] Before the birth of Christ this fiery place of judgment had become a common belief, and while the earliest Christian writings (the Pauline epistles) do not mention damnation, in the synoptic Gospels Jesus speaks often of the hell of fire (or Gehenna, a valley outside the walls of Jerusalem where children were once burned as sacrifices to a pagan god). These verses from Matthew 18 are representative:

> If your hand or your foot causes you to stumble, cut it off and throw it away; it is better for you to enter life maimed or lame than to have two hands or two feet and to be thrown into the eternal fire. And if your eye causes you to stumble, tear it out and throw it away; it is better for you to enter life with one eye than to have two eyes and to be thrown into the hell of fire.[7]

In Matthew 25, in which Jesus describes the last judgment, he says that this place of judgment predates humankind: "Then he will say to those at his left hand, 'You that are accursed, depart from me into the eternal fire prepared for the devil and his angels.'"[8]

Islam too describes a place for the punishment of wrongdoers and disbelievers, Jahannam, derived from Gehenna. The Qu'ran describes Jahannam as a place of hellfire, where miscreants will find their skin eternally burning away and replaced to burn again, find themselves in garments made of fire, and find boiling water that will scald inside and out.[9] As Gai Eaton notes, Muslims understand that "none escape judgment," and those who are flung into the abyss for punishment enter a place of roaring flames, filled with scorpions the size of mules and enormous serpents that flay the damned from head to toe.[10] (Versions of hell as a place of judgment may also be found in other faiths; devout Hindus and Buddhists join Christians, Muslims, and Jews in believing in an actual hell.)

The Abrahamic tradition thus is full of references to this place of eternal torment for those who rebel against God, and they have been further developed by later theologians. Augustine wrote in *On the Trinity* that the devil and all those who have chosen their own desires over God's will burn in the eternal fire of hell.[11] Moreover, he argues in *City of God* that fire and worm alike will afflict those in hell.[12]

Other authorities agree. Thomas Aquinas argues in his supplement to the *Summa Theologica* that all the elements, including heat and cold, "conduce to the torture of the damned."[13] And while Calvin's *Institutes* contain little on hell as a place of punishment, he does include this affirmation that whatever it may be, it exists, and that its torments are real: "As language cannot describe the severity of the divine vengeance on the reprobate, their pains and torments are figured to us by corporeal things, such as darkness, wailing and gnashing of teeth, inextinguishable fire, the ever-gnawing worm (Matthew 8:12; 22:13; Mark 9:43; Isaiah 66:24). It is certain that by such modes of expression the Holy Spirit designed to impress all our senses with dread."[14] Whatever hell is, it is a place of punishment for sinners, and it is horrible.

In America, hell has been imagined often as a place of fire and brimstone, perhaps in part because of the preaching of the Puritan divines and of Jonathan Edwards, whose image of sinners dangling over the flames of hell in "Sinners in the Hands of an Angry God" is still read as both history and literature. Evangelical Christians today continue to preach hellfire and brimstone, that is, that those who do not accept Christ and serve God are doomed to hell. Among the many who believe this are superstar Seattle pastor Mark Driscoll, who recently preached that "it makes perfect sense to me that a convicted criminal goes to prison. Similarly, it makes perfect sense that a condemned sinner goes to hell."[15] Those who die in their sins go to hell; where else would they go?

Many mainstream American Christians still consider hell an actuality; my colleague Roger Olson notes that contemporary evangelical theologians believe hell "is a necessary aspect of God's justice and human sinfulness."[16] But while all evangelical theologians believe hell is real and eternal, some disagreement exists on the nature of the punishment in hell. Best-selling author Francis Chan, for example, isn't sure where the consensus lies these days: "There are some good, godly men—and maybe even the majority—that seem to take the annihilation view. I was surprised because all I was brought up with was conscious torment."[17] If evangelicals, long noted for their insistence on the reality of hell, no longer agree on what that reality is, it should not be surprising that many

Christian theologians think of hell not as a physical place but as a spiritual condition, although judgment remains a part of the equation.

Dostoevsky's Zosima, in *The Brothers Karamazov,* describes hell as an inability to love. Christopher Garrett argues that this is typical of Dostoevsky's theology. Dostoevsky's greatest characters (the Underground Man, Raskolnikov, and Ivan Karamazov) "each experience an inner hell caused by their pride, rebellion, and naturalistic worldview."[18] They are, like Milton's Satan, carrying hell around with them. C. S. Lewis wrote in *Surprised by Joy* that "union with that Nature [of God] is bliss and separation from it horror. Thus Heaven and Hell come in. But it may well be that to think much of either except in this context of thought, to hypostatize them as if they had a substantial meaning apart from the presence or absence of God, corrupts the doctrine of both and corrupts us while we so think of them."[19] In *The Great Divorce*, Lewis dramatizes this by depicting hell as self-chosen exile, with ever-growing distances between individuals, and between them and God.

Karl Barth concurs. Hell should still be considered a place of judgment, but it need not be splashy flaming punishment. Separation is sufficient torment:

> That man is separated from God means being in the place of torment. "Wailing and gnashing of teeth"—our imagination is not adequate to this reality, this existence without God. The atheist is not aware of what Godlessness is. Godlessness is existence in hell. What else but this is left as the result of sin? Has not man separated himself from God by his own act? "Descended into hell" is merely confirmation of it, God's judgment is righteous—that is, gives man what he wanted.[20]

Still there remains little question among theologians who believe in hell that its primary purpose is to punish the wicked, and imaginative literature is also filled with examples of hell as a punitive locale. Milton's *Paradise Lost* begins just moments after the fallen angels led by Satan have been cast out of heaven, and we find them floating in the lake of fire. Satan raises his head, surveys the scene, and discovers the prison created for him and all those who rebel against God:

A dungeon horrible, on all sides round,
As one great furnace flamed; yet from those flames
No light; but rather darkness visible
Served only to discover sights of woe,
Regions of sorrow, doleful shades, where peace
And rest can never dwell, hope never comes
That comes to all, but torture without end
Still urges, and a fiery deluge, fed
With ever-burning sulphur unconsumed.
For those rebellious; here their prison ordained
Such place Eternal Justice had prepared
For those rebellious; here their prison ordained
In utter darkness, and their portion set.[21]

It is indeed a prison ordained, as Satan learns: he can exit hell, but he cannot leave hell behind. In book 4, Satan discovers "the hell within him" that he can no more fly from than from himself: "Me miserable! Which way shall I fly infinite wrath and infinite despair? / Which way I fly is hell; myself am hell."[22]

Although Satan begins the epic as our most sympathetic character, his character is debased continuously after we are introduced to our human heroes, Adam and Eve. Satan is shown squatting like a toad, whispering temptation into the ear of the sleeping Eve, and taking on the form of the surface-crawling snake to consummate his temptation of her. Satan and his demons are later forced into that form after Satan returns to the city of Pandaemonium to boast of his accomplishment: "He hears / On all sides, from innumerable tongues / A dismal universal hiss, the sound / Of public scorn."[23] His punishment is complete. He who had sought to be master of his own fate is forced against his will into another shape, at least for a time; he who had prided himself on the eloquence that had seduced a third of the angels is, like his fallen comrades, reduced to hissing; and he who had been the beautiful and radiant servant of God becomes the repugnant and reviled snake. The punishment is complete.

Milton benefited from the depiction of hell in Dante's *Inferno*, and most certainly Dante believed that hell was a place of punishment. In fact, in

Dante's hell, the punishments devised for the damned are not generic hell-fire and brimstone, but much worse and much more fitting. Using the principle of *contrepasso* (that is, "the punishment fits the crime)," Minos the dreadful assigns torments exquisitely appropriate to each class of sinner. As John Casey notes, with Dante we have an imaginative rendering of hell and its punishments that exceeds anything preceding it in Christian theology, in the works of Tertullian, Origen, or even Augustine: "a philosophical structure that is fully worked out and exactly imagined to its smallest details."[24] Where religion left us unsatisfied and hell incomplete, Dante and other imaginative souls have filled in the gaps, giving us a place of punishment that makes sense and satisfies our senses.

So for Dante in the second circle of hell are those who succumbed to lust, and who now are tossed about by hellish tempests just as they were buffeted in life by their own desire:

> As winter starlings riding on their wings
> Form crowded flocks, so spirits dip and veer
> Foundering in the wind's rough buffetings,
> Upward or downward, driven here and there
> With never ease from pain nor hope of rest.[25]

Those in the first round of the seventh circle, who committed acts of violence against their neighbors, are immersed in boiling rivers of blood, as their blood boiled and drove them to rage and mayhem. In the second round of the seventh circle, where those who committed violence against themselves reside, we find spirits denied a body and able to speak only when they are torn, for "justice must forbid / Having what one has robbed oneself of."[26] Throughout Dante's hell, in fact, we find perfect punishments devised for sinners, whether those sins are those of lust, greed, gluttony, or betrayal.

The once-radiant Satan himself is punished by his imprisonment, frozen and naked, in humiliating ugliness. As Dante writes,

> If he was truly once as beautiful
> As he is ugly now, and raised his brows

Against his maker—then all sorrow may well
Come out of him.[27]

Just like Milton's more dynamic Satan, who begins beautiful and ends cast down into a grotesque form, Dante's Satan is another sinner subjected to punitive contrepasso. Hell is a place of universal punishment and a warning to all who would transgress against God.

But hell can also be used a place of warning for those that would transgress against the state, the threat of punishment that helps maintain an orderly society. In the science fiction novel *Surface Detail*, Iain Banks imagines a cosmos in which cultures create virtual afterlives for their citizens. Some virtual souls luxuriate in sybaritic heavens after death, but many are bound for hell. The characters Prin and Chay, Pavuleans, humanoid pachyderms, are trapped in their society's hell. Prin still believes that they are experiencing a reality that they can escape; his lover, Chay, has lost faith and believes that they are lost forever, that this is their destiny. She tells him, "This is what is real, not anything we might think we remember from before. That memory is itself part of the torment, something to increase our pain.... This is all there is, all there ever was, all there ever will be."[28]

If Chay is correct, this eternity will be filled with unbelievable pain and unrelievable despair. It may be digital, but it is a proper hell, all right: "A seemingly infinite realm of torture presided over by slavering, wild-eyed devils, a never-ending world of unbearable pain, humiliation beyond imagining and utter, unending hatred."[29] But Prin is correct. There is a possibility of escape. As he tells Chay, however they might feel their suffering at that moment, they are code, not flesh and blood, and their memories of what they had been before are true. They had volunteered to investigate the existence of hell and discovered that all the rumors were founded on fact. The hells (every culture creates its own) do exist, and are intended to keep people afraid and in line: "The Hells existed because some faiths insisted on them, and some societies too, even without the excuse of over-indulged religiosity."[30] Without the threat of eternal torment, why would people be faithful? And even in secular societies, without the threat of torture, even after death, why would people toe the line?

The authorities finally acknowledge that the virtual Pavulean hell does exist—and insist that it *must* exist. Senator Errun, an old and powerful male, encourages a whistle-blower to give up her quest. "We need threat to keep us honest," he tells her. "We need the threat of punishment in the afterlife to keep us from behaving like beasts in this existence.... All that matters is that people are frightened into behaving properly while they are alive."[31] Later, Errun tries to induce Prin not to testify about what he knows. He goes on at length about "the need for useful lies, pretend worlds, and keeping those that made up the lumpen herd in one place," but when Prin rejects his offer, he turns angry: "You conceited, presumptious little shit-head!...We need the Hells! We're fallen evil creatures!" Prin, Errun says, knows only a tiny world, where people are nice and civilized and reasonable and polite and noble. He has no idea "what would happen if we didn't have the threat of Hell to hold people back!"[32]

To this way of thinking, it is the threat of punishment that compels good behavior, just as fear of a supernatural hell drives a person of faith toward good. In our culture, debate continues as to the efficacy of punishment. Some years ago, the needle swung away from punishment of evildoers and in the direction of rehabilitation, but there is still a part of us that believes punishment is not only appropriate but necessary, either in this life or in the next. Take Ariel Castro, who pled guilty in 2013 to kidnapping three women and repeatedly raping them for a decade. Castro escaped any possibility of earthly punishment by committing suicide in jail; responding to a question about the afterlife on my Facebook feed, several people said that his case was why they believed in a hell, because they wanted there to be justice somewhere for such heinous acts. My wife, Jeanie, put it like this: "When people like Ariel Castro die, we like to imagine him suffering somewhere. Whether it's real or not, maybe it makes us feel better."[33] We want to believe that evil is punished, in this life or the next, and hell also exists to give the living the sense that this takes place.

Events and localities intended to punish the guilty and torment the innocent—earthly hells—cluster in stories across human history. We find prisons, concentration camps, genocides, mass rape, mutilations, and many other such horrors. Our imaginative literature takes supreme advantage of these dramatic hells, as discussion of just a few will demonstrate. The prison story is one genre that revolves around the notion of a place of punishment and torment. In novels, films, and other forms of storytelling, inmates are subjected to sadistic guards, brutal fellow inmates, and harrowing conditions that may include solitary confinement, cold, heat, and maybe even zombies (in "Mob of the Dead," a module for *Call of Duty: Black Ops II*, players must fight the undead as they attempt their escape from Alcatraz). The threat of punishment may be used to keep the populace in line—and these stories offer cautionary tales to those who run afoul of the law. Far better to be compliant than to be subject to these human hells.

At the beginning of *Les Miserables*, Jean Valjean is a prisoner of the state doing twenty years of hard labor for stealing a loaf of bread to feed his family. His condition and that of his fellow inmates is expressed as being one of eternal torment: "Look down, look down / You'll always be a slave." The landscape of the film is appropriately hellish. Waves crash over long lines of sodden prisoners who stand waist deep in freezing water, hauling ashore a huge ship, a task seemingly beyond human strength, while high above, an imperious overseer (Russell Crowe) watches their suffering without pity. When Valjean is paroled, the meaning of his punishment is summed up by Crowe's Javert, who tells him "You will starve again / Unless you learn the meaning of the law." The hideous punishment we have witnessed is intended to deter him and others from any future wrongdoing.

In *Cool Hand Luke*, Paul Newman plays Luke, a free spirit who runs afoul of the state for a bit of drunken mayhem—cutting the heads off parking meters because he believes parking ought to be free—and winds up on a work farm. There, he constantly rebels against the system and ends up locked in a box to suffer, digging and filling a grave-sized hole over and over, and fitted with leg irons like a slave. Roger Ebert said that the film is notable for being "wall-to-wall with physical punishment, psychological cruelty, hopelessness and equal parts of sadism and masochism"—a good working definition of hell.[34] Certainly the mirror sunglasses and casual cruelty of Boss Godfrey (Morgan

Woodward) make him seem inhuman, demonic. Like Javert, Boss God-frey is implacable, unmovable, and sadistic: so devoted to justice that he becomes unjust.

The overseer of Luke's work camp, the Captain, explains the signif-icance of these punishments to the others watching Luke rebel: "What we've got here is failure to communicate. Some men you just can't reach. So you get what we had here last week, which is the way he wants it. Well, he gets it. I don't like it any more than you men." Punish-ment for the sake of punishment is a hallmark of hell. Although some Christian thinkers (beginning with St. Paul and Origen) seem to suggest that those in hell may someday be redeemed, the majority of Christian thought through the ages affirms that hell serves only one purpose: the eternal punishment of those who have sinned and rejected God, the torture of those who are lost through their own choices.

Andy Dufresne (Tim Robbins) is the person chosen for punishment in *The Shawshank Redemption* (the film version of Stephen King's no-vella *Rita Hayworth and the Shawshank Redemption*). He has been convicted of murdering his wife and her lover, and his incarceration looks to Red (Morgan Freeman) as though it will be more than he can bear. He wagers that Andy will be the "new fish" who ends up crying on his first horrible night in prison: "The first night's the toughest, no doubt about it. They march you in naked as the day you were born, skin burning and half blind from that delousing shit they throw on you, and when they put you in that cell…and those bars slam home…that's when you know it's for real. A whole life blown away in the blink of an eye. Nothing left but all the time in the world to think about it." Red records the abuse of sadistic guards, the attacks of brutal homosexuals known as "the Sisters," and Andy's time in solitary. Hope is dangled in front of Andy in the form of the truth about the actual killer of his wife and her lover, and then that hope is brutally ripped away from him. Andy's time in prison could lead him to despair, and certainly it is calculated to. That it doesn't we will consider later, but let us con-clude that Shawshank Prison has every appearance of hell, including a cruel warden who knows his Bible: "I believe in two things: discipline and the Bible. Here you'll receive both. Put your trust in the Lord;

your ass belongs to me. Welcome to Shawshank." Shakespeare tells us in *The Merchant of Venice* that "the devil can cite Scripture for his purpose," without accepting it as normative, and in Matthew 4, Satan forms temptations for Jesus by twisting scripture.[35] "It's a terrible thing to live in fear," a character says, and Andy and the other inmates of Shawshank are subject to such incredible violence and abuse that they could easily give up hope, which as the movie repeats, is too dangerous in such a world.

In the Batman mythos, Arkham Asylum is also notably intended as a place where the evil are confined and which offers an object lesson about punishment and despair. Like Dante's hell, Arkham in its various iterations might have this motto emblazoned above its gate: "Abandon all hope, ye who enter here." Over decades, hundreds of dangerous and presumably insane criminals have been taken to the asylum where, one might hope, they will be given help and emerge cured. Somehow, they never do. Criminals do emerge, released, or more likely escaped, but they return to their crimes, if anything, madder and more horrible than ever. In *Batman Begins* (and other stories of Gotham City), Arkham is a horrible place run by a madman, Dr. Jonathan Crane (Cillian Murphy), better known to fans of the mythos as the Scarecrow. In *Arkham Asylum* and *Arkham City*, two of the most popular games of all time, players playing as Batman must make their way through prison areas now controlled by mad overlords and filled with evildoers, and not only escape, but foil their plots. As is typical in gameplay, as part of his quest, Batman must fight a number of bosses who we might think of as equivalent to demon lords (Bane, Szasz, Killer Croc) on the way to the climactic confrontation with the lord of hell—the Joker, naturally. Only then, with the Joker defeated, can he emerge from the prison.

I have mentioned the real-life genre of the Holocaust story, but while these stories of death camps filled with torture and cruelty certainly engendered (and still engender) fear, the question of deterrence seems more complicated. While one might conceivably be frightened enough by the threat of this hell to stop being a dissident out to undermine the government, or stop being a practicing homosexual, one cannot stop being a gypsy, Jew, or homosexual. No account of the concentration camps would have served the societal function of deterring aberrant identity in Nazi Germany. Such stories did, however, enforce fear—and if fear rather than deterrence is a societal good, then the camps served a powerful function. They enforced compliance even with hateful policies, and might indeed have deterred behaviors the state found hateful. Hell can strike fear into the hearts of many, even as it convinces some few to behave.

The Nazis were no innovators in coming up with a policy that struck fear into the heart and encouraged people to bow down before the power of the state; stories of such actions go back into the twilight of human history. According to the ancient myth of Theseus, King Minos of Crete held the city of Athens responsible for the murder of his son and demanded that every seven years a tribute be sent regularly to Crete of seven handsome young men and seven beautiful virgins. These young people would be sent into the labyrinth constructed for Minos by his brilliant craftsman Daedalus, and there, they would all be killed and eaten by the half-human monster, the Minotaur. According to another version Minos had defeated Athens in battle and demanded this sacrifice as tribute. In both versions, at regular intervals, Athens culled fourteen young people and sent them to their deaths. In return for consigning their children to hell, the culture had peace.

Battle Royale, a best-selling 1999 novel by Japanese author Koushun Takami (later a manga series and acclaimed film), recasts this situation in contemporary terms. A repressive government (the Republic of Greater East Asia) regularly throws junior-high classes into something called the Program (the "Battle Royale Millennium Act" in the film), and these students are required to fight to the death. The program is initiated in response to the breakdown of order—especially among the young—and so it is the young who are chosen to pay for the growing chaos in society. As the *Guardian*'s critic Peter Bradshaw noted it is a brilliantly conceived idea involving "the fictional conceit of a violent game being at once the safety-valve for endemic violence and a violent response on the part of the government: an act of capital punishment, arbitrarily decided upon and sub-contracted to its victims by the state: they have to kill and terrify each other."[36] The children in *Battle Royale* are thrown onto a horrible island full of booby traps, then they are forced to kill each other or be killed themselves. It is as if the damned were condemned to hell and forced at the same time to be both demons and victims.

The Hunger Games offers an American version of the Minotaur story that seems to have developed independently from the similar story by Takami. (While the blogosphere has charged author Suzanne Collins with ripping off *Battle Royale*, she told the *New York Times* she was unfamiliar with either book or film, and despite the similarities, her story and fictional world are more complex and fully developed.)[37] In Panem, the outer provinces starve, shiver, or sweat while their overseers enjoy food, gorgeous clothing, and everything they desire, but the fullest expression of hell is the games themselves, the cruel annual event in which people suffer—and the fear of which serves to keep even starving people under the Capitol's thumb.

As in the decree of King Minos and the Battle Royale Millennium Act, the Hunger Games are both a punishment and a warning. In the film *The Hunger Games*, the Reaping is preceded by a propaganda film, narrated by President Snow, that creature who smells of blood and roses, and how sanctimoniously narrates the Capitol's rationale for the Hunger Games: "War. Terrible war.... Then came the peace. Hard-fought. Sorely won." The defeated districts were ordered to offer up "in tribute" two young people every year who would fight in a "pageant of honor, courage, and sacrifice" to remember the past and safeguard the future.

The hero of the saga, Katniss Everdeen, understands things differently. As she narrates it in book 1, the Hunger Games are a yearly reminder to the provinces of how their rebellion against the Capitol failed, and "how totally we are at their mercy. How little chance we would stand of surviving another rebellion." Whatever words they use, the real message is clear: "Look how we take your children and sacrifice them and there's nothing you can do. If you lift a finger, we will destroy every last one of you. Just as we did in District Thirteen."[38]

In the Hunger Games saga, the children of the twelve remaining provinces (the Capitol claims that District 13 was destroyed in the rebellion, although freedom seekers make their way toward the lost district hoping to find a bastion of resistance) are thrown into arenas that could be "anything from a burning desert to a frozen wasteland," and there, over the course of the competition, they try to kill each other, and to avoid being killed by the arena itself, for the games makers are not content to let the action simply unfold. In the arena, contestants might encounter mutated insects and animals, poisonous fog, fire, tidal wave. The very landscape rises up against the contestants. And all of it, the violence, the mayhem, is televised for the Capitol to enjoy, for the provinces to endure.

The games do serve the function of striking fear into the intended victims. In the film *The Hunger Games*, the slow entry into the Square for the Reaping is heart-rending. Katniss's sister Prim (Willow Shields) is terrified (a scene not described in the book), and Gary Ross and his editors flash around the crowd of likewise frightened children and young adults gathered in the square to watch the president's film and wait for Effie Trinket (Elizabeth Banks) to announce which of them will be sacrificed as the tributes from District 12. The irony, of course, is that this terror inflicted on the districts and on the tributes particularly is entertainment for the wealthy in the Capitol. "To make it humiliating as well as torturous," Katniss says, "the Capitol requires us to treat the Hunger Games as a festivity, a sporting event pitting every district against the others."[39] The games are shown to huge ratings, the opening pageantry and interviews enacted in front of enormous crowds. Those who survive to "win" the games receive riches and celebrity. The losers receive death, usually painful, always premature.

The Hunger Games create a hell that induces fear and punishes enemies, and it is so clearly good at its function that in book 3 when the leaders of the rebellion see the possibility of victory, they suggest punishing the Capitol with a new Hunger Games. Let the people of the Capitol live in fear, they suggest; let's entertain ourselves with the deaths of *their* children for a change. It is a chilling moment; Katniss says that whatever the outcome of the rebellion, "Nothing has changed…nothing will ever change."[40]

The second designer and administrator of the Hunger Games we meet, Plutarch, acknowledges the draw of punishing our enemies by subjecting them to torments—and the diabolical appeal of those torments. "We're fickle, stupid beings with poor memories and a great gift for self-destruction," he acknowledges. But maybe, just maybe, this time things will be different. Maybe because of the heroism and eloquent witness of Katniss, "this time it sticks. Maybe we are witnessing the evolution of the human race." Of course he goes on to undercut his hopeful argument by immediately telling Katniss about his new singing contest show—and his invitation to her to appear on it: because she is a two-time Hunger Games champion, people would tune in to see her by the millions. Entertainment trumps enlightenment.[41]

When we consider the popularity of the Hunger Games, *Battle Royale*, and of the many modern-day reality shows set in hellish locales or torturing or debasing their contestants, we are, as uncomfortable as I hope it makes us, looking at the prospect of hell as entertainment. As the *Onion*'s review of *The Cabin in the Woods* notes, the film is "entertaining, while asking the same question of viewers and characters alike: Why come to a place you knew all along was going to be so dark and dangerous?"[42] In the twice-a-year Hunger Games we know as *Survivor* (after premiering in 2000, it is presently at twenty-nine seasons), a group of people is marooned in some challenging location and forced to undergo deprivation and psychological torture, all in hopes of winning a prize. And all for our enjoyment. Similar challenges apply to other games such as *Fear Factor*, where contestants were tested physically, mentally, and emotionally. *Fear Factor* was probably best known for its second stunt, in which contestants truly were subjected to the tortures of the damned. In order to win the challenge, contestants were asked to eat sheep eyeballs, giant spiders, pureed rat, or a pizza made of bile, blood, rancid cheese, and live worms. They were covered in rats, or zipped into a body bag with worms, stink beetles, crickets, and giant cockroaches. Almost no torment was too hideous. Almost. In 2012, after considerable handwringing, NBC executives nixed an episode in which contestants would be asked to drink twenty-four-ounce glasses of donkey semen and urine (the episode later aired in Denmark).[43] But seemingly every other abuse of contestants was fair game, and Americans watched them suffer.

Fictional versions of these reality shows (*The Hunger Games*, *Battle Royale*, *The Running Man*, *Death Race 2000*, and *Death Race*) often parody our attraction to hell as entertainment, but their extremes are not so far-fetched, considering the physical and emotional trials of contestants in such shows as *Fear Factor*, *Survivor*, and *Wipeout*. The only difference is the lethality of our fictional hells, and in many cases, their use, as Peter Bradshaw noted of *Battle Royale*, as simultaneous entertainment, cautionary tale, and capital punishment. Why would people tune into such things? Why do we?

The Hunger Games suggests one justification for turning hell into entertainment: the success of the policy of bread and circuses. The name of the nation Panem is important. In book 3 (or if you know a little Latin, or Roman history) we discover that "Panem" is drawn from the Latin word for bread and is a reference to the Latin phrase "panem et circenses," *bread and games*, a policy implemented in imperial Rome to keep the masses fed and entertained. The policy was decried by the satirist Juvenal, who noted how the populace of Rome had given up their rights and responsibilities because of bread and circuses and didn't even seem to have realized it. But we cannot condemn them, for like the Romans, we too are drawn to spectacle, even if that spectacle is other humans offering up their lives, health, and psychological well-being for our entertainment.

We do have our own gladiators who enter the arena and risk life and limb. In August 2013, the National Football League—the most popular sports league in America—attempted to settle a class-action lawsuit out of court. Without admitting fault, it agreed to a $765 million settlement on the question of concussions and possible brain damage to past players. When the popular all-pro defender Junior Seau committed suicide in 2011, his brain, like those of many football players who have been concussed, showed evidence that he was suffering from chronic traumatic encephalopathy. It was perhaps the final straw. The NFL's eighteen thousand retired players have suffered an inordinate number of cases of dementia, Alzheimer's, brain damage, and early death, over and above the torn ligaments, broken bones, and other injuries inflicted on any given Sunday. As the league has worked to reduce concussions, it has directed hits from the head to the legs and in the process caused a rash of injuries to the knees of marginal and star players alike. Many writers say that anterior cruciate ligament (ACL) injuries are now ravaging the NFL, and certainly there is ample evidence of this.[44] The 2012 rookie of the year Robert Griffin III was badly hurt on national television when his ACL was torn in the 2012 playoffs. On the day when I drafted this section, Houston Texans linebacker Brian Cushing and Los Angeles Rams quarterback Sam Bradford were among the star players carted off the field with season-ending knee injuries in a season that saw such injuries increase by 64 percent.[45] When we watch the NFL now, we do so with conscious awareness that even the NFL realizes that the game harms its players, sometimes for the rest of their lives.[46] Nonetheless, record numbers of us tune in, play fantasy football, and increase the ratings of sports radio programs whenever they discuss the NFL. Football may be hell, but it is still entertainment to us.

In addition to professional sports, we find hell as entertainment in other reality programming. On Thursday nights, my girls, Lily and Sophie, like to watch *Wipeout*, a game where contestants take on a ridiculously unforgiving obstacle course that batters and bruises and embarrasses and (for all I know) concusses them beyond the worth of any prize money. Some readers may watch *The Voice*, or *Dancing with the Stars*, or *Survivor*, or *The Bachelor*. Some may be fans of *Jersey Shore*, or *Duck Dynasty*, or *Here Comes Honey Boo Boo*. The point, really, is this: at any given moment we can tune in to television, YouTube, or a multitude of media sources and watch as the hearts of real people get broken, real dreams get shattered, real bodies abused, real lives exposed, and all for our viewing pleasure.

The perverse love we have for reality programming was actually responsible for *The Hunger Games*. Suzanne Collins told *School Library Journal* that one night during the Iraq War she was channel surfing, and what she saw simultaneously disturbed and inspired her to write *The Hunger Games*. It was the crazy combination of lots of reality shows and lots of coverage of combat: "On one channel, there's a group of young people competing for I don't even know; and on the next, there's a group of young people fighting in an actual war. I was really tired, and the lines between these stories started to blur in a very unsettling way."[47] That strange dichotomy helped her develop the concept; the two seemed entirely too closely linked for her liking. She went on to explain this further to the *New York Times*:

> The Hunger Games is a reality television program. An extreme one, but that's what it is. And while I think some of those shows can succeed on different levels, there's also the voyeuristic thrill, watching people being humiliated or brought to tears or suffering physically. And that's what I find very disturbing. There's this potential for desensitizing the audience so that when they see real tragedy playing out on the news, it doesn't have the impact it should. It all just blurs into one program.[48]

Suzanne Collins is making a spiritual point about our fascination with our reality programming, not as extreme as the Hunger Games, perhaps, yet operating in the same ways. What does it do to us when we take pleasure in real people offering up their lives for our entertainment? The second-century African theologian Tertullian wrote an entire treatise, *On the Spectacles*, about why Christians should avoid the gladiatorial games, and perhaps his reasoning still applies. Like the crowds Tertullian described at the Roman entertainments, our own pursuit of mindless spectacle and amusement can make our "ignorance linger and bribe [our] knowledge."[49]

In *The Confessions*, Augustine added his condemnation of his age's Hunger Games: he described the sad tale of his friend Alypius, who got caught up in the "madness of the gladiatorial games."[50] Alypius went, innocently, to the games, believing he had the moral fortitude to distance himself from the action in the arena, but upon watching a gladiator struck down, Alypius was

> struck in the soul by a wound graver than the gladiator in his body. Thus he fell more miserably than the one whose fall had raised that mighty clamor which had entered through his ears and unlocked his eyes to make way for the wounding and beating down of his soul....

As soon as he saw the blood, he drank in with it a savage temper, and he did not turn away, but fixed his eyes on the bloody pastime, unwittingly drinking in the madness— delighted with the wicked contest and drunk with blood lust. He was now no longer the same man who came in, but just one of the mob he came into.[51]

Experts continue to disagree about the effects of watching violent spectacles in person, on television, in the movies, and in other media. Certainly most people who watch them, or who play violent video games, do not go on to commit their own violence. But Collins, Tertullian, and Augustine—all Christian writers—are making the same point: consuming torture as entertainment is sure somehow to be bad for the soul.

Whatever the moral consequences of witnessing spectacle and human lives offered for our entertainment, there is one last element of hell in literature and culture worth our exploration. Characters in a hellish environment and beset by the demonic make for compelling stories. For Daredevil, a regular-guy superhero stuck in Hell's Kitchen, any success he enjoys beating back the force of darkness is a victory. For Batman, trapped in Arkham Asylum or Arkham City, coming out on top is a dramatic coup. Who expects good to triumph in hell?

Hell has always provided a dramatic environment within which characters might struggle. During the early books of *Paradise Lost* when Satan appears to be the hero, part of his striving is against the landscape of his new domain, which he must traverse and at last escape. Although Dante's poet is not menaced by the damned or by demons, his pity and faith are engaged throughout his journey through hell; it is an internal adventure if not an external conflict. In hearing Francesca tell how she was drawn to Paolo and fell into adultery, Dante's pity is first drawn forth:

All the while the one shade spoke,
The other at my side was weeping; my pity
Overwhelmed me and I felt myself go slack:

Swooning as in death, I fell like a dying body.

Upon my mind's return from swooning shut
At hearing the piteous tale of those two kin,
Which confounded me with sadness at their plight,

I see new torments and tormented ones again
Wherever I step or look.[52]

Although it would be better for Dante—simpler, easier to maintain his faith, less disturbing for his future—to avoid engagement with the damned, to remind himself that they are where they are because of their own choices, he cannot simply disengage the higher engagement of compassion. There is something heroic about this. Some Christian sages have speculated that the sight of souls in hell should be satisfying or even delightful to the faithful. Tertullian wrote at length on the prospect of seeing pagans in hell in his diatribe against the Roman games:

How vast a spectacle then bursts upon the eye! What there excites my admiration? What my derision? Which sight gives me joy? Which rouses me to exultation? As I see so many illustrious monarchs, whose reception into the heavens was publicly announced, groaning now in the lowest darkness with great Jove himself, and those, too, who bore witness of their exultation; governors of provinces, too, who persecuted the Christian name, in fires more fierce than those with which in the days of their pride they raged against the followers of Christ.

What world's wise men besides, the very philosophers, in fact, who taught their followers that God had no concern in ought that is sublunary, and were wont to assure them that either they had no souls, or that they would never return to the bodies which at death they had left, now covered with shame before the poor deluded ones, as one fire consumes them!

Poets also, trembling not before the judgment-seat of Rhadamanthus or Minos, but of the unexpected Christ! I shall have a better opportunity then of hearing the tragedians, louder-voiced in their own calamity; of viewing the play-actors, much more "dissolute" in the dissolving flame; of looking upon the charioteer, all glowing in his chariot of fire; of beholding the wrestlers, not in their gymnasia, but tossing in the fiery billows; unless even then I shall not care to attend to such ministers of sin, in my eager wish rather to fix a gaze insatiable on those whose fury vented itself against the Lord.[53]

For Tertullian, seeing souls deservedly consigned to hell was the ultimate and most edifying spectacle of all. In an age in which Christians were regularly martyred in the arena, perhaps we might expect this satisfaction from one of the saints, although it does seem the slightest bit unchristian to glory in the torments of others.

Augustine and Aquinas, too, believed that the saints in heaven would have awareness of the souls in hell, and Aquinas goes so far as to say that the perfect happiness of those in heaven is at least partly based on their awareness of the punishment of the damned: "In order that the happiness of the saints may be more delightful to them and that they may render more copious thanks to God for it, they are allowed to see perfectly the sufferings of the damned."[54] Aquinas further argues that seeing and affirming the punishments of those in hell will not—cannot—involve pity. "Whoever pities another," he argues, "shares somewhat in his unhappiness. But the blessed cannot share in any unhappiness. Therefore they do not pity the afflictions of the damned."[55]

Jonathan Edwards, called by religious historian George Marsden and others "the American Augustine," goes further than either Augustine or Aquinas: like Tertullian, he seems to delight in the punishment of the damned.[56] On numerous occasions he speaks of the joy caused to the blessed by the torments of the damned. If all that God does is glorious, then how can God's justice not be an occasion of joy? As Edwards says, "When [the redeemed] shall see the smoke of their torment, and the raging of the flames of their burning, and hear their dolorous shrieks and cries, and consider that they in the meantime are in the most blissful state, and shall surely be in it to all eternity; how will they rejoice!"[57]

Marsden argues that "like him or not, [Edwards] remains a looming presence in the American heritage," for his reactions and reasoning shaped and continue to shape the American mind.[58] Thus, those reactions and that reasoning may have some share in our response to Dante and his pity, condemned by the theology of Edwards and the others as inappropriate at best and faithless at worst. When, later in their journey, Dante and Virgil encounter the fraudulent and the false prophets, who are twisted so that their heads face backward, Dante cannot help but respond to "our human image so grotesquely reshaped." He implores the reader, "Try to imagine, yourself, how I could have kept / Tears of my own from falling."[59]

Bur Virgil, although not a Christian or a theologian, responds as Tertullian, Augustine, Aquinas, and Edwards do to the torments of the souls in hell. He condemns Dante's pity. "Who could be more impious," he asks, "than one who'd dare / To sorrow at the judgment God decrees?"[60] And yet isn't there something truly heroic about Dante's unwillingness to withhold his Christian compassion from even these lost souls? For Dante to "share somewhat in the unhappiness" of souls in hell is a mark of his humanity and more. If, as Pope Benedict argued in his encyclical *Caritas in Veritate*, love (or "caritas") is "the principal driving force behind the authentic development of every person and of all humanity…an extraordinary force which leads people to opt for courageous and generous engagement," then Dante in hell may be responding as a Christian in the face of a Christian tradition, heroically offering a courageous and generous engagement even with those whom God has condemned.[61]

A more contemporary epic based on *Inferno* finds our so-called hero engaged in external conflict as well as spiritual, with the odds stacked just as high against him. In the storyline "Down in the Ground Where the Dead Men Go," John Constantine, the protagonist of the comic *Hellblazer*, must return to Hell to reclaim the soul of his sister Cheryl. Instead of the poet Virgil, Constantine's guide is the demon Nergal, an old enemy who now shares a common enemy, his daughter Rosacarnis, who has taken his throne in hell. Together, Constantine and Nergal pass into hell over a bridge of souls in limbo, past countless dangers, and finally into hell itself. "I'd forgotten what it was like," Constantine says. "The air with its varied perfumes of decay. The pathways paved with screaming mouths."[62]

Although he has a guide, Constantine is not protected against external threat as Dante was, and he remains in constant danger of losing not only his life but his soul. In order to survive, Constantine allows Nergal to merge with him, taking on the very real risk that Nergal will not release him. But Nergal abandons Constantine after they arrive at the palace, where Rosacarnis has appeared in front of the assembled lords of hell to request that she be legally installed by the first of the fallen as the lawful ruler of House Nergal. Constantine strides into the assembly and, as is his way, works some magic there, not through literal magic, but through his cunning and intelligence. He sides with Rosacarnis against her father and when Nergal arrives in an indestructible body, Constantine is prepared to offer his life to thwart him and regain Cheryl's soul. Because of Nergal's previous possession, a connection still exists between them; if Constantine is harmed, Nergal is harmed. But the first of the fallen steps in and changes the rules of the game. He kills Rosacarnis, calls up Cheryl's soul, and offers her the option to remain in hell, damned, with the soul of her husband.

All of Constantine's courage and cunning are undone in an instant as Cheryl, out of love for her husband, elects to remain in hell. The first of the fallen sends Constantine back to earth in a flash, heartbroken but alive. Although not protected against any of hell's perils, Constantine goes head to head with the lord of hell and lives to fight another day. Rosacarnis and Nergal are dead, as are most of the lords of hell. Constantine tries to view this as victory: "I'm back. I went to Hell, and I came back. In one piece. More or less. While my enemies burned black and crispy. So I won, didn't I?" But the images accompanying these words give the lie to Constantine's bravado: his face, shattered with regret, his fleeing form as he runs out into the streets.[63] He survived but he lost his sister, who doomed herself to eternal torment, and his pity for her overwhelms any possible triumph.

Sometimes surviving hell is a victory. But it might not feel like winning, particularly for those who feel for the souls who remain in agony.

This is as true in figurative hells as literal; the stakes are much higher in an environment where death and destruction lurk at every corner, where powerful evil forces rule. In *The Silence of the Lambs*, Clarice

Starling's victory over Jame Gumb in his basement is so cathartic because we know that she too could have been another victim. For her to come out of that hell alive, to rescue Gumb's intended victim, and to put an end to his menace count as overwhelming victories against insuperable odds. Her supervisor, Jack Crawford, knows it and congratulates her. The TV news knows it. "Dungeon of Horrors," the news calls Gumb's basement, which it can't even depict as it is: "The film was edited to exclude some of the more grisly objects. In the far reaches of the basement, the cameras could show only the low, lime-sprinkled thresholds of the chambers holding Gumb's tableaux. The body count in that part of the basement stood at six so far."[64]

Like Dante, like Constantine, Starling is driven by her pity for the damned. Although she has rescued Gumb's last victim and ended his terror, Hannibal Lecter knows that it will not be the end of her pity. Just as she was moved by the screaming of the lambs in slaughter, she will be moved again: "You'll have to earn it again and again, the blessed silence. Because it's the plight that drives you, seeing the plight, and the plight will not end, ever."[65] Lecter believes Starling, like Constantine, will reenter hell to save lost souls. It is a dreadful task, but no worthier challenge can be found in any of the worlds, above or below. As Paul Asay wrote, "For millennia heroes have gone to hell and back—often quite literally—to reclaim a loved one and/or find new life. Gods and men alike have made the trip....But the most powerful...of these stories is that of Jesus, who died and (as is written in the Apostle's Creed) descended into hell, and rose again to bring us all the possibility of new life."[66]

Being stuck in or entering hell offer challenges enough, even without the thought of rescuing souls trapped there. Hell can be trackless heat, as on the planet Arrakis, central setting of the *Dune* saga, where Paul Atreides faces treachery and death in a barren landscape as he strives to revenge his father's death, recover his holdings, and simply survive. It can be confinement in one's own body, as the bride (Uma Thurman) discovers in *Kill Bill* after she is shot and left for dead by her beloved Bill, delivered of a child who is taken from her, and raped by hospital attendants. It can be the frigid vista of outer space, as in *Gravity*, where newly minted astronaut Dr. Ryan Stone (Sandra Bullock) finds herself alone, abandoned in orbit, lost in every way a person can be lost, before a miracle leads her to find her way back home. In each of these stories, the physical conflicts against incredible odds are stirring. But each of these stories of hell and many more beside outline spiritual recovery as well as physical victory. Souls are rescued from hell every day in our stories and, perhaps, in our lives.

My first creative writing teacher, Hansford Martin, was one of Flannery O'Connor's professors in the creative writing program at the University of Iowa. He said many things to me as a young writer that I still recall as an old writer, critic, and reader. He told us that the storyteller's most important job was to dig the deepest hole possible for the main character, and the story that followed would be the character's attempt to dig his or her way out of that hole. Although Hansford never used the word hell to name that hole, he clearly believed that our characters had to go through hell if our stories were going to be worthwhile, and there is both narrative and theological truth to this. Our stories are better when they take place in the deepest possible hole, and characters and souls alike value their redemption more when they know what a struggle it has been for them to emerge into the light.

In a recent Batman story, Bruce Wayne deals with the concept of Gotham City as hell and accepts all that is awful about it. But then he goes on to explain (at some length) why he loves it and why we love stories about such places.

> What do you love about Gotham City?...I mean, it's an awful place to live. Right? I mean, it's terrible. It's unaffordable, dangerous, and full of rain. It's a monster. So why? Why do you love it?...I can tell you why I love it. I love it because it's a city people come to because they want to become something more than what they are.... We come here, to Gotham, because it's transformative, this place. We come here with our dreams and the city, it looks at us with its unblinking stone eye—an eye that sees all our faults, everything we're afraid's true about ourselves—and it says: "Try. I dare you."...If you stand up to the challenge, if you walk through the fire, you will emerge changed. Burned down to that self you knew was there all along. The one you came here to be. The hero.[67]

What Bruce Wayne/Batman understands about Gotham City is universally true of our dramatic experiences of hell. Paradoxically, our stories of hell, the region of the damned, are often stories of redemption, hard-won redemption, involving great courage and moral fiber, and more than a bit of luck or grace, however you understand the term.

Only by going into hell can we emerge changed, as heroes.

Literature and culture give us lots of examples of people who emerge from hell changed, we hope, for the good. By the end of the Hunger Games saga, Katniss Everdeen emerges from not one, not two, but three violent arenas alive, and like Clarice Starling, despite all she has seen and done, she may one day recover from the hells she has known. In the world of *The Walking Dead*, Rick wakes up to discover that the dead are walking and everything he has known and loved is gone, but that he must go on and attempt to create order and meaning in a world that suddenly lacks it. In *Gravity*, astronaut Ryan Stone stops mourning her daughter's death and stops being dead to the world as she faces a worse hell. As Red might say in *The Shawshank Redemption*, Rick and Ryan both are faced with the decision to get busy living or get busy dying, and both ultimately choose life, however challenging that might be.

Speaking of *The Shawshank Redemption*, that story offers us Andy Dufresne, who never gives up hope in that hope-killing Shawshank Prison. He makes his escape from his cell and from the prison walls, but in escaping from hell, he also manages to bring Red to a place of healing where bad memories can wash away in the Pacific waves. It was Red who argued that hope was a dangerous thing, but Andy's example has changed his mind. In the final words of the movie, as Red sets out and arrives, he says, "I find I'm so excited, I can barely sit still or hold a thought in my head. I think it's the excitement only a free man can feel, a free man at the start of a long journey whose conclusion is uncertain. I hope I can make it across the border. I hope to see my friend and shake his hand. I hope the Pacific is as blue as it has been in my dreams. I hope."

Hell is horrible, the testing ground of heroes, the domain of the fallen, the home of evil and despair, but it also offers us a useful metaphor for the pain and casual violence we encounter in our own lives.

None of us hopes to go to hell at the end of our life, but many of us would say that we have had some acquaintance with it, and in our stories of characters entering and overcoming hell, we are offered powerful conflict and high adventure at the same time we are also offered soothing analogues to our own suffering and loss, to the challenges we face and will face in our own lives. Hell can be overcome; this is, again, narrative and theological truth.

This leads us directly to our consideration of the last of the realms of the afterlife. What uses do we make of purgatory, that murky realm where souls are tested and tried before passing on to whatever comes next? In stories of those tested in the flames of adversity (or cold of outer space) and even of people sunk in their everyday lives, we find truths at work. We'll turn our attention now in our final chapter to the realms of purgatory, where people find themselves stuck, waiting and hoping to grow into their final destinies.

CHAPTER FIVE

PURGATORY

Working Out Our Salvation

"It's not going to stop
Till you wise up."
AIMEE MANN, "WISE UP"

"A wrong sum can be put right: but only by going back till
you find the error and working it afresh from that point."
C. S. LEWIS, *THE GREAT DIVORCE*

The ghostly word Lost floats across the screen as a dissonant chord grows in volume, crescendos. The word vanishes as we cut to an eye in extreme close-up. The eye opens, and then we see what it sees, the tops of tall bamboo. The camera pulls away and we are with Jack, who is lying on the floor of a forest. He clearly doesn't know where he is any more than we know where he is. He gets to his feet, runs through the jungle to the beach, and stands there for a moment. Then he hears the sounds of disaster, turns, and sees the airplane or rather what is left of the airplane. And then he is running down the beach and into that horrific landscape of fire and screaming and shrieking jet engine noise, into the first episode of the TV series *Lost*.

After the wounded are stabilized, the dead are buried, Jack's own wounds are momentarily tended to, the survivors of Oceanic Flight 815 begin to reflect on where they are, and why. At the end of "Tabula Rasa," the first episode following the pilot, Jack and Kate sit on the beach. This episode has centered on Kate and has been filled with flashbacks from her traumatic life. At the conclusion, she wants to tell Jack what she has been through, about why she was a fugitive from the law. He tells her it doesn't matter.

"Three days ago, we all died," Jack says. "We should all be able to start over."

The plane crash, their arrival on the mysterious island, should offer them all a blank slate—a tabula rasa. Kate nods, and a song begins playing (on Hurley's headphones, we discover as the scene changes), Joe Purdy's "Wash Away": "I got troubles, lord, but not today / Cause they're gonna wash away."

In this new life, the old sins are being washed away.

Jack's words spawned a plethora of fan theories that the Island was purgatory—a theory espoused by Stephen King, among others—because this is a narrative we believe. *Lost* was always retelling a story of people working out their salvation, so why not think of it in traditional religious terms? As King put it in *Entertainment Weekly*, for Jack and the others, "the island is their purgatory, a place where they can put paid to sins of omission and commission before going on."[1] On the island, in this new phase of their existence, however difficult it may be, these characters should be able to leave behind their past, filled with sin and misery, and seek something better.

In this place, among these people, they should be able to find themselves, to finally reach the point where they will no longer be lost.

In October 2012, I interviewed *Lost*'s co-creator and executive producer, Damon Lindelof, at the Austin Film Festival.[2] Amid a conversation that touched on *Star Trek*, *Prometheus*, and *Lost*, in front of a crowded room full of screenwriters and film buffs, we somehow ended up talking about purgatory. "One of the things that we were really, really interested in, and passionate about and crazy enough to take on was this idea of purgatory," Lindelof said. "It was very much in the DNA of the show from the word 'Go.'" Those lines in "Tabula Rasa" were spoken metaphorically, but many fans took them literally, believing that the island in *Lost* was actually purgatory. That was never the idea for the island itself; everything that happened on the island was "real life," so to speak, but the writers of the show really wanted to tell the purgatory story, and that entered the picture literally in the "Sideways world" segments of the show's final season.

"We didn't call it 'The Sideways' in the writer's room," Lindelof told me. "We referred to it as 'The Bardo.' Which, for those of you who haven't read *The Tibetan Book of the Dead*, it's essentially a concept where when you die, you don't know you're dead. It's sort of like Bruce Willis in *The Sixth Sense*. And your journey is about coming to the revelation that you have died. And once you come to the revelation that you have died, then you are ready to move on." In spiritual terms—and *Lost* never shied away from the spiritual element—Bardo is about liberation from the temptations of the temporal world and attaining enlightenment, a sort of Buddhist purgatory where the soul finds release from the worldly notions that have held it down.

As Damon Lindelof indicated, purgatory was in the DNA of *Lost,* and literary explorations of purgatory are also in his artistic DNA. Lindelof read Dante's *Divine Comedy* in high school and was entranced by it. He returns to it often: "In the laundry list of things that I will pull from, either consciously or subconsciously in my storytelling, it's definitely one of the ingredients. Right next to cayenne pepper is where Dante is."[3] So perhaps it's not surprising that *Lost* used the story of purgatory to wrestle with the show's central concept: these characters (Jack, Hurley, Sawyer, Kate, Locke, Ben, et al.) were all lost in every way that human beings could be lost: physically, emotionally, spiritually. Only through the trauma of their plane crash and their battle to survive could they find themselves and community.

Their story is our story too, and one of the reasons we return to an operative narrative of purgatory even if we don't believe in it as an item of faith. What the story of purgatory tells us is this: When suffering and pain have burned away everything that doesn't matter, we can at last be found in every way that human beings can be found.

PURGATORY AS PURIFYING FLAME

"Great men are formed in fire."
THE WAR DOCTOR (JOHN HURT),
"THE DAY OF THE DOCTOR," *DOCTOR WHO*

Anything worth having is worth suffering for, whether it's redemption or your art, or so goes a popular narrative. Suffering ennobles human-kind (or at least it can, according to this narrative; in real life, terrible suffering and pain is as likely to turn you into a snarling beast or a worthless cynic as a saint). But plenty of stories deal with characters who face suffering and are transformed by it. Psalm 23 speaks of passing through the Valley of the Shadow of Death to a place of safety and joy, and many of our best and best-known secular narratives deal with one who suffers as part of a purifying movement from the person she or he had been to the person she or he was meant to become. It is a story that goes like this: in suffering, the former person eventually falls or is cast away, and the new, improved version can emerge, changed by that physical and emotional suffering, perhaps, but more important, changed in his or her inmost soul. What she or he was incapable of now becomes possible, whether that thing is love, or compassion, or courage, or human connection.

In *Lost*, the story looks something like this: Jack, who could not connect to his father or anyone else, becomes a hero who loves; Kate, who has always run away, becomes a hero who holds on; Benjamin Linus, who put his ambition above everything, becomes a hero who sacrifices. Each of the characters on the island who had been lost finds her- or himself transformed through suffering and deprivation into something new, better, beautiful. Perhaps the experience itself may look like hell, but it brings you, ultimately, to heaven.

Take the movie *127 Hours*, nominated for six Academy Awards. In it, James Franco plays Aron Ralston, an outdoorsman who falls into a crevasse while hiking alone and is trapped there for days until he cuts his arm off to free himself. Ralston is a person who doesn't believe he needs others, who believes that he is sufficient to himself, and his plight and subsequent suffering are a direct result of this. He has gone off can-yoning on his own, without leaving word of what he intends to do or where, and when he plummets into a canyon and is pinned there by a boulder, not another person on the planet besides him knows where he is. After a week of pain, environmental extremes, and isolation, Ralston makes the horrific choice to break and cut off his own arm to free himself. But as appalling as that suffering sounds, screenwriter Simon Beaufoy uses the theological word grace to describe Ralston's movement in the story because of his suffering: "The received opinion is that [life is] about one person doing extraordinary things, but it's not, really. It's about all of us. It's about people, about crowds, about humanity. And he's turned his back and said, 'I don't need them.' It's his movement towards grace, if you like. You do need people. You can't live without them. We're all interconnected in some way."[4]

Director Danny Boyle also saw Ralston's suffering serving the same purpose. It teaches him to become the person he ought to become, one who experiences life fully with others instead of the radical individual he has always been. At the beginning of the film, he has turned his back on others: Ralston "doesn't need anybody. And he climbs solo. And he didn't tell anybody where he's going." But his ordeal changes him, burns away his pride in his own self-sufficiency, and leads him to become a compassionate and whole human being, as the film's conclusion, which depicts the actual Aron Ralston, his wife, and child, demonstrates. The emotional or spiritual lesson learned in this journey through suffering, Boyle says, is that "not only does he need those people, those people will pull him back if he will let them."[5] It is a terrible way to learn a lesson—days of intense suffering and belief that he is going to perish, and even more intense pain as he amputates his crushed arm to leave that useless part of himself behind. But it changes Aron for the better.

He has, so to speak, gone through hell to get to heaven.

This is also the popular religious understanding of purgatory, as a place of suffering much more closely attuned to hell than to the heaven where its inhabitants are ultimately headed. Official Catholic dogma simply describes purgatory (to this day) as the state of being after death in which Christian souls are purged of their sin so that they may at last enter heaven, and Dante, our foremost imaginer of purgatory, understood it as "a place of hope, an initiation into joy, of gradual emergence into the light," but in the popular religious notions of purgatory, developed over centuries, its torments make this intermediate state all but indistinguishable from the hell where none of its inhabitants are ultimately bound.[6]

In the early Church, as historian Peter Brown has observed, even before a formal doctrine of purgatory was formulated, the need for something like purgatory became clear: there must be this intermediate state, somewhere between heaven and earth, where unpurged souls wait to be perfected. As Gregory the Great wrote, "a shoddy unfinished soul" is not prepared to meet God; what would refine that soul, would cleanse it of even the minor blemishes that even the well-lived Christian life would leave?[7] That question preoccupied thinkers throughout the church, and general agreement came that some form of suffering is required to purge the soul of blemishes. An early (seventh-century) story of a protopurgatory in the Irish *Vision of Fursa* suggested that every sin that is not purged on earth must be corrected in heaven, and Fursa's vision of a near-death experience and the accounts (and arguments) of those who followed suggest that this purgation must come through blistering flames.[8] We find Augustine and later Aquinas agreeing that the punishments of purgatory must be fierce and fiery, and the fifteenth-century poet Thomas Hoccleve writing about the pains of a soul in purgatory, agony so intense that if your future soul could call to you from its imprisonment, it would beg you to amend your ways for your own future sake.[9] But our most important understanding of purgatory comes from Dante.

Unlike heaven and hell, which Dante and Milton may have helped us understand but which they hardly invented, Dante's *Purgatorio* follows the development of the doctrine of purgatory by mere decades. Jacques Le Goff notes how the concept of purgatory "benefited from an extraordinary stroke of luck: the poetic genius of Dante," and he then goes on to trace in detail how Dante shaped forever our understanding of this state.[10] Jeffrey Schnapp agrees; despite the power of Dante's *Inferno* and *Paradiso*, he argues that "purgatory is Dante's most original creation." The poet took on the job of imagining purgatory into being, and because of the *Purgatorio*, "Purgatory bears a universally recognized structure" down to this very moment.[11]

For Dante, as for the earlier writers, purgatory was a place of punishment for a set (if unknown) time where one's sins could be purged. It was a place of pain but also one of hope. In the *Purgatorio*, the character

Dante observes how souls advance, slowly, toward the light, their trials endured in the hope of future redemption, as canto 1's invocation suggests: "And what I sing will be that second kingdom, / in which the human soul is cleansed of sin, / becoming worthy of ascent to Heaven."[12]

Unlike in Dante's experience in heaven and hell, the souls in purgatory mark their time with the rhythms of sun, stars, and planets. Here, time matters. "You laggard spirits," Cato castigates Dante and others listening to a singer, "What negligence, what lingering is this? / Quick, to the mountain to cast off the slough / that will not let you see God show himself!"[13] Once on the mountain, the souls being purged must "do their time" on each level before progressing to the next. Since their experience in purgatory is transitory, time for those here is important in ways it never can be in heaven or hell, where time stretches out before the saved and the lost into all eternity. Dante's guide—still Virgil at this point—often speaks of time passing, and prompts them onward. "He who best discerns the worth of time / is most distressed whenever time is lost," he says at one point, and at another he encourages Dante to use their time "more fruitfully."[14] It is a reminder that however painful the time in purgatory, however it may seem to stretch, time for souls in purgatory is finite, and when each has been purified it will at last be fit for heaven.

Thus, as in the popular religious imagination, Dante understands purgatory to be similar to hell yet in other ways a reversal of it. Hell and purgatory are similar in that in both souls are subjected to punishment, but they are a mirror image of each other in that punishment's duration—the souls in purgatory will endure their testing for a season, but those in Hell will be subject to it through all eternity—and in its purpose—the souls in purgatory are being purged and cleansed for heaven, not simply punished for their sins on earth. The mountain of purgatory is formed by the earth Satan displaced in his fall from heaven; both literally and metaphorically, purgatory is the result of the fall. Hell is a city where one presses downward for egress, whereas purgatory is a city where one passes through punishments but ever upward toward heaven.

Still, the sinners in Dante's account are being purged by punishments, and as in *Inferno*, he assigns contrepasso punishments to fit each individual sin dramatically: the proud are crushed under stones, the slothful are forced to run and run, the lustful are tormented with actual flames. But the landscape of *Purgatorio*, on the whole, seems less dark and painful, less fraught with torture and terror than many other versions of purgatory. Demons constitute the work force in purgatory in many visions and theological texts, but Dante places radiant angels on each of the seven cornices. Instead of experiencing the individual torment found in many purgatory narratives, souls in Dante's purgatory sing hymns together and together share the suffering apportioned. However, as thoughtful and beautiful a purgatory as Dante created, the idea of a dark and frightening purgatory persisted. It was probably too valuable to the church as an incentive to assist those suffering in purgatory and as a spur to good behavior in this life to relinquish, even in the face of Dante's masterpiece.

A nineteenth-century Jesuit text, *Purgatory Surveyed*, which translates and updates a French study from 1625, admonishes us to imagine purgatory in these most frightening terms: "You must, then, conceive Purgatory to be a vast, darksome and hideous chaos, full of fire and flames, in which the souls are kept close prisoners until they have fully satisfied for all their misdemeanours, according to the estimate of Divine justice." Those prisoners are devoured by flame, suffer torments that surpass all the agonies of mortal life, and are "lodged in the very suburbs of hell" (probably in substandard housing).[15] In these accounts purgatory seems all but identical to hell, and as with narratives of hell itself, clearly intended to alter the behavior of people in this life by warning them about the possible lives to come.

Not all narratives of purgatory contain a burning fire, of course, but even such a thoroughgoing modern Anglican as C. S. Lewis (beloved of American evangelical Christians who reject purgatory) had a sense that a process of purgation was necessary for redemption, and that it would involve some sort of suffering. Although there is some disagreement among Lewis devotees, he seems to have believed in purgatory: "Our souls *demand* Purgatory, don't they?" he asked. Would the sinner whose clothes and body reek (literally or metaphorically) really expect to walk into heaven without being cleansed first, even if grace operates? Certainly not; we would demand to be purified first.[16]

In his *Letters to Malcolm, Chiefly on Prayer*, Lewis wrote on the necessity of suffering in whatever serves as purgatory:

> I assume that the process of purification will normally involve suffering. Partly from tradition; partly because most real good that has been done me in this life has involved it. But I don't think the suffering is the purpose of the purgation. I can well believe that people neither much worse nor much better than I will suffer less than I or more....The treatment given will be the one required, whether it hurts little or much.[17]

From the early fathers, then, to twentieth-century Protestants and all the way to the present, purgatory has in popular religious thought been a place of pain where one's impurities are burned away. According to these understandings, Paul J. Griffiths writes, hell and purgatory alike "are simply places of torment."[18] So what function does purgatory—and stories of purgatory—serve if the place is indistinguishable from hell? The primary difference, both theologically and in artistic representations, seems to be this: hell is torment unending; purgatory is torment with an expiration date.

In art and literature, purgatory may look like hell and feel like hell, and experts agree that the soul being purified suffers beyond any earthly pain. But at some point, the punishment ends. Stephen Greenblatt notes in his study of purgatory in the Renaissance imagination that religious art often depicts hell and purgatory identically, with only tiny representational differences: "The principal device is to reproduce the traditional imagery of Hell but to add an image of rescue."[19] Thus in illustrations of purgatory a tormented soul might climb out of a boiling cauldron, or an angel offer a rescue from billowing flames, and in stories, characters might suffer all the pains of hell but ultimately be delivered of them. We might need to return to those stories we considered as representative of hell to reassess precisely how they function. The last chapter discussed *The Shawshank Redemption* as a journey into hell, but we could also say that in Red's part of the story, Shawshank Prison might be read as purgatory. Hellish though it might be, ultimately Red departs it a changed man. For Sandra Bullock's character in *Gravity*, likewise, her frozen hell offers an escape hatch so ultimately it is a tale shaped like purgatory.

We also looked at Gotham City as hell, for it certainly seems to be intentionally and consistently represented as such, and here we find some interesting narrative problems. In the ongoing Batman metanarrative, of course, Bruce Wayne will never be rescued from Gotham. Batman will always be in hell to contest against the powers of darkness. But in the movie *The Dark Knight Rises*, Bruce/Batman actually escapes the cleansing atomic fire at the movie's end and becomes a new man. He falls in love and retires from crime fighting. We can certainly read Gotham City in the conclusion to Christopher Nolan's Batman trilogy (if not in the larger mythos) as a tale of purgatory, since in this version of the story our hero is at last free of his torments, free of his pain, and actually filled with joy.

What makes a story smack of purgatory instead of hell is that its suffering is finite—and that, in most of our stories, their characters emerge changed and even redeemed. Unlike the Beatles' "Eleanor Rigby," where despite suffering, "no one was saved," generally our stories of purgatory show us a test passed successfully. The Old Testament story of Job again offers a narrative model for us in this regard, although it is more ambiguous than many of our secular narratives (Is Job rescued?), and of course it precedes Christianity and the development of an actual doctrine of purgatory.

As we saw earlier in the book, in the opening scene of the book of Job Satan, or the accuser, shows up at a roll call of the heavenly beings, and God asks him to note the righteous Job:

> The LORD said to Satan, "Have you considered my servant Job? There is no one like him on the earth, a blameless and upright man who fears God and turns away from evil." Then Satan answered the LORD, "Does Job fear God for nothing? Have you not put a fence around him and his house and all that he has, on every side? You have blessed the work of his hands, and his possessions have increased in the land. But stretch out your hand now, and touch all that he has, and he will curse you to your face."[20]

In the story that follows, God allows Satan to test Job, taking away all he possesses, killing his children, and racking his body with pain. Job suffers, but he passes Satan's test. He never curses God. That test, however, is followed by another: Job's friends, amateur theologians that they are, attempt to get him to admit to some secret sin that would explain why he has been afflicted. Job continues to maintain his righteousness and that somehow, although he does not understand it, God is just. At last, God ends this story with a final test. He speaks to Job out of a whirlwind and says, essentially, "My ways are not for such as you to understand or question," and Job responds with deep humility: "I had heard of you by the hearing of the ear, / but now my eye sees you; / therefore I despise myself, / and repent in dust and ashes."[21] While it seems unfair to us that Job should suffer all this and the humiliation of prostrating himself in dust and ashes, it is a theophany—an encounter with God—we are talking about, and it is the final test he must pass.

Job is not destroyed by his pain, by his theological dispute with his friends, or by his direct encounter with God. All of that is finite, and in an ending that may not be original to the story but has the virtue of at least being dramatically fitting, Job is rewarded for his faithfulness by receiving new possessions, new servants, and new children. He has, in the story's terms, passed the test. This story is understood to be the great ordeal of Job's life, the test that once passed, prepared him for all that came next. It also at least suggests that he lives happily ever after ("And Job died, old and full of days") without other purgatories to endure, although this is not necessarily true of our own lives, or of many of the narratives we consume.[22] The ongoing nature of our lives and of many ongoing stories, as the Batman example suggests, militates against our understanding of a single purgatory narrative as definitive.

BIG PURGATORIES, SMALL CHANGES

"Someone put me out my misery
I can't do this again."

"GROUNDHOG DAY," EMINEM

Lost notwithstanding, continuing stories often put their characters through hell only to return them to something like the status quo. Until recently, we did not expect to see dramatic changes in long-running characters, did not expect that they would ever be substantially altered, grow old, or die. *Lost, Mad Men, Breaking Bad, The Walking Dead, House of Cards,* and *Game of Thrones* have helped to reshape our understanding of TV narratives as always essentially unchanging, but many of our most popular shows continue for year after year and the characters don't change too much. This is for both artistic and commercial reasons: producers don't want to alter successful formulas.

Unlike movies and novels, which screenwriter-director Shane Black says chronicle the single most important things ever to happen to their characters, ongoing or serial narratives are instead marked by what TV writers and producers call "deep characterization," the sense that a TV show is, say, a two-hundred-hour narrative, not a series of twenty-two- or forty-five-minute stories in each of which characters experience a radical movement.[23] This also applies to comics and other serial storytelling, including the trend to stretch films into multipart epics, and to the ongoing story of our lives. But even if characters generally experience only incremental change, it is common to see them go through some sort of purgatorial testing and be altered by it, if only in a small way or for a short time.

On *House, M.D.*, for example, pain and its determinative functions were foregrounded throughout the show's eight-year run. Gregory House (Hugh Laurie), the irascible title character, suffers constant pain in his leg and has become addicted to Vicodin as a result. In the Emmy-, Humanitas-, and Peabody-winning first-season episode "Three Stories," we learn that before the action of the show began, House refused to allow his leg to be amputated, and so today he walks with a cane and suffers almost continuously, or would if not for his reliance on medication.

House's physical pain is symbolic of other pain. House suffers constant emotional pain from the loss of his mobility and the ways his handicap visibly sets him apart ("They all assume I'm a patient because of this cane," House complains in the pilot episode; "People don't want a sick doctor"), from the loss of his girlfriend, Stacy Warner (Sela Ward), and from the loss of who knows what else on top of that. He is also, I would venture, in substantial spiritual pain. What else would make a man so unhappy, so difficult to be around?

Whatever has shaped him, this much is certain: House is misanthropic and touchy and has cut himself off from almost all human contact except the occasional tendentious conversation with his one friend, the oncologist James Wilson (Robert Sean Leonard). A popular trope on the show from that pilot episode is that House doesn't want to talk to patients, even his own patients. But even in the midst of all this suffering, sometimes his pain becomes exponentially larger. On numerous occasions, House's various pains spike and he experiences some sort of change or transformation, however momentary, as a result. Within the limits of serial drama formulas, *House, M.D.*'s writers employ the narrative of purgatorial pain and testing on multiple occasions to show their main character moving through the major moments in his life and emerging in some way different.

In the two-part finale to the fourth season, House calls Wilson to come fetch him because he has once again had too much to drink. Wilson's girlfriend, Amber (Anne Dudek), comes instead. On the way home, their bus is involved in an accident and Amber dies. House is wracked with guilt over her death and especially over the pain he has caused Wilson. When his addiction to Vicodin causes him to begin hallucinating (in the fifth season), his subconscious coughs up Amber as his constant companion, the painful situation rendered even more painful by her presence. He attempts to give up Vicodin cold turkey so he can lose the hallucinations and continue to practice medicine, but in the season finale, it is revealed that what we and he had thought to be a happy ending—successful detoxification and a long-desired love affair with hospital administrator Lisa Cuddy (Lisa Edelstein)—was nothing but more hallucinations. If House is ever going to be better, he will need more than medication and delusion: he will have to go through something difficult and real.

So in "Broken," the opening episode of the sixth season, House checks into drug rehabilitation at the Mayfield Psychiatric Hospital, a residential program where he endures the agony of detoxification for real this time. He also suffers the emotional pain of being away from the job that gives him meaning and worth, and the emotional pain of misdiagnosing Stevie (Derek Richardson), a mentally ill fellow patient he likes, resulting in the man's serious injury. He endures the emotional pain of realizing that his attending psychiatrist, Dr. Nolan (Andre Braugher), is right in his scathing dismissal ("You don't care about getting out. You don't care about him. You don't even care about the truth. You don't care about anything, House"), and the emotional pain of falling in love with Lydia (Franka Potente), a married woman who ultimately can never be his. The result of all this pain is House's realization that he can't go on the way he has since his injury and subsequent addiction.

After Dr. Nolan charges him with not even caring about the truth, House makes what feels like a groundbreaking admission: "I need help." And by the end of the episode, he has taken some small steps in response to his suffering. Dr. Nolan quantifies them, when he tells House that he'll write a letter recommending he be reinstated as a physician: "Well, two things just happened. You got hurt, which means you connected to someone else strongly enough to miss them. And more important…you recognized the pain and came to talk to me, instead of hiding from it in the Vicodin bottle. The fact that you're hurting and you came here, the fact that you're taking your meds and we're talking right now." House is released from this purgatory having passed through the flames. He boards a bus (the side of which sports an ad: "Prepare to Succeed!"), and in an echo of the final scene of *The Graduate*, he takes a seat in the back of the bus as it pulls away from Mayfield. Unlike the deeply ambivalent ending of *The Graduate*, however, the ending of "Broken" allows House a rare smile. For the moment, he emerges from his trial as something healthier, more whole.

The finale of the series, "Everybody Dies," shows House moving into a new life in an even more substantial fashion. House fakes his own death in a burning house, his sins metaphorically being consumed by literal flames. Like the plane-wrecked characters in *Lost*, at the end of the series he steps out of the life he's lived up until now and begins again. Now he is going to be something else, starting with becoming the friend he has never really been, embarking on a road trip with Wilson, who now is dying of cancer. Unlike the season 4 episode "Under My Skin," in which the hallucinated version of Amber offers a chilling rendition of the song "Enjoy Yourself," the series ends its run with a feel-good version of the same song rendered by Louis Prima. Because of the hell we know he has been through, the words resonate: "Enjoy yourself, enjoy yourself / It's later than you think." Because (as House tells Wilson) he is now dead, he can be whatever he wants to be. In the season 5 episode that followed Amber's death, House spoke these words: "Almost dying changes nothing; dying changes everything." Perhaps now—finally—that House, M.D., is dead, Gregory House can complete his evolution into a new and better person.

Despite the static nature of his seventy-year-old character, Batman also offers us stories of painful testing that aim to remake him into something new, or as new as the narrative will permit. Given the conventions of superhero comics, Batman foils a villain's plot virtually every time he leaves the Batcave, but some of those plots have a longer-lasting influence on Bruce Wayne, Batman, or both. A prime example is the 2013 Joker story "Death of the Family" (the title is a reference to the Joker's murder of Robin/Jason Todd in the late 1980s in "Death in the Family"), which ran for twenty-three issues across nine Batman-connected titles. In "Death of the Family," the Joker (like Satan in the story of Job) takes it upon himself to test an upright man by taking away everything that matters to him, although being a Joker, he does it for reasons that don't make much sense to us.

Joker believes that Batman's love for his "family"—the various Robins, Batgirl, Alfred, and Catwoman—has made Batman weak, has subverted the grim crime fighter he has battled for decades, and has changed him into something feeble. The Joker has taken a year away from Gotham City, a year in which he has watched and planned. Now he puts his plan into action. He creates a purgatory experience for Batman in order to burn away all the things that seem to him to prevent Batman from being Batman, in the hope that a new Caped Crusader will emerge cleansed, renewed, the dangerous Dark Knight with whom the Joker loves to play.

In the course of the story, Joker tells each of the various characters something like what he says to Catwoman during their battle: "Stop loving The Bat. Your love makes him weak. Be his greatest adversary and he'll be stronger."[24] Without his human encumbrances, the Joker believes, Batman will be a greater nemesis; we know, however, that without them the Batman would be no better than the Joker, a psychopath cut off from humanity. As a way of dramatically (and gruesomely) illustrating what he's shooting for, the Joker has cut off his own face, making his already tenuous connection to humanity even more so. Through this storyline, he appears with his face held on like a mask, as though this stark white human face covers something completely inhuman—and that is what he hopes to make Batman as well.

While designating "Death of the Family" a purgatory story, we must also acknowledge some of its strange twists and turns. The Joker is a malevolent God who creates the mad funhouse through which he runs Batman and his allies, just as he does in *Batman: The Killing Joke* (a classic storyline referenced in *Death of the Family*) when Batman and Commissioner Gordon are subjected to the ordeal of a deadly trial in a literal carnival. The Joker's desire to purge Batman of his so-called weakness and the "sin" of surrounding himself with those he cares about is diabolical, not divine. But the element of testing and purification, however twisted, rings true to the purgatorial narrative, as does the limited time frame and Batman's eventual escape into some new form of life. Purgatory is often imagined to be populated by devilish tormentors; the Joker is a properly devilish character (especially now that he has removed his face), and his purgatory functions in the same hellish fashion: the Joker imposes punishment and pain, leading (he hopes) to Batman's transformation.

At the close of the story, Joker has gathered the family together and they are all captive: Batman (Bruce Wayne), and his friends and family: all four past and present Robins (Dick Grayson, Jason Todd, Bruce Wayne's adopted son, Tim Drake, and his biological son, Damian), Batgirl (Barbara Gordon), and Bruce Wayne's butler, Alfred. They sit, heavily bandaged, at a banquet table, where the Joker purports to have sliced off their faces and prepares to serve them that main course. Batman certainly believes the Joker capable of such a gruesome act: "I hate nothing more on this earth than you, Joker." The Joker responds with more emotional and spiritual testing, asking why, in that case, time and time again Batman has allowed the Joker to live, to escape to kill again, to torture, when he might have put an end to his threat and saved the lives and sanity of those he seems to *love* more than anything on earth.[25]

In capturing, punishing, and yes, finally killing Batman's friends and family, Joker says, he is doing what Batman most needs: returning him to his solo roots. "They make you everything you want to forget that you are," Joker tells him, "everything you're afraid of. And you were afraid, when you took them in....But you don't have to be afraid anymore, don't you see? Because Joker's here now! He carried out your orders, and he's here to rescue you, finally, from this nightmare."[26] Purgatory, as artistic depictions suggest, seems identical to hell, but with the element of rescue. The world does indeed shift for Batman and his family, but not in a uniformly positive direction, as the purgatory narrative would ordinarily have us hope. Of course this dark time of punishment and trial has been ordained not by a loving God but by a madman, so the result is not a transcendent experience leading to redemption, but a desperate attempt by Batman to emerge from this purgatory still clinging to the status quo.

That Batman does escape and is still Batman is something to celebrate, but it feels in many ways a dark victory. Perhaps part of the darkness is Batman's, however, for this story does not always end in this fashion even in other superhero narratives. In "Born Again," a similar storyline written by Frank Miller in *Daredevil* in the 1980s, the criminal mastermind known as the Kingpin tries to destroy the life of Daredevil (Matt Murdock), and his test is so extreme that our hope for Daredevil (as it was for Batman) is simply that he somehow claw his way free without losing his life, his soul, or his honor. To remain a hero when tested by flame and suffering can be a significant victory, but "Born Again" offers us more. One of the individual issues in this storyline is actually called "Purgatory," and "Born Again" seems a more positive rendering of the purgatory narrative and thus one worth exploring.

The villainous Kingpin is the criminal mastermind who drives the plot. He uncovers Matt Murdock's secret—that he is Daredevil—and he attempts to destroy Matt in every way possible. For a time, Matt loses his mind, so gripped by paranoia that he beats up not only a mugger on a subway but the cop who tries to intervene. The Kingpin's grip on Matt's "civilian" life is relentless: he causes Matt to lose his girl-friend, his home, his livelihood as a lawyer, and his reputation. When Matt confronts the mountainous villain himself, he is beaten within an inch of his life and left for dead. So far, this story has the ring only of hellish punishment to it. What makes it a slightly more hopeful version of a purgatorial narrative is that Matt is found by his mother, Maggie (who left his father and is now a nun, Sister Maggie), and she ministers to his body and soul, praying that he will live and recover to serve the light:

> *His soul is troubled. But it is a good man's soul, my Lord.*
> *He needs only to be shown your way. Then he will rise as your own*
>   *and bring light to this poisoned city. He will be as a spear of*
>   *lightning in your hand, my Lord.*
> *If I am to be punished for past sins, so be it.*
> *If I am to be cast into Hell, so be it.*
> *But spare him.*
> *So many need him.*
> *Hear my plea.*[27]

Like Batman, Matt survives, but in the chapter of the story that immediately follows Maggie's impassioned prayer Matt begins to recover in mind and soul as well as body, to become again the hero we expect him to be. Daredevil ultimately defeats the Kingpin without killing him. Using his wits instead of simply his fists, he turns the tables on the Kingpin, robbing him of his business and his reputation. In a graphic novel filled with shadows and darkness, the final panel of the book is a full page set in bright sunshine: Matt and his love interest, Karen Page (a fan favorite who has recovered from the hell of heroin addiction in her own purgatorial storyline), walk though the streets of Hell's Kitchen in broad daylight. In "Born Again," the Kingpin's plan does not leave the hero scrambling to try and hold onto his old life, as the Joker's plan did with Batman. It results in a character who has had his old life burned away and who has arisen from the ashes a stronger and more resilient hero. It's not too much to argue that Daredevil is now the spear of lightning in the hand of God that his mother prayed might emerge as a result of his ordeal.

The purgatory model is one that can be central to dramatic narrative. Many stories we love are based on testing and trial that lead to redemption, whether that story is the trials of the journey home in *The Odyssey*, the perilous twists and turns of love in *Pride and Prejudice*, or the battle with mental illness in *Silver Linings Playbook*. Many such stories are primarily about the suffering and growth of their characters—whether Greg House, Katniss Everdeen, Harry Potter, Elizabeth Bennet, or Batman—but some not only impel us to identify with the suffering of the characters but by their nature cause us actually to take on suffering ourselves. We'll consider two variations on the story of ennobling suffering before we turn to other popular notions of purgatory. *Schindler's List* and *12 Years a Slave*, movies about hideous systematic evil and human responses to it, both suggest powerful new ways to understand the function of stories of purgatory.

Schindler's List (adapted from the nonfiction novel by Thomas Keneally, which functions in a very similar fashion), begins with a prayer, as hands are seen lighting a Sabbath candle. We are then introduced to a succession of images of a man who will turn out to be the charming swindler Oskar Schindler (Liam Neeson). Schindler dresses with confidence; however, the way he pulls currency out of various nooks and crannies in his hotel room argues that here is a person who looks impressive, but who has gathered up every last cent he possesses to go out and put on a good show. At last, he affixes a gold Nazi swastika pin to his lapel; now he is dressed up and ready to go to work.

The story of *Schindler's List* is quickly told: Oskar is a German capitalist who hopes to grow rich in Poland after the Nazi takeover. But for reasons never fully explained, he develops a sympathy for the suffering Polish Jews and begins saving them from the concentration camps by hiring them for his factory. Along the way, he faces a chilling bureaucracy that intends to condemn the Jews, the suspicion of the Jews themselves, and an inhuman SS camp commandant, Amon Goeth (Ralph Fiennes), who enjoys killing Jews by his own hand. Why might we say this story functions as a purgatory narrative instead of a story of hell? *Schindler's List* is a tale of trials and sufferings for the Jewish characters and it tests the ingenuity and courage of Schindler himself. But the hell of Nazi rule is temporary, and as in all good tales of purgatory, the characters prepare to emerge changed as the story leads us through the end of World War II, when Schindler, as a Nazi war profiteer, must flee the Jewish friends he has cared for throughout the story.

Schindler has been altered in this story (at least as he is depicted in Steven Zaillian's script). As he prepares to flee, Itzhak Stern (Ben Kingsley) and the other Jewish leaders give him a gold ring "like a wedding ring," and he has a splashy breakdown in which he laments how his selfishness and his love of creature comforts kept him from doing more:

SCHINDLER (to himself)
       I could've got more...if I'd just...I don't
       know, if I'd just...I could've got more...

STERN   Oskar, there are twelve hundred people who
       are alive because of you. Look at them.
       He can't.

SCHINDLER If I'd made more money...I threw away
       so much money, you have no idea.
       If I'd just...

STERN   There will be generations because of
       what you did.

SCHINDLER I didn't do enough.

STERN   You did so much.

Schindler starts to lose it, the tears coming. Stern, too. The look on Schindler's face as his eyes sweep across the faces of the workers is one of apology, begging them to forgive him for not doing more.[28]

Oskar is certainly no longer the ardent capitalist we met at the beginning of the movie, and the ripping of the swastika from his lapel is a sign of that reversal. The Jewish characters too undergo a transformation in the course of the story. They go from being frightened victims to masters of their own fate, and ultimately to Oskar Schindler's caretakers instead of vice versa. The novel, too, sees this giving of the golden ring as a profound event and relates how in the moment in which Oskar solemnly put it on his finger, "Though nobody quite understood it, it was the moment in which they became themselves again, in which Oskar Schindler became dependent on gifts of theirs."[29]

But just as the main characters undergo change because of their trials, something similar happens to the viewers of *Schindler's List*, something that has the potential to be transformational. Few films are so difficult to watch; if I am a representative example (and I have been studying and writing about films for thirty years), *Schindler's List* is a movie of such power and emotion that I can scarcely bear to view it again in its entirety—and rarely have. The casual cruelty and pervasive racism, and harrowing scenes like Amon Goeth's casual murders, the clearing of the Krakow Ghetto, and the arrival of the Schindler women in the showers at Auschwitz, make the film impossible to look away from—but almost impossible to watch.

It may be that stories like this insist on taking their readers or viewers through a transformative journey as they are offering their characters a chance to transcend their own purgatories. A recent film that seems to support this theory is *12 Years a Slave*, British director Steve McQueen's adaptation of the slave narrative of free black man Solomon Northrup, who was kidnapped in 1841 and taken to be sold in the slave market in New Orleans. While this most assuredly resembles a story of purgatory such as we have come to understand it—Solomon is tried and tested, beaten and starved, overworked and in every way treated as though he has had the misfortune to find himself in hell—the title itself indicates that Solomon's sojourn in that realm has limits. However, although we have been primed by the purgatory archetype to expect redemption, it cannot be said that Solomon experiences anything so positive as a result of his time in purgatory. There is no happy ending to his story except that he receives his freedom and becomes again his own master; indeed, as in the case of Job, no happy ending could ever really compensate him for the suffering he has experienced. Solomon returns home to find that his family has moved on, and the slaveholders in the story neither repent of their individual cruelty nor of their complicity in a corrupt and corrupting system. Unlike other films that offer similar emotional and spiritual challenges to their viewers (*Schindler's List, Magnolia, Apocalypse Now, A Clockwork Orange*), *12 Years a Slave* uses the purgatory ordeal not to shape the future narrative of its main characters, but to shape the future narratives of those who encounter the story—the audience.

My son Chandler and I saw *12 Years a Slave* with an audience of hundreds of avid filmgoers when it was showcased at the 2013 Austin Film Festival. The experience of watching the movie reminded me of the experience of watching *Schindler's List*. Sometimes I had to turn away from the screen; sometimes the scenes of rape, violence, and torture brought tears to my eyes; sometimes the sheer hopelessness of Solomon's plight led me to remind myself, "twelve years. The poster says it's only twelve years." The audience was silent and intensely focused throughout the film, and when the closing credits were over, many of us sat silent, stunned by what we had witnessed. It was as if we had been more than witnesses; it felt as though we too had undergone suffering on the way to whatever meaning we might now find. It was clearly not simply another movie, for me or for any of the others in attendance. Although the movie was beautifully made, it was certainly not enjoyable.

So why did we watch, why did I recommend it so strongly to others, why am I still thinking about it? Perhaps because, in some small way, I have been transformed by that experience of suffering in ways that the movie's characters could never be. Wesley Morris argues that the reason to see this film goes beyond the usual arguments about enjoyment and aesthetics. In this film, he says, viewers have "an opportunity to bear witness to grim matters of fact. No one goes to the movies to feel this upset."[30] But perhaps we are moved to the point of change as a result of the story we've seen, and we will never be quite the same again.

Besides the many literary and cultural narratives of punishment and struggle that can bring about a transformational change, a move toward heaven if you will, we should also consider one last popular narrative of purgatory: the idea that purgatory is a sort of limbo in which humans are frozen in place in a life that seems interminable as we seek to figure it out—or find some way out of it. Finally, we'll look at what we lose when we try to set aside all narratives of purgatory as wrongheaded or irrelevant—in addition to a great story pattern, we lose the recognition that we are linked together, the living and the dead.

OTHER USES OF PURGATORY

"Those that are dead are not dead
They're just living in my head."

"42," COLDPLAY

We have been exploring stories that illustrate the notion of purgatory as a place of dramatic suffering that refines the characters who suffer. Popular usage of the term *purgatory*, however, rarely suggests a dramatic locale marked by purifying flame. Instead it might be more like molasses, or the suburbs. In popular culture, the narrative of purgatory is often invoked when a character is stuck in place, working out his or her own salvation (one hopes) through a succession of all-but-identical days, months, or years. Like Phil Connor in *Groundhog Day* who wakes up every morning to an identical day, like the characters cast away in limbo in *Inception*, like the narrator in the Beatles' "A Day in the Life" who has his usual cup of tea, reads the newspaper after getting out of bed, and looks up to realize he is late, again, like the members of the chorus in T. S. Eliot's *Murder in the Cathedral*, who keep repeating that they are "living and partly living," characters in literature and popular culture may find purgatory less a place of elaborate suffering (although every story must have some sort of suffering and conflict) than a place like ordinary life where they are stuck trying again and again until they get it right.

This narrative of purgatory, as Griffiths notes, may look more similar to earthly life than to either hell or heaven. It has a familiar narrative: things go on as they always have, but after a while, at last, things change.[31] Heaven and hell are final destinations. Purgatory is like Paradise City in the movie *Defending Your Life*, where souls hang around awaiting the verdicts of their hearings—up or down (or, perhaps more properly in that film, onward or back). Or it is a train station like King's Cross Station at the close of *Harry Potter and the Deathly Hallows* where you may sit for a while talking with Dumbledore, but you could eventually get on a train and depart for places beyond. In this iteration, purgatory is not some burning suburb of hell, but more like a gray vista of life passing off into the unknown distance, something like the gray town described as the starting point for C. S. Lewis's ghosts in *The Great Divorce*. That gray town is purgatory if you depart it at some point; it only becomes hell if you remain there forever.

The film *Groundhog Day* is often taught in courses on religion and literature. Some have remarked on its lesson of Buddhist mindfulness— be where you are, completely—but it also works as a popular story of purgatory, of doing one's time like the souls in Dante's *Purgatorio*, of repeating the same thing over and over again until (as in Eminem's "Groundhog Day") it becomes a misery. As a result of his sins (pride, lechery, gluttony, and selfishness almost to the point of solipsism) weatherman Phil Connor wakes up every morning in a place he doesn't want to be. He goes through the motions of his day: he meets an old friend from high school, broadcasts a news report on Groundhog Day as everyone waits to see if winter is going to continue for another six weeks, eats, attempts to sleep with attractive women, goes to bed. Then he wakes up, groans, and does it all over again.

Screenwriter Danny Rubin describes the movie in this way: Phil is repeating the same day over and over, the worst day of his life, but ultimately it has the potential to be the best day if he can simply persevere and live into it. It's a story about how, given enough time, even the worst of us can change: "Here's a guy who is having a terrible day and he's kind of a horrible person and just through the act of repetition and paying attention and remembering, he is forced to change who he is, and by changing who he is, he changes the life that he experiences [and] the world around him."[32] The suffering is mundane but real, the change certain. *Groundhog Day* offers ice, snow, and insurance salesmen instead of flames or demons, but it still clearly operates as a story of purgatory.

At the beginning, Phil is a certain kind of person, cocksure, egotistical, insufferable. In the middle of the story, he is in despair, facing the gray forever, one day after another, no hope of change. Then he realizes that the only hope of change is to change himself. In *Groundhog Day*'s final act, we see Phil rescuing a carload of ladies with a flat tire, catching an ungrateful boy who daily slips and falls from a tree (and never thanks him for rescuing him), learning to play the keyboard with art and flair, and speaking to Rita, his producer and the woman he has grown to love, with the honesty and affection he has never been capable of before. Even those things he cannot change—the town's old homeless man still dies, every day, however Phil tries to care for him—have become a part of the compassionate new Phil, who serves and loves and demonstrates his transformed nature on one perfect day: which turns out to be his last day in purgatory.

The next morning he wakes up, Rita at his side, transformed and launched into the next phase of his life, whatever that will be.

Had he remained caught in Groundhog Day forever, that would have been hell. But since he escapes Punxsutawney, Pennsylvania, changed and ready for heaven, that almost-eternal Groundhog Day is ultimately revealed as purgatory. Many of our secular purgatory narratives follow this model: we work out our salvation through long-repeated days that lead to hard-won self-knowledge so that we are ultimately freed to new life. My colleague Roger Olson sees this immersion in instructive repetition as a kind of purgatory that even Protestants could perhaps accept as possible and necessary. Imagine, he says, those great saints—Augustine, Calvin, Zwingli—who were filled with theological insight, and yet also displayed great hatred toward those who disagreed with them or in their eyes transgressed against the true faith. Can we imagine Calvin in hell? Certainly not. But, he asks, can we imagine Christian haters being taken immediately into heaven? That too seems unjust. "What's wrong with a Protestant believing that upon entering paradise a hate-filled Christian leader of the past who condoned torture and even murder (I don't know what else to call [Calvin's] burning of Servetus even though it was technically legal—we still call 'legal' stonings of women in certain countries 'murder') has to take a spiritually therapeutic 'class' of correction?"[33] As Olson suggests, there is room in even a Protestant understanding for the idea that all Christians—even famous ones—die imperfect, and thus require an infusion of holiness before they can be admitted into the presence of the Most Holy. Perhaps the experience is boot camp, perhaps holy companionship, but in any case, this purgatory isn't about searing flames and agony so much as it's about change, growth, and wisdom earned over a span of days, months, or years. Through the process of time rather than through explicit suffering, some individuals who need to be purged of their past attitudes and beliefs might be brought closer to perfection. That's a narrative that also works for the living.

My second novel, *Cycling*, was originally published in 2003. It is a book whose main character, Brad Cannon, doesn't know he's in purgatory, but actually is. He seeks to avoid suffering—he's already experienced enough of that—and instead repeats his days as exactly as he can to avoid any conflict or drama. The point of the story became clearer and clearer to me as I wrote: Brad's understandable desire to avoid suffering is fruitless, and his attempt to cycle through the same events over and over again—lunch with the same friends or relatives at the same places on the same days, the same grueling thirty-five-mile bike ride every time he goes out—nonetheless leads to unexpected drama and to growth. Against his will, even though he is trying to walk in his same footsteps day after day after day, Brad changes. Many stories—most of them, thankfully, with more dramatic conflict than the one I wrote—show an unwilling character caught in a cycle of pain or loneliness or boredom who at last emerges from that repetition with self-knowledge and even a possibility of redemption.

Often that cycle of the repetitive everydayness is broken by a stranger who comes to town and cracks open a closed system. (Writer and filmmaker Bill Witliff once said in my hearing that there are only two stories: a person goes on a journey and a stranger comes to town.) In *Stranger Than Fiction*, Will Farrell plays an IRS agent who knows exactly how many steps he takes to the bus stop and counts how many times he brushes his teeth, but a strange voice that only he can hear (Emma Thompson) and a beautiful baker he is assigned to audit (Maggie Gyllenhaal) turn him outward from his closed-in world. In *Silver Linings Playbook*, Pat (Bradley Cooper) has decided that he is going to pursue his jogging, his reading, his tenuous hold on sanity, and his estranged wife. Then he meets Tiffany (Jennifer Lawrence), and she begins to break into his patterned life. She begins to jog with him, to follow football with him, and ultimately she helps him emerge from his limited patterns, just as he helps her.

The purgatory model can function in any kind of storytelling, in any genre. In Marilynne Robinson's Pulitzer Prize–winning literary novel *Gilead*, pastor John Ames has lived a sad and very small life until a young woman walks in the back door of his church and he falls in love with her in his old age. Although he continues to pastor a small church in a small town, to structure his life around Sunday sermons, now he is accompanied on this journey by one who loves and admires him, who gives him a beloved child, and who helps him see past another long-established pattern in his life, his tendency to denigrate his godson John Boughton, who admittedly has piled up more than a few negatives on his ledger.

Gilead is a story set in small-town Iowa and its most dramatic present action is a conversation at a bus stop. Some might regard these stories of everyday purgatory as dull or repetitive, but stories of the everyday can also be filled with conflict and dramatic interest. It depends on the character and the type of story. Superhero comics have a metanarrative: Batman goes out every night and fights a supervillain, and for him, that is his humdrum routine. A day in which he had a conversation at a bus stop would actually be novel. One of the best new comics, *Hawk-eye*, features the Avengers' archer in his off hours, and almost every story somewhere includes the words "Okay...this looks bad" and displays Hawkeye/Clint Barton covered in bandages from the minor and major injuries he incurs in the course of his average day.

For Hawkeye, whether he is falling off a building, being shot at by criminals, or opening the door to three women who are now or have been his love interests, each day looks the same at its heart: Hawkeye expects bad things to happen to him, and they do. So it is that by issue 3, we find the splash page featuring Hawkeye, his sidekick, Kate, and some unnamed and naked woman together in a hot rod being shot at by four cars full of goons with semiautomatic weapons. "Okay," Hawkeye says, "This looks bad. Really really bad. But believe it or not, it's only the third most-terrible idea I've had today and today I have had exactly nine terrible ideas."[34] Hawkeye's Groundhog Day is more filled with violent action than Phil Connor's, but what makes Hawkeye learn what little he seems to learn comes in the course of the everyday, the sheer volume of events. As he looks back over his recent life at one point and realizes he has screwed up, he expresses it to Kate like this: "Look at me. Look at all these things I've done."[35]

The exotic can also feel like everyday. I'll close by considering *In Bruges*, where hitmen Ray (Colin Ferrell) and Ken (Brendan Gleeson) find themselves in hiding after Ray accidentally kills a child in their bungled last job. Their boss, Harry (Ralph Fiennes), orders them to hide for two weeks in Bruges and wait until the furor blows over; later, Harry will order Ken to kill Ray because he believes that the murder of a child, even by accident, cannot be forgiven. Ray is not, shall we say, overwhelmingly happy to be in Bruges, and the thought of spending two weeks there makes it seem like eternity, even with the sightseeing. Maybe especially with the sightseeing. Ken is enamored with Bruges, but the script repeatedly has Ray looking at him blankly as he expresses his enthusiasm for the history and architecture. "Ken!" he complains early on, "It's all just old buildings!"[36]

While in Bruges seeing the sights, Ray and Ken visit the Groeningemuseum, where the camera dwells lovingly on the fifteenth-century

Last Judgment triptych attributed to Hieronymus Bosch. The painting becomes an important symbolic touchstone for the film. Ray asks Ken what the painting is about, and Ken tells him it is "the final day on earth when mankind will be judged for all the crimes they have committed. And that." The day of judgment is when it is decided who gets into heaven and who gets into hell.

"And what's the other place?" Ray asks.

"Purgatory."

"Purgatory. Purgatory's kind of like the in-betweeny one. 'You weren't *really* shit, but you weren't all that great either.'"

Seeing the painting jolts Ray into introspection. He asks Ken if he actually believes in the afterlife; this question emerges because he can't get over shooting the boy, that it will never go away. He suggests he might kill himself (and does attempt to later in the film) but he says "and even *then* it mightn't go away," referring back to the last judgment. Purgatory would actually be an improvement for Ray at this point, and perhaps he too hopes for the in-betweeny state, that he's not a terrible person even though he's done some terrible things. Ken too addresses this thought, and perhaps he attempts to make Ray feel better by describing his own situation: "And at the same time, at the same time as trying to lead a good life, I have to reconcile that with the fact that, yes, I have killed people. Not many people. And most of them were not very nice people. Apart from one person."

Ray's guilt—and his dislike of Bruges—are clear purgatorial elements in a movie that invites you to think of Ray as being in purgatory. When Harry comes to Bruges to punish Ken for refusing to kill Ray, Ken argues that despite his sins, there is still a chance for Ray's redemption: "The boy has the capacity to change. The boy has the capacity to do something decent with his life." When Ray wants to kill himself, Ken stops him, takes away his gun, and advises him, "Just go away somewhere, get out of this business, and try to do something good. You're not going to help anybody dead. You're not going to bring that boy back. But you might save the next one." And while Harry disagrees with him—violently—Ken continues to offer Ray every chance to change, ultimately giving his own life to save him from Harry's judgment.

The movie ends with Ray having been shot by Harry and being carted away into an ambulance, but it seems very possible that he might survive. Certainly Ray repeats that hope several times, which marks a dramatic change from the person who wanted to kill himself. And if he does survive, he says, he will go back to London, to the mother of the boy he shot, and tell her what he did, and ask her forgiveness, and accept whatever punishment she deems just. Prison? Death? At least he wouldn't be in Bruges.

"Maybe that's what Hell is," he thinks as they carry him through the falling snow to the ambulance. An eternity spent in Bruges.

But if Ray escapes Bruges—and more, escapes Bruges in one piece, and with the clarity to do the right thing, with the capacity to do something decent with his life—then hard as it was to be in Bruges, it truly was only purgatory, and maybe the best thing that could ever happen to a sinner.

The last dimension of the purgatory narrative that we will explore has been largely forgotten by non-Catholics but appears occasionally in literature and popular culture, the idea that the souls in purgatory remain connected to the believers on earth, and that the prayers of the living can have an effect on the fate of the dead. Jesuit writer W. H. Anderson speaks in *Purgatory Surveyed* about all the pains of purgatory, of fire and worm, of distance from God. By beginning with this rhetorical sally he wants to spur his readers to consider the importance of compassion toward those souls in between. Given the horrors of their present condition, could there be, he asks, "a more eminent or prudent act of fraternal charity, than to help the souls in Purgatory?"[37] Since these creatures are suffering the greatest torments imaginable, there can be no greater Christian love than to ease their pain and shorten their passage. The living have a responsibility to the dead in this final purgatory narrative, and the connection between the living and the dead is closer than we imagine.

Sometimes that connection seems to flow only from the dead to the living; I have discussed ghosts and other departed forms reaching out to the living, and the many scenes in the Harry Potter saga where Harry has a kind of contact with his departed friends and family. The theology of purgatory, however, suggests the converse: we are reaching out to the dead and having some sort of influence on their existence, rather than the other way round. A concrete way to understand this theological point is to consider how in video and console shooter games like *Gears of War* and *Call of Duty*, players in a cooperative game may be hit and fall to the ground. Although "dead," they remain aware of what is going on, but without the help of their teammates, they will be unable to return to the game. But a sympathetic teammate—or a pragmatic one—can rush over to a "dead" soldier and revive him or her; the connection between the living and the dead doesn't get much more tangible than this. The narrative of purgatory likewise suggests that the living can be of good service to the dead, that the dead still exist somewhere, and that their stories are not yet fully told.

In "The New Man in Charge," the *Lost* epilogue released with the DVD set, Benjamin Linus tells Walt (Malcolm David Kelley) that he needs to come back to the island because he has work to do, starting with his father.

"My father's dead," Walt responds. Normally this would be our stopping point, but Ben knows, as do we, that on *Lost*, being dead is no bar to continued evolution.

"Doesn't mean you can't help him," Ben says, and at last Walt agrees to return to the island to do just this in a story that presumably we will never know, since the show no longer exists. But in the world of *Lost*, particularly in its final season, it seems entirely possible that living characters might be helping dead characters through the purgatory of the Sideways world (I say "might" because the actual chronology of who is dead when is a bit confusing; as a character says in the series' finale, here there is no such thing as "now"). The motto of the series from its first episodes was "Live together or die alone," and ultimately that focus on the necessity of community doesn't stop even at death. During the sixth season, Desmond (Henry Ian Cusick) continually brings people who had known each other on the island back together in the Sideways world in hopes of spurring their recollections of each other. Desmond and his allies are reaching out to the dead to help them move on to their next phase, and that assistance—even in a world where meaningful coincidence reigns—is essential. In "The End," Jack's father, Christian Shephard (no subtlety to the symbolism there, as Kate notes), puts it succinctly when he and Jack speak at the church in the series' final scene. Inside the sanctuary, the dead all await the chance to move on, and before that happens, Christian sums up the series' message and its final take on purgatory: "No one does it alone, Jack. You needed all of them. And they needed you."

The dead need the help of the living? It may not be a belief we live out in our active theologies, but we certainly understand it through stories we consume. We have seen it in *Hamlet*, where the ghost asks Hamlet to act for justice in this world so that he can move on from his purgatorial torments in the next. We have seen it in the movie *Ghost*, where Oda Mae (the medium played by Whoopi Goldberg) finds herself in just such a helping position in respect to Patrick Swayze's suffering ghost Sam. His torment isn't flame, as in the religious narrative of purgatory, but all the same he remains in between, unable to move ahead while his murder goes unavenged and his beloved Molly remains in danger. He cannot affect the outcome of the story directly, cannot be seen or heard by anyone except Oda Mae, and without her intercession on his behalf, his torment would be extended. But like the faithful Christians who pray for the poor souls in purgatory, Oda Mae takes on the responsibility of aiding Sam. She goes to Molly and tries to explain the situation: "He's stuck, that's what it is. He's in between worlds." She helps Molly understand where Sam is now, and why he can't move on and, in the process, helps make it possible for him to complete his time in between and take the next step into the blinding light.

In the classic comedy *Topper*, stodgy banker Cosmo Topper (Roland Young) also has friends in between worlds, his deceased clients the fun-loving Kerbys (Cary Grant and Constance Bennett), and they need his help if they're going to move on. As we learned in the section on haunting, he needs them as well; if he's ever going to truly live, he has something to learn from the dead. The movie's original trailer describes the persona of actor Roland Young as America's leading Babbitt (a reference to Sinclair Lewis's now-forgotten novel about the emptiness of middle-class respectability), and the ghostly Kerbys—ironically—must "convert" Topper from boring banker to fun-loving playboy if they're ever to be angels. They are ultimately successful: Topper affirms toward the end of the film, "I want to drink, I want to dance, I want to sing. I want to have fun," and when, like the Kerbys, he suffers a car accident that might be fatal, he announces, "I'll get up in the morning and have some fun." But unlike them, he returns to his earthly existence, where his wife demonstrates her own willingness to be less stodgy and more sexy, and the Kerbys move on happily to heaven.

We have seen this relationship between living and dead—with a twist—in the movie *The Sixth Sense*, where the psychiatrist Malcolm believes he is helping the psychic boy Cole, who sees dead people, to become better adjusted to his strange and frightening talent. He encourages Cole not to recoil from the specters he encounters, but to engage them. Maybe, he tells Cole, "These people…People that died and are still hanging around. Maybe they weren't ready to go…. Maybe they wake up that morning thinking they have a thousand things to do and a thousand days left to do them in…. And then all of a sudden, it's all taken away. No one asked them. It's just gone."

Although he doesn't know it yet (and neither do we), Malcolm is in this very state; he has been dead since the opening scene, and although he is here to help Cole, clearly Cole also has a role to play for him.

"What do those ghosts want when they talk to you?" Malcolm asks Cole.

"Just help," Cole says, and together they agree that Cole will try to help those lost souls, the dead who can't move on. Together, they bring justice for a little girl poisoned by her mother and prevent the same terrible fate for her little sister. Cole is able to reconcile his mother with her mother, even though the latter has been dead for years:

COLE   She said, you came to her where
       they buried her. Asked her a
       question…. She said the answer is
       "Everyday."
       Lynn covers her face with her hands. The tears roll out
       through her fingers.

COLE   (whispers)
        What did you ask?
        Beat. Lynn looks at her son. She barely gets the words out.
LYNN   (crying)
        Do I make her proud?[38]

And at last, we realize in retrospect that Cole has always known that Malcolm was dead, was one of those ghosts who doesn't know that he's a ghost. Even before the two of them agreed that Cole's job was to help the dead move on, he was doing that very thing, acting as a patient to the ghost of a doctor who needed to know that he had done something right before he could pass on to what's next, who needed to know how to communicate his love to the wife who might have feared she came second to his work. Cole's intercession in Malcolm's story makes it possible for Malcolm too to find peace.

In this, as in other narratives, the relationship between living and dead is fluid, not fixed. The dead need the living; the living need the dead. And all of us need to work through the trials and tribulations of our story in order to reach a happy ending, whatever that possibility might be.

CONCLUSION

The Dead and the Living

"We are all going, McKinley said to his wife, and we sure are. There's your labyrinth of suffering. We are all going. Find your way out of that maze."
JOHN GREEN, *LOOKING FOR ALASKA*

I closed with narratives of purgatory, because, in the end, this theologically challenging myth turns out to be in some ways our most relevant realm of the afterlife. The purgatory story plays itself out in three ways in our literature and culture. Purgatory is perhaps our primal plot, in which through suffering and trial human beings reach the fates they are supposed to achieve. A popular version of purgatory also tells us that if we persevere through our everyday tasks, we will eventually attain wisdom. And purgatory, as we saw, suggests that the link between the living and the dead is tangible, and that we still may have a part to play in the fates of those who are no longer with us.

When we consider this last belief about the connectedness of the saints in this world and in the next, we come full circle to the book's original concerns about the line between life and death. Why is it that we are drawn to stories about how the living can affect the fates of the dead—and vice versa? Perhaps because, as I have postulated all along, these stories of life, death, and what comes after life are among our most important stories and among the most powerful ways that we wrestle with these big questions.

Am I gone after I die? Not if my soul survives in some state, or my memory prompts people to pray for me.

Will people get what they deserve in the next life, if not in this one? Perhaps, if our stories of heaven and hell—and purgatory—have some truth to them. But we also are comforted to know that grace and mercy operate in our stories as well, that people who may not deserve a second chance get one, and that people who suffer have the opportunity to escape that labyrinth of suffering.

In "City of Blinding Lights," which U2 performed at President Barack Obama's inauguration concert on January 18, 2009, we hear how blessings come "not just for the ones who kneel / Luckily." The narrative of ultimate grace that we categorize as stories of purgatory offers us hope that whatever our own circumstances, whatever troubles assail us, perhaps we too may find blessings in the end. At the close of *House, M.D.*, an unhappy man finds joy and lives into the friendship he has never before valued properly. At the close of the Hunger Games saga, despite everything she has lost and all she has gone through, Katniss receives the essential grace of love and family. At the close of *Harry Potter and the Deathly Hallows*, those characters we love (and even some who have been enemies like Draco Malfoy) are granted entry to community and acceptance. At the close of *Lost*, we are encouraged to note that even Benjamin Linus (also once a series villain) is offered the chance to move on with redeemed souls Jack, Kate, and John Locke, although he declines, saying there is still further work to do on himself—more purgation.

I agreed to write this book above all because I was intrigued by our attraction to these purgatory narratives. Why, my editor, Cynthia Read, asked me, do most American Christians disclaim any theological belief in purgatory, but hope and pray that all our stories of suffering will ultimately end in redemption, mercy, and grace? After spending two years thinking and writing about these stories, I believe the reason is that redemption, mercy, and grace are the things we most desire, and in the turmoil of our own lives and loves we are drawn to stories in which suffering is redeemed, in which even those who were not quite good enough—which is almost all of us—may still be granted amazing grace in the end.

In *The Great Divorce*, one ghostly character tells another, "You weren't a decent man and you didn't do your best. We none of us were and we none of us did. Lord bless you, it doesn't matter."[1] The story of purgatory, formally abandoned as it may be by many in their faith lives, is alive and well in the culture, and it continues to argue that beyond this existence and these current difficulties or boredoms is another reality, even more beautiful, even more full of possibility. And who doesn't hope for that?

All of these stories of heaven, hell, purgatory, and their inhabitants serve vital purposes for us. They assure us that the universe has ultimate meaning and order, even if we may not perceive it around us in our everyday lives. They tell us that our existence is not limited to this one, that one way or another we will go on. They require us to live with compassion and justice now, for someday there will be compassion for those who suffered in this life, and justice for those who made others suffer. They offer us the possibility that we are not completely responsible for the evil we do, since outside agents may have forced our hands—and may be more able to do the good we want to do, since outside agents may accompany and even guard us along our paths. Stories of the afterlife offer us this and more, whether we encounter them in our faith traditions or in our stories, art, and music, and without them, our lives in this existence would be impoverished.

I hope this exploration of how we understand the afterlife has encouraged you to think—and prompted you to rethink—and that it has helped to explain the lasting dramatic power of many of our favorite stories. Above all, I hope that because of our conscious consideration of these stories, your suffering might be shorter and your wisdom increased, in this life and whatever might follow it.

APPENDIX

Literary and Cultural Works Consulted

While no study of literature and culture could claim to be encyclopedic, I wanted to indicate the wide scope of materials considered for this study of the afterlife in literature and culture. I chose these works based on their popularity, their critical acclaim, or their applicability to the topic—and often a combination of all three. I tried to skew toward more contemporary work, since little of it will have been studied seriously elsewhere. In some cases in *Entertaining Judgment* I've done a close reading of these texts; in others, I've relied on my thirty years of study—and forty years as a consumer—of literature and culture to summarize a work's cogent qualities and themes in support of a larger point. I haven't identified every scrap of material culture, every advertisement, and every piece of pop art I encountered while I worked, but this appendix should give you a good sense of the database for this study—and offer resources for your own further engagement.

Art and Architecture
Blake, William, works in various media (engravings, watercolor, oil, tempera), 1784–1827
Bosch, Hieronymous, various works, ca. 1480–1515
Burne-Jones, Edward, works in various media (oil, tempera, watercolor, stained glass, tapestry), 1861–98
Butcher, Samuel J., Precious Moments Chapel, 1989
Dore, Gustave, *The Bible*, 1866; *Paradise Lost*, 1866; *The Vision of Hell*, 1866; *Il Purgatorio ed il Paradiso*, 1867
Kinkade, Thomas, "Heaven on Earth," 2004
Rossetti, Dante Gabriel, *Ecce Ancilla Domini!/The Annunciation*, 1849–50

Comics and Graphic Novels

30 Days of Night, 2002
Action Comics, 1938–
American Vampire, 2010–
Batman, 1940–
Batman: Hush, 2005
Batman: The Killing Joke, 1988
Batman: Year One, 1987
Blade, 1973–
Buffy the Vampire Slayer, 1998–
*Captain Britain and MI-13: Vampire
    State,* 2009
Constantine, 2013
Daredevil, 1964–
The Dark Knight Returns, 1986
Death of the New Gods, 2008
Detective Comics, 1937–
Fantastic Four, 1961–
Final Crisis, 2009
From Hell, 1999
A Game of Thrones, 2011–14
Green Arrow, 2000–
Green Arrow: Quiver, 2000
Hawkeye, 2012–
Hellblazer, 1988–2013
Hellboy, 1994–
Hellboy in Hell, 2012–
I, Vampire, 2011–13
The Joker: Death of the Family, 2013
Justice League, 1960–
Lucifer, 2000–6
Marvel Zombies, 2005–
New Gods, 1971–95
Planetary/Batman: Night on Earth, 2003
The Sandman, 1989–96
Smallville, 2012–
Superman for All Seasons, 1999
Superman: Secret Origin, 2010
Thor, 1962–
Vampirella, 1969–

The Walking Dead, 2003–
X-Men, 1963–

Computer and Console Games

The Arkham series, 2009–13
Baldur's Gate: Shadows of Amn,
    2000 and 2013
The BioShock series, 2007–13
Bloodrayne, 2002
The Call of Duty series, 2003–
Dark, 2013
The Diablo series, 1996–2012
The Gears of Wars series, 2006–
Legacy of Kain, 1996
The Walking Dead, 2012

Drama

Abbott, George, et al., *Damn Yankees,*
    1955
Eliot, T. S., *Murder in the Cathedral,*
    1935
Goethe, Johann Wolfgang von, *Faust,*
    1808
Kushner, Tony, *Angels in America,*
    1993
Marlowe, Christopher, *The Tragicall
    History of the Life and Death of
    Doctor Faustus,* 1592
Sartre, Jean-Paul, *No Exit,* 1944
Schönberg, Claude-Michel, et al.,
    Les Miserables, 1980
Shakespeare, William, *Hamlet,* ca.
    1599–1602
———, *The Merchant of Venice,* ca.
    1596–98
———, *Twelfth Night; or, What You
    Will,* ca. 1602
The Wakefield Master, *The Second
    Shepherd's Play,* ca. 1475
The York Mystery Plays, ca. 1376–1569

Movies

12 Years a Slave, 2013
28 Days Later, 2002
30 Days of Night, 2007
127 Hours, 2010
The Alien films, 1979–97
Angels in the Outfield, 1951, 1994
Apocalypse Now, 1979
Bambi, 1942
Batman, 1989
Batman Begins, 2005
Batman Returns, 1992
Battle Royale, 2000
Battle Royale II, 2003
Bedazzled, 1967, 2000
Big Night, 1996
Bill and Ted's Bogus Journey, 1991
The Bishop's Wife, 1947
Blade, 1998
Blade II, 2002
Blade: Trinity, 2004
Blue Lagoon, 1980
Bram Stoker's Dracula, 1992
Buffy the Vampire Slayer, 1992
The Cabin in the Woods, 2012
Charlie and the Chocolate Factory,
   2005
Children of Men, 2006
City of Angels, 1998
A Clockwork Orange, 1971
The Conjuring, 2013
Constantine, 2005
Cool Hand Luke, 1967
The Corpse Bride, 2005
Crash, 2004
Damn Yankees, 1958
Daredevil, 2003
The Dark Knight, 2008
The Dark Knight Rises, 2012
Dark Shadows, 2012

Dawn of the Dead, 1978
Death Race, 2008
DeathRace, 2000, 1975
Defending Your Life, 1991
The Devil and Daniel Webster, 1941
The Devil's Advocate, 1997
Dracula, 1931
Elysium, 2013
The Exorcist, 1973
Field of Dreams, 1989
From Dusk Till Dawn, 1996
From Hell, 2001
The Hunger Games series, 2012–15
Ghost, 1990
Gladiator, 2000
The Godfather, 1972
The Godfather II, 1974
Gravity, 2013
Groundhog Day, 1993
The Harry Potter saga, 2001–11
Heaven Can Wait, 1978
Hellboy, 2004
Hellboy II: The Golden Army, 2008
Here Comes Mr. Jordan, 1941
The Hunger Games series, 2012–
I Am Legend, 2007
In Bruges, 2008
Inception, 2010
Interview with the Vampire, 1994
It's a Wonderful Life, 1946
Kill Bill, Parts 1 and 2, 2002–3
Les Miserables, 2012
The Lion King, 1994
Love at First Bite, 1979
The Lovely Bones, 2010
Magnolia, 1999
Man of Steel, 2013
The Matrix trilogy, 1999–2003
Michael, 1996
Night of the Living Dead, 1968

Nosferatu, 1922

O Brother, Where Art Thou, 2000

Only Lovers Left Alive, 2013

The Passion of the Christ, 2004

Pet Sematary, 1989

The Pirates of the Caribbean: At World's End, 2007

The Pirates of the Caribbean: Dead Man's Chest, 2006

Places in the Heart, 1984

The Preacher's Wife, 1996

Prometheus, 2012

The Prophecy series, 1995–2005

Pulp Fiction, 1994

The Return of the King, 2003

Rosemary's Baby, 1968

The Running Man, 1987

Shaun of the Dead, 2004

The Shawshank Redemption, 1994

The Silence of the Lambs, 1990

Silver Linings Playbook, 2012

The Sixth Sense, 1999

South Park: Bigger, Longer, and Uncut, 1999

Star Wars: A New Hope, 1977

Stranger Than Fiction, 2006

Superman, 1978

Superman Returns, 2006

Titanic, 1997

Topper, 1937

Tree of Life, 2011

The Twilight Saga, 2008–12

Underworld, 2003

Unforgiven, 1992

Vampire Hunter D, 1985

What Dreams May Come, 1998

Wings of Desire, 1988

Wonder Bar, 1934

World War Z, 2013

Music

Aerosmith, "Angel," 1988

Bad English, "Ghost in Your Heart," 1989

Baker, Anita, "Angel," 1983

The Beatles, "A Day in the Life," 1967

———, "Eleanor Rigby," 1966

Benatar, Pat, "Hell Is for Children," 1980

Carlisle, Belinda, "Heaven Is a Place on Earth," 1987

Cloud Cult, *Love*, 2013

Cohn, Marc, "Saving the Best for Last," 1991

Coldplay, *Mylo Xyloto*, 2011

———, *Viva la Vida*, 2008

Cole, Keyshia, "Sent from Heaven," 2008

Def Leppard, "Heaven Is," 1992

Diddy (Sean Combs), "Angels," 2010

Diddy-Dirty Money with Skylar Gray, "Coming Home," 2010

Dinning, Mark, "Teen Angel," 1959

Dion, Celine, and R. Kelly, "I'm Your Angel," 1998

Eminem, "Groundhog Day," 2013

Fabares, Shelly, "Johnny Angel," 1962

Fleetwood Mac, "My Little Demon," 1997

Foreigner, "I'll Get Even with You," 1980

Hill, Lauryn, "To Zion," 1998

Judas Priest, "Angel," 2005

LL Cool J, "Paradise," 2003

Los Lonely Boys, "Heaven," 2004

MacLachlan, Sarah, "Angel," 1997

Madonna, "Angel," 1985

Mann, Aimee, *Magnolia: Music from the Motion Picture*, 1999

Morrison, Van, "A Town Called Paradise," 1986

Mozart, Wolfgang Amadeus, *The Magic Flute*, 1791

Mumford and Sons, *Babel*, 2012

My Chemical Romance, *The Black Parade*, 2006

OK Go, "Oh Lately It's So Quiet," 2006

Orbison, Roy, "In Dreams," 1963

Presley, Elvis, "Angel," 1962

Seal, "Future Love Paradise," 1991

Snoop Dog, "Eyez Closed," 2011

Tavares, "Heaven Must Be Missing an Angel," 1976

Thompson Square, "I Can't Outrun You," 2013

2Pac Shakur, "I Wonder If Heaven's Got a Ghetto," 1997

U2, "City of Blinding Lights," 2004

———, "If God Will Send His Angels," 1990

Various, "Angel of the Morning," 1968–

Various, "Cheek to Cheek," 1935–

Various, "Crossroads Blues," 1937–

Various, "I'll Fly Away," 1929–

Various, "Let Zion in Her Beauty Rise," 1835

Various, "Marching to Zion," 1707–

Various, "My Blue Heaven," 1928–

Various, "Woodstock," 1969

Various, "Zion's Hill," ca. nineteenth century–

Wilson, Ann, and Mike Reno, "Almost Paradise," 1984

Nonfiction

Burpo, Todd, and Lynn Vincent, *Heaven Is for Real: A Little Boy's Astounding Story of His Trip to Heaven and Back,* 2010

Byrne, Lorna, *Angels in My Hair*, 2011

Coulter, Ann, *Demonic: How the Liberal Mob Is Endangering America*, 2011

Eadie, Betty J., *Embraced by the Light*, 1992

Gilbert, Elizabeth, *Eat, Pray, Love*, 2006

Graham, Billy, *Angels: God's Secret Agents*, 1976

Moody, Raymond, *Life after Life*, 1975

Rawlings, Maurice S., *Beyond Death's Door*, 1985

Sports Illustrated, 1972–

Virtue, Doreen, *How to Hear Your Angels*, 2007

Novels and Short Fiction

Albom, Mitch, *The First Phone Call from Heaven*, 2013

———, *The Five People You Meet in Heaven*, 2007

Atkinson, Kate, *Life after Life*, 2013

Atwood, Margaret, *The Blind Assassin*, 2001

Austen, Jane, and Seth Grahame-Smith, *Pride and Prejudice and Zombies*, 2009

Banks, Iain, *Surface Detail*, 2010

Benét, Stephen Vincent, "The Devil and Daniel Webster," 1937

Brooks, Max, *World War Z*, 2006

———, *The Zombie Survival Guide*, 2003

Collins, Suzanne, The Hunger Games series, 2008–10

Cronin, Justin, *The Passage*, 2010

Dickens, Charles, *A Christmas Carol*, 1843

Dostoevsky, Feodor, *The Brothers Karamazov*, 1880

Enger, Leif, *Peace Like a River*, 2001

Garrett, Greg, *Cycling*, 2003 and 2014

Green, John, *The Fault in Our Stars*, 2012

———, *Looking for Alaska*, 2005

Hansen, *Mariette in Ecstasy*, 1991

Harris, Thomas, *Hannibal*, 1999

———, *Red Dragon*, 1981

———, *The Silence of the Lambs*, 1988

Herbert, Frank, et al., The Dune series, 1965–

Hilton, James, *Shangri-La*, 1933

King, Stephen, *Pet Sematary*, 1983

———, *Rita Hayworth and the Shawshank Redemption, Different Seasons*, 1982

———, *Salem's Lot*, 1975

———, *The Stand*, 1978

Jacobs, W. W., "The Monkey's Paw," 1902

James, Henry, "The Jolly Corner," 1908

James, P. D., *Children of Men*, 1992

Joyce, James, *Portrait of the Artist as a Young Man*, 1916

Kostova, Elizabeth, *The Historian*, 2005

Lewis, C. S., The Chronicles of Narnia, 1950–56

———, *The Great Divorce*, 1946

———, *The Last Battle*, 1956

———, The Space Trilogy, 1938–45

Martin, George R. R., A Song of Ice and Fire series, 1991–

Matheson, Richard, *I Am Legend*, 1954

McCarthy, Cormac, *The Road*, 2006

Meyer, Stephanie, The Twilight series, 2005–8

Morrison, Toni, *Beloved*, 1987

O'Connor, Flannery, *Everything That Rises Must Converge*, 1965

Pearson, T. R., *Gospel Hour*, 1991

Percy, Walker, *The Moviegoer*, 1961

Polidori, John William, *The Vampyre*, 1819

Robinson, Marilynne, *Gilead*, 2004

Rowling, J. K., The Harry Potter novels, 1997–2007

———, *The Tales of Beedle the Bard*, 2008

Sebold, Alice, *The Lovely Bones*, 2002

Steinbeck, John, *The Grapes of Wrath*, 1939

Stoker, Bram, *Dracula*, 1897

Takami, Koushun, *Battle Royale*, 1999

Tolkien, J. R. R., *The Hobbit*, 1937

———, *The Lord of the Rings*, 1954–55

Trussoni, Danielle, *Angelology*, 2010

———, *Angelopolis*, 2013

Radio

Pet Sematary, BBC radio serial, 1997

The Rush Limbaugh Show, 1998–

Salem's Lot, BBC radio serial, 1995

Television

Angel, 1999–2004

Angels in America, 2003

The Bachelor, 2002–

The Bachelorette, 2003–5, 2008–

Batman: The Animated Series, 1992–95

Being Human, 2008–13

Breaking Bad, 2008–13

Buffy the Vampire Slayer, 1997–2003

Charmed, 1998–2006
Dancing with the Stars, 2005–
Dark Shadows, 1966–71
Doctor Who, 2005–
Doomsday Bunkers, 2012
Doomsday Preppers, 2012–
Duck Dynasty, 2012–
Fantasy Island, 1978–84
Fear Factor, 2001–6, 2011–12
The Flip Wilson Show, 1970–74
Futurama, 1999–2013
Game of Thrones, 2011–
Hannibal, 2013–
Here Comes Honey Boo Boo, 2012–
House, M. D., 2004–12
Jersey Shore, 2009–12
Lost, 2004–10
Mad Men, 2007–15
The Monkees, 1966–68
Resurrection, 2014–
Salem's Lot, 1979
Sam Kinison: Breaking All the Rules, 1987
The Simpsons, 1989–
Smallville, 2001–11
South Park, 1997–
The Stand, 1994

Strictly Come Dancing, 2004–
Supernatural, 2005–
Survivor, 2000–
Touched by an Angel, 1994–2003
True Blood, 2008–14
The Vampire Diaries, 2009–
The Voice, 2011–
The Walking Dead, 2010–
Wipeout, 2008–

Verse

Barrett Browning, Elizabeth, "The Cry of the Children," 1842
Browning, Robert, "Andrea del Sarto," 1855
Dante, *The Divine Comedy*, ca. 1308–21
Homer, *The Iliad*, ca. eighth century BCE
———, *The Odyssey*, ca. eighth century BCE
Langland, William, *Piers Plowman*, ca. 1367
Milton, John, *Paradise Lost*, 1667
Rilke, Rainer Maria, *Duino Elegies*, 1922
Virgil, *The Aeneid*, 19 BCE

ACKNOWLEDGMENTS

I have been the beneficiary of considerable encouragement and substantial resources during the planning, research, and writing of this book, and it would be at best, ungracious, and at worst, delusional, to allow anyone to believe I wrote this book with only myself to thank. As I suggested in the final chapter, Cynthia Read, my editor at Oxford University Press, was essential to the writing of this book. It is only the purest truth to say that this book would not exist without her enthusiasm for it. Her suggestions of possible texts to consider and her continuous engagement through the process of proposal, research, and writing made the task of working on several books at once (my happy and unhappy fate over the past two years) mostly a happy one. It is a joy to work with a dynamic and talented editor—and with all the professionals at Oxford University Press.

Baylor University, my teaching home for a quarter century, supported this work with a 2012 research leave and with the award of the 2013 Baylor Centennial Professorship. I used the award funds to travel in England, France, and Wales doing research and speaking on this topic, and consulting with theologians, clergy, and consumers of literature and culture about this topic. I am grateful for the continued support of former provost Elizabeth Davis, of my dean, Lee Nordt, and of my department chair, Dianna Vitanza. I was blessed by meaningful conversations with and by the support of my Baylor colleagues Tom Hanks, Hulitt Gloer, and Richard Russell, and by the graduate and undergraduate students from whom I learn daily. I am also indebted to Hulitt Gloer for the use of his cabin at Turtle Creek, outside of Kerrville, Texas, where much of this book was drafted. The gift of solitude was essential to completing a substantial book during a teaching semester. Vanessa Snodgrass located and discussed many of these sources with me during her time as my research assistant, yet another resource Baylor offered me. I am grateful, as always, for all Baylor is and does.

The Episcopal Theological Seminary of the Southwest provides me with an office in Austin as writer in residence that serves as home base for my writing and for my service to the larger church. I am grateful to Dean Cynthia Kittredge and academic dean Scott Bader-Saye for their support, and to them, Anthony Baker, and other faculty and seminarians for talks that had a bearing on the writing of the book. My continued affiliation with the faculty, students, and alumni of the Seminary of the Southwest, where I received my MDiv, is a great blessing to me, and I hope, something positive for them as well.

Gladstone's Library in Wales supported my research by several terms as residential scholar, and the library's warden, Peter Francis, offered counsel and insight on my research and many other topics. So did the ever-changing array of scholars, writers, clergy, and visitors to the library during my visits. My thanks must go to Peter, Chef Alan Hurst, and all the staff of that great institution who feed and take care of their guests as they write and read.

The Lanier Theological Library in Houston, Texas, gave me the run of the library as residential scholar as I finished drafting this book. I am grateful to library director Charles Mickey, head librarian Sharon Cofran, and Susie Brooke, who made my stay effortless, and to Mark Lanier, who built this amazing research center and gave me the keys to the kingdom.

Chris Seay fed and housed me during the final writing of the book at Lanier Library and has been a partner with me on virtually everything I've ever written thanks to our shared affinity for religion and culture. Thanks, Chris, again, for all you are and all you do.

Along with Chris, I am grateful for other friends including Rowan Williams, Tim Ditchfield, and Greg Rickel who discussed this work with me and who supported it from near and far.

Most especially, I give thanks for my family. My boys, Jake and Chandler, helped with the research for this book, sometimes knowingly, and my girls, Lily and Sophie, were instructive in their own ways, although I did not find a way to work *My Little Pony* or *Powerpuff Girls* into these pages. Finally there is my precious wife Jeanie, who makes it possible to balance my lives as husband, father, writer, speaker, teacher, and preacher. Jeanie, you inspire me daily. Thank you for pushing me to go out and accomplish more—and for making home my favorite destination anywhere.

NOTES

INTRODUCTION

1   John Green, *Looking for Alaska* (New York: Penguin, 2005), 100.

2   Lynn Schofield Clark, *From Angels to Aliens: Teenagers, the Media, and the Supernatural* (New York: Oxford University Press, 2003), 160.

3   N. T. Wright, *Surprised by Hope: Rethinking Heaven, the Resurrection, and the Mission of the Church* (New York: HarperOne, 2008), 18.

4   Matthew 12: 32 (NRSV).

5   Wright, *Surprised by Hope*, 18.

6   Stewart M. Hoover, "Religion, Media, and Identity: Theory and Method in Audience Research on Religion and Media," *Mediating Religion: Conversations in Media, Religion and Culture*, ed. Jolyon Mitchell and Sophia Marriage (London: T&T Clark, 2003), 16.

7   Jon Meacham, "Heaven Can't Wait," *Time*, April 16, 2012, accessed at www.time.com/time/magazine/article/0,9171,2111227,00.html.

8   Leah Rozen, "Perspective: A Little Splice of Heaven," *Los Angeles Times*, June 12, 2011, accessed at http://articles.latimes.com/2011/jun/12/entertainment/la-ca-movie-heaven-20110612.

9   Katherine Viner, *Guardian*, August 24, 2002, accessed at http://www.guardian.co.uk/books/2002/aug/24/fiction.features.

10   Alice Sebold, *The Lovely Bones* (London: Picador, 2002), 12.

11   Margaret Atwood, *The Blind Assassin* (London: Virago, 2001), 632.

12   The primary point of Stanley Fish's *Surprised by Sin: The Reader in Paradise Lost* (Cambridge, MA: Harvard University Press, 1998) is that Milton intended for us to be seduced by the energetic and even-noble Satan and then to recognize our mistake and, presumably, to amend our ways.

13   Warren Ellis, *Planetary/Batman: Night on Earth* (New York: DC Comics, 2003), 2.

14   Frank Miller, *The Dark Knight Returns, 1987* (New York: DC Comics, 1997), 8–10.

15 Mike Mignola, "Pancakes," *Hellboy: The Right Hand of Doom* (Milwaukie, OR: Dark Horse Comics, 2004), 12–14.

16 "The Final Purification, or Purgatory," the Catechism of the Catholic Church, accessed at http://www.vatican.va/archive/ENG0015/__P2N.HTM.

17 "Editorial: Clemens in Baseball Purgatory," *Newsday*, June 18, 2012, accessed at http://www.newsday.com/opinion/editorial-clemens-in-baseball-purgatory-1.3790608.

18 Steve Buckley, "Buckley: A-Rod Destined for Baseball Purgatory," *Boston Herald*, November 22, 2013, accessed at http://bostonherald.com/sports/columnists/steve_buckley/2013/11/buckley_a_rod_destined_for_baseball_purgatory.

19 Eileen Marable, "Rockstar Games Traps Cheating Players in Their Own Little Purgatory," *Dvice*, June 15, 2012, accessed at http://dvice.com/archives/2012/06/rockstar-games.php.

20 "A Stock Market in Purgatory," *Albany Times-Union*, June 5, 2012, accessed at http://www.timesunion.com/business/article/A-stock-market-in-purgatory-3611682.php.

21 "Finance in Purgatory," *Economist*, February 15, 2014, 67.

22 "Purgatory," *Lostwiki*, May 31, 2008, accessed at http://www.losttvfans.com/page/Purgatory.

23 Bill Keveney, "Lost in 'Lost,'" *USA Today*, May 10, 2006, accessed at http://usatoday30.usatoday.com/life/television/news/2006-05-09-lost_x.htm.

24 Jeff Jensen, "'Lost': The Final Word," *Entertainment Weekly*, August 6, 2010, accessed at http://www.ew.com/ew/article/0,,20313460_20412951,00.html.

25 Hank Steuver, "Lost or Not, We're Still at Loose Ends," *Washington Post*, May 21, 2010, accessed at http://www.washingtonpost.com/wp-dyn/content/article/2010/05/20/AR2010052003181.html.

26 Henry Taylor, "'Jedi' Religion Most Popular Alternative Faith," *Telegraph*, December 11, 2012, accessed at http://www.telegraph.co.uk/news/religion/9737886/Jedi-religion-most-popular-alternative-faith.html.

27 Matthew Sweet, "Live Like a Time Lord," *Telegraph*, November 23, 2013, R33.

28 Clive Marsh, "On Dealing with What Films Actually Do to People: The Practice and Theory of Film Watching in Theology/Religion and Film," *Reframing Theology and Film: New Focus for an Emerging Discipline*, ed. Robert K. Johnson (Grand Rapids, MI: Baker, 2007), 155.

29 C. S. Lewis, "On Stories," *Essays Presented to Charles Williams*, ed. C. S. Lewis (1947; Grand Rapids, MI: Eerdmans, 1966), 103, 105.

30 Diane Winston, Introduction, *Small Screen, Big Picture: Television and Lived Religion*, ed. Diane Winston (Waco, TX: Baylor University Press, 2009), 6.

31 Jeremy Begbie, Introduction, *Sounding the Depths: Theology through the Arts*, ed. Jeremy Begbie (London: SCM, 2002), 1.

32 Nigel Forde, "The Playwright's Tale," Begbie, *Sounding the Depths*, 63.

CHAPTER ONE

1   The Book of Common Prayer, *Prayerbook and Hymnal* (New York: Church, 1986), 465.

2   William Shakespeare, *Hamlet* 3.3.78–79.

3   Gary Scott Smith, *Heaven in the American Imagination* (Oxford: Oxford University Press, 2011), 196–97.

4   T. R. Pearson, *Gospel Hour* (New York: Avon, 1991), 44.

5   Joseph Harris, "Beowulf's Last Words," *Speculum* 67 (1992): 1.

6   Shakespeare, *Hamlet* 5.2.352–58.

7   Thomas Harris, *The Silence of the Lambs* (New York: St. Martin's, 1989), 347–48.

8   J. R. R. Tolkien, *The Letters of J.R.R. Tolkien*, ed. Humphrey Carpenter (New York: Houghton Mifflin, 2000), 201.

9   Fran Walsh, Philippa Boyens, and Peter Jackson, *The Return of the King*, accessed at http://www.imsdb.com/scripts/Lord-of-the-Rings-Return-of-the-King.html.

10 Leif Enger, *Peace Like a River* (New York: Grove, 2001), 299.

11 Kate Atkinson, *Life after Life* (New York: Reagan Archer, 2013), 7.

12 Psalm 146:3–4 (NRSV).

13 Psalm 90:10 (NRSV).

14 Job 14:1–2, 7–12 (NRSV).

15 Catechism of the Catholic Church 1.2.2.11, 1013, accessed at http://www.vatican.va/archive/ccc_css/archive/catechism/p123a11.htm#1012.

16 "Cloud Cult's 'Love' Channels a Life Tested by Loss," *Morning Edition*, National Public Radio, March 6, 2013, accessed at http://www.npr.org/2013/03/06/173518074/cloud-cults-love-channels-a-life-tested-by-loss.

17 John Green, *The Fault in Our Stars* (New York: Dutton, 2012), 168.

18 J. K. Rowling, *The Tales of Beedle the Bard* (New York: Children's High Level Group, 2008), 78–79.

19 J. K. Rowling, *Harry Potter and the Deathly Hallows* (New York: Scholastic, 2007), 427.

20 Pearson, *Gospel Hour*, 33.

21 Such proscriptions may be found in numerous passages of the Hebrew Testament, including Deuteronomy 18:9–12, Leviticus 19:31, and Isaiah 8:19–22.

22 John Casey, *After Lives: A Guide to Heaven, Hell, and Purgatory* (New York: Oxford University Press, 2009), 17–18.

23 1 Samuel 28:8–20.

24 Matthew 14:25–27 (NRSV). A parallel passage appears in Mark 6:48–50.

25 Luke 24:37 (NRSV).

26 Toni Morrison, *Beloved* (New York: Knopf, 1987), 9.

27 Shakespeare, *Hamlet* 1.1.21–29.

28 Catherine Belsey, "Shakespeare's Sad Tale for Winter: Hamlet and the Tradition of Fireside Ghost Stories," *Shakespeare Quarterly* 61.1 (2010): 2.

29 John Caputo and Gianni Vattimo, *After the Death of God*, ed. Jeffrey W. Robbins (New York: Columbia University Press, 2007), 48.

30 Harold Bloom, *Shakespeare: The Invention of the Human* (New York: Riverhead, 1998), 430.

31 Charles Dickens, *A Christmas Carol* (1843; Oxford: Oxford University Press, 2006), 11, 13–14, 16.

32 Ibid., 12.

33 Ibid., 22–24.

34 Ibid., 80.

35 Henry James, "The Jolly Corner," *Selected Tales*, ed. John Lyon (New York: Penguin, 2001), 555.

36 *Buffy the Vampire Slayer: Season 8*, library ed. vol. 2 (Milwaukie, OR: Dark Horse Books, 2012), 59–60.

37 Bram Stoker, *Dracula* (Oxford: Oxford University Press, 1996), 38.

38 Alexia Elejalde-Ruiz, "The Vampire's Allure," *Chicago Tribune*, April 28, 2012, accessed at http://articles.chicagotribune.com/2012-04-28/ entertainment/ct-prj-0429-vampires-20120428_1_vampire-genre-director-guillermo-del-zombie.

39 Ashley Fetters, "At Its Core, the 'Twilight' Saga Is a Story about _____," *Atlantic*, November 15, 2012, accessed at http://www.theatlantic.com/ entertainment/archive/2012/11/at-its-core-the-twilight-saga-is-a-story-about/ 265328/.

40 See, among other references, Leviticus 3:17 and, from the Qur'an, Al-Ma'ida (5:3) on dietary law, and Leviticus 15:19 and from Sahih Al-Bukhari, vol. 1, book 6, Hadith 303, on menstruation.

41 Polidori's novella emerged from one of the most famous literary gatherings of all time, the ghost story competition at Lake Geneva in 1816, which also produced Mary Shelley's *Frankenstein; or, The Modern Prometheus*.

42 Miles Doyle, "*Twilight*'s Early Light: The Vampire Stories of Charles Nodier," *Fordham Magazine*, December 2009, accessed at http://www .fordham.edu/campus_resources/enewsroom/fordham_magazine/fordham_ online/twilights_early_ligh_73857.asp.

43 Stoker, *Dracula*, 162, 168, 200.

44 Stephen King, *Salem's Lot* (New York: Doubleday, 1975), 169, 321.

45 "Welcome to the Hellmouth," *Buffy the Vampire Slayer*, aired March 10, 1997, WB Network.

46 Stephanie Meyer, *Twilight* (New York: Little, Brown, 2005), 19.

47 1 Corinthians 15:42–44 (NRSV).

48 Justin Martyr, *Dialogue with Trypho,* chapter 124, accessed at http://www.newadvent.org/fathers/01288.htm.

49 Augustine, *Exposition on the Book of Psalms*, Psalm 50, accessed at http://www.newadvent.org/fathers/1801050.htm.

50 Roger E. Olson, *The SCM Press A–Z of Evangelical Theology* (London: SCM Press, 2006), 197.

51 "Chapter 47: Exaltation," *The Church of Jesus Christ of Latter-Day Saints*, accessed at http://www.lds.org/manual/gospel-principles/chapter-47-exaltation?lang=eng.

52 Stephenie Meyer, *New Moon* (New York: Little, Brown, 2008), 526–27.

53 Russell M. Nelson, "Celestial Marriage," *Liahona*, November 2008, accessed at http://www.lds.org/liahona/2008/11/celestial-marriage?lang=eng.

54 Matthew 22:30 (NRSV); Joseph Smith, *Doctrine and Covenants* 131:1–4.

55 Elizabeth Kostova, *The Historian* (New York: Little, Brown, 2005), 172–73.

56 "The Harvest," *Buffy the Vampire Slayer*, aired March 10, 1997, WB Network.

57 "The Prodigal," *Angel*, aired February 22, 2000, WB Network.

58 Mike Mignola, *Hellboy: Wake the Devil* (Milwaukie, OR: Dark Horse Comics, 1997), n.p.

59 Stoker, *Dracula*, 217.

60 King, *Salem's Lot*, 351–52.

61 Max Brooks, "Zombies: Doomsday Attack," *Washington Post*, October 30, 2009, accessed at http://www.washingtonpost.com/wp-dyn/content/discussion/2009/10/30/DI2009103000942.html.

62 Daniel W. Drezner, "How the Zombie Apocalypse Affects Interest Group Politics," *Foreign Policy*, March 11, 2013, accessed at http://drezner.foreignpolicy.com/posts/2013/03/11/how_the_zombie_apocalypse_affects_interest_group_politics; Daniel W. Drezner, "Metaphor of the Living Dead," *Sex, Tech and Rock 'n Roll*: TedX, Binghamton, NY, February 24, 2013, accessed at http://drezner.foreignpolicy.com/posts/2013/03/05/this_is_me_at_tedx_on_zombies?wp_login_redirect=0.

63 "Preparedness 101: Zombie Pandemic," *Centers for Disease Control*, accessed at http://www.cdc.gov/phpr/zombies_novella.htm.

64 Max Brooks, "A Conversation with Max Brooks," *Max Brooks' Zombie World*, accessed at http://www.maxbrookszombieworld.com/.

65   John Gray, *Black Mass: Apocalyptic Religion and the Death of Utopia* (London: Penguin, 2008), 2.

66   Jonathan Kirsch, *A History of the End of the World: How the Most Controversial Book in the Bible Changed the Course of Western Civilization* (New York: HarperOne, 2006), 5.

67   Daniel Wojcik, *The End of the World As We Know It: Faith, Fatalism, and Apocalypse in America* (New York: New York University Press, 1999), 2; Lee Quinby, *Anti-Apocalypse: Exercises in Genealogical Criticism* (Minneapolis: University of Minnesota Press, 1994), ii.

68   Max Brooks, "Zombie Wars," *Washington Post*, October 6, 2006, accessed at http://www.washingtonpost.com/wp-dyn/content/discussion/2006/10/03/DI2006100300686.html.

69   Sam Kinison, *Breaking All the Rules*, HBO, aired April 17, 1987.

70   1 Kings 17:21b–22 (NJB).

71   Jane Austen and Seth Grahame-Smith, *Pride and Prejudice and Zombies* (Philadelphia: Quirk, 2009), 237–38.

72   Kim Paffenroth, *Gospel of the Living Dead: George Romero's Vision of Hell on Earth* (Waco, TX: Baylor University Press, 2006), 10.

73   Adam Chodorow, "Death and Taxes and Zombies," *Iowa Law Review* 98 (2013): 1214.

CHAPTER TWO

1   Alice Azania-Jarvis, "Why Do So Many Celebs Think an Angel Is Watching over Them?" *Daily Mail* July 22, 2013, accessed at http://www.dailymail.co.uk/news/article-2372991/Bond-actress-Gemma-Arterton-Gloria-Hunniford-stars-believe-supernatural-intervention.html#ixzz2ZmafvU9F.

2   Bosley Crowther, "The Bishop's Wife," *New York Times* December 10, 1947, accessed at http://movies.nytimes.com/movie/review?res=9A0DE4DB103CE13BBC4852DFB467838C659EDE.

3   Richard Woods, "Angels," *Encyclopedia of Christianity*, ed. John Bowen (Oxford: Oxford University Press, 2005), 44.

4   "Precious Moments Park and Chapel," preciousmoments.com, accessed at http://www.preciousmoments.com/park-chapel/.

5   Gabriel Fackre, "Angels Seen and Devils Heard," *Theology Today* 51.4 (1994): 345.

6   Joseph Campbell, "Mythological Themes in Creative Literature and Art," *The Mythic Dimension: Selected Essays, 1959–1987*, ed. Antony Van Couvering (San Francisco: HarperSanFrancisco, 1987), 180–82.

7   Fiona MacCarthy, "Wings of Desire," *Guardian*, December 23, 2006, accessed at http://www.guardian.co.uk/artanddesign/2006/dec/23/art.

8 Ibid.

9 Billy Graham, *Angels: Gods Secret Agents* (London: Hodder & Stoughton, 1976), 25–26.

10 Greg Garrett, "Christ Isn't Missing From 'The Voice'—Just the Biblical Jargon," *Huffington Post*, April 24, 2012, accessed at http://www.huffingtonpost.com/greg-garrett/christ-isnt-missing-from-the-voice-bible-translation_b_1435008.html.

11 Catechism of the Catholic Church, accessed at http://www.vatican.va/archive/ccc_css/archive/catechism/p1s2c1p5.htm.

12 A. Leo Oppenheim, *Ancient Mesopotamia: Portrait of a Dead Civilization* (Chicago: University of Chicago Press, 1964), 199.

13 Malcolm Godwin, *Angels: An Endangered Species* (New York: Simon & Schuster, 1990), 13.

14 Psalm 34:7, 91:11 (NRSV).

15 Exodus 3:2, 14:19, 23:20.

16 2 Kings 19:35–37 (NRSV).

17 Genesis 18, 19.

18 Matthew 4:11 (NRSV); Acts 12:11 (NRSV), Acts 5:19–20.

19 Acts 12:23; Revelation 15–16, 12:7–9.

20 Luke 1:11–64; Matthew 1:20 (NRSV).

21 Luke 2:8–14 (NRSV).

22 Acts 8:26; Acts 27:21–26; Revelation 1:1–2 (NRSV).

23 Ayat al-Birr 2:177. Other credal statements from the Qur'an affirming belief in angels may be found in 4:136, 2:285.

24 Qur'an 2:97.

25 Karen Armstrong, *Muhammed: Prophet for Our Time* (London: HarperPress, 2006), 96.

26 Qur'an 32:11.

27 Woods, "Angels," 42.

28 Danielle Trussoni, *Angelology* (New York: Penguin, 2010), 168.

29 D. Densil Morgan, *The SPCK Introduction to Karl Barth* (London: SPCK, 2010), 89.

30 Karl Barth, *Church Dogmatics* 111, 3, 486. Ed. G. W. Bromiley and T. F. Torrance, Trans. G. W. Bromiley (Bellingham, WA: Logos Bible Software, 2004), CD-ROM.

31 Dante, *Paradiso, The Divine Comedy*, cantos 28.16 to 29.145.

32 Helene Wecker, "Cracked," *New York Times*, May 3, 2013, accessed at http://www.nytimes.com/2013/05/05/books/review/angelopolis-by-danielle-trussoni.html.

33 Roger Ebert, "City of Angels," *Chicago Sun-Times*, April 10, 1998, accessed at http://www.rogerebert.com/reviews/city-of-angels-1998.

34 Nancy Gibbs, "Angels Among Us," *Time*, December 27, 1993, accessed at http://www.time.com/time/subscriber/article/0,33009,979893,00.html.

35 David Van Biema, "Guardian Angels Are Here, Say Most Americans," *Time*, September 18, 2008, accessed at http://www.time.com/time/magazine/article/0,9171,979893,00.html#ixzz2ZljsmFbH.

36 John Milton, *Paradise Lost* (Oxford: Oxford University Press, 2005), 2.1033.

37 Ibid., 4.786.

38 Ibid., p. 285.

39 Ibid., 11.349–60.

40 Ibid., 12.557–58.

41 "Angel," *Buffy the Vampire Slayer*, aired April 14, 1997, WB Network.

42 Stephanie Meyer, *Twilight* (New York: Little, Brown, 2005), 56.

43 Godwin, *Angels*, 203.

44 Milton, *Paradise Lost*, 4.790.

45 Ebert, "City of Angels."

46 Matthew 22:30; Genesis 6:2–4.

47 Veronika Bachmann, "The Book of the Watchers (1 Enoch 1-36): An Anti-Mosaic, Non-Mosaic, or Even Pro-Mosaic Writing?" *Journal of Hebrew Scriptures* 11.4 (2011): 15.

48 Rita Kempley, "Wings of Desire," *Washington Post*, July 1, 1988, accessed at http://www.washingtonpost.com/wp-srv/style/longterm/movies/videos/wingsofdesirepg13kempley_a0ca02.htm.

49 "Cinema: The New Pictures," *Time*, December 8, 1947, accessed at http://www.time.com/time/subscriber/article/0,33009,934178-2,00.html.

50 Trussoni, *Angelology*, 272.

51 Danielle Trussoni, *Angelopolis* (New York: Viking, 2013), 5.

52 Ibid., 5.

53 Ibid., 29.

54 Rainer Maria Rilke, "*Duino Elegies: A Bilingual Edition*, trans. Stephen Cohn (Evanston, IL: Northwestern University Press, 1989), 21, 27.

55 "Neil Gaiman: My Top 10 New Classic Monsters," *Entertainment Weekly*, July 23, 2008, accessed at http://www.ew.com/ew/gallery/0,20214359,00.html#20485035.

56 Richard Corliss, "Movies: Caught between Heaven and Hell," *Time*, February 14, 2005, accessed at http://www.time.com/time/magazine/article/0,9171,1027514,00.html#ixzz2cHNpp4IG.

57 Milton, *Paradise Lost*, 1.45, 61, 63.

58 N. T. Wright, *Evil and the Justice of God* (Downers Grove, IL: InterVarsity Press, 2006), 43, 109.

59 Elaine Pagels, *The Origin of Satan* (London: Allen Lane, 1996), xviii.

60 Leszek Kolakowski, "*Mephistopheles: The Devil in the Modern World* by Jeffrey Burton Russell," *Journal of Modern History* 59.4 (1987): 803.

61 Canon One, Twelfth Ecumenical Council: Lateran IV 1215, accessed at http://www.fordham.edu/halsall/basis/lateran4.asp; Number 2851, Catechism of the Catholic Church, accessed at http://www.vatican.va/archive/ENG0015/__PAC.HTM.

62 Adrian Hastings, "Devil," *The Oxford Companion to Christian Thought*, ed. Adrian Hastings, Alistair Mason, and Hugh Pyper (Oxford: Oxford University Press, 2000), 164.

63 Job 1:9–11 (NRSV).

64 John 1:1–9 (NRSV). The Johannine epistles also employ light and darkness as ruling images for this cosmic struggle between good and evil: "If we say that we have fellowship with him while we are walking in darkness, we lie and do not do what is true; but if we walk in the light as he himself is in the light, we have fellowship with one another, and the blood of Jesus his Son cleanses us from all sin" (1 John 1:6–7 [NRSV]).

65 The Book of Common Prayer (London: Everyman's Library, 1999), 95.

66 "Publick Baptism of Infants," 1662 Book of Common Prayer website, accessed at http://www.eskimo.com/~lhowell/bcp1662/baptism/index.html.

67 Joseph Baker, "Who Believes in Religious Evil? An Investigation of Sociological Patterns of Belief in Satan, Hell, and Demons," *Review of Religious Research* 50.2 (2008): 206, 211.

68 Dante, *Inferno*, The Divine Comedy, 34.34–36.

69 Jeff Labrecque, "Hannibal's Mads Mikkelsen: 'Lecter Is the Devil…but I Kind of Like Him,'" *Entertainment Weekly*, April 4, 2013, accessed at http://insidetv.ew.com/2013/04/04/hannibal-mads-mikkelsen/.

70 Christopher Partridge and Eric Christianson, "Introduction: A Brief History of Western Demonology," *The Lure of the Dark Side: Satan and Western Demonology in Popular Culture*, ed. Christopher Partridge and Eric Christianson (London: Equinox, 2009), 13.

71 Mike Mignola, *Hellboy: Wake the Devil* (Milwaukie, OR: Dark Horse Books, 1997), n.p.

72 Mike Mignola, *Hellboy: The Chained Coffin and the Right Hand of Doom* (Milwaukie, OR: Dark Horse Books, 2008), 271.

73 Mignola, *Hellboy: Wake the Devil*, n.p.

CHAPTER THREE

1 Hebrews 12:22–24 (NRSV).

2 Luke 23:43 (NRSV).

3   "China: Guilin," *Sports Illustrated*, February 15, 2013, 76–77.

4   John Steinbeck, *The Grapes of Wrath* (1939; New York: Penguin, 1992), 112.

5   Alexander Pope, *Epistle to Dr. Arbuthnot*, 308, accessed at http://rpo.library
    .utoronto.ca/poems/epistles-several-persons-epistle-dr-arbuthnot.

6   Homer, *The Odyssey*, trans. Robert Fagles (New York: Penguin, 1996),
    4.632–41, p. 142.

7   Walker Percy, *The Moviegoer* (1961; New York: Random House, 1988), 235.

8   "Earthquake near China's Shangri-La Kills at Least 5," news.com.au,
    September 1, 2013, accessed at http://www.news.com.au/world/earthquake-
    near-chinas-shangri-la-kills-at-least-5/story-fndir2ev-1226708359346.

9   Jon Meacham, "Heaven Can't Wait," *Time* April 16, 2012, accessed at www
    .time.com/time/magazine/article/0,9171,2111227,00.html.

10 Gary Scott Smith, *Heaven in the American Imagination* (Oxford: Oxford
    University Press, 2011), 1.

11 Rodney Stark et al., *What Americans Really Believe: New Findings from
    the Baylor Surveys of Religion* (Waco, TX: Baylor University Press, 2008),
    69–73.

12 Robert Browning, "Andrea del Sarto," accessed at http://www.poetryfoundation
    .org/poem/173001.

13 Facebook message, September 15, 2013.

14 John Milton, *Paradise Lost* (Oxford: Oxford University Press, 2005), 4.56–64.

15 N. T. Wright, *Surprised by Hope: Rethinking Heaven, the Resurrection, and
    the Mission of the Church* (New York: HarperOne, 2008), 18.

16 John 14:2–3 (NRSV).

17 Meacham, "Heaven Can't Wait."

18 Frederick Buechner, *The Magnificent Defeat* (1966; San Francisco:
    HarperSanFrancisco, 1985), 91.

19 Flannery O'Connor, "Revelation," *Everything That Rises Must Converge*
    (New York: Farar, Straus, and Giroux, 1965), 217.

20 1 Corinthians 13:1–6 (NRSV).

21 Ben Child, "Sean Penn on *The Tree of Life*: 'Terry Never Managed to
    Explain It Clearly,'" *Guardian*, August 22, 2011, accessed at http://www
    .theguardian.com/film/filmblog/2011/aug/22/sean-penn-tree-of-life.

22 J. K. Rowling, *Harry Potter and the Sorcerer's Stone* (New York: Scholastic,
    1998), 213–14.

23 "Rowling Answers 10 Questions about Harry," *Time*, December 19, 2007,
    accessed at http://content.time.com/time/specials/2007/personoftheyear/
    article/0,28804,1690753_1695388_1695569,00.html.

24 J. K. Rowling, *Harry Potter and the Deathly Hallows* (New York: Scholastic,
    2007), 698–99.

25   Ibid., 700.

26   Ibid., 758.

27   Shawn Adler, "'Harry Potter' Author J. K. Rowling Opens Up about Books' Christian Imagery," *MTV News*, October 17, 2007, accessed at http://www .mtv.com/news/articles/1572107/jk-rowling-talks-about-christian-imagery .jhtml.

28   Rowling, *Harry Potter and the Deathly Hallows*, 759.

29   Facebook message, September 13, 2013.

30   Basil, *On the Holy Spirit*, 9.23, accessed at http://www.newadvent.org/ fathers/3203.htm.

31   Augustine, "Exposition on Psalm 145," 3, accessed at http://www.newadvent .org/fathers/1801145.htm.

32   Rowan Williams, *The Lion's World: A Journey into the Heart of Narnia* (New York: Oxford University Press, 2012), 115.

33   C. S. Lewis, *The Last Battle* (1956; New York: HarperCollins, 1994), 193.

34   Williams, *The Lion's World*, 117.

35   Leif Enger, *Peace Like a River* (New York: Grove, 2001), 300, 302.

36   Ibid., 300.

37   Ibid., 303.

38   Leah Rozen, "Perspective: A Little Splice of Heaven," *Los Angeles Times* June 12, 2011, accessed at http://articles.latimes.com/2011/jun/12/ entertainment/la-ca-movie-heaven-20110612.

39   Milton, *Paradise Lost*, 4.690.

40   Facebook message, September 15, 2013.

41   *Eat, Pray, Love, Rotten Tomatoes*, accessed at http://www.rottentomatoes .com/m/eat_pray_love/.

42   Barbara Fisher, "Short Takes," *Boston Globe*, February 19, 2006, accessed at http://www.boston.com/ae/books/articles/2006/02/19/short_takes_boston_ globe/

43   Elizabeth Gilbert, *Eat, Pray, Love: One Woman's Search for Everything across Italy, India and Indonesia* (New York: Viking, 2006), 114–15.

44   Matthew 6:19–21 (NRSV).

45   Neil Genslinger, "Doomsday Has Its Day in the Sun," *New York Times*, March 11, 2012, accessed at http://www.nytimes.com/2012/03/12/arts/ television/doomsday-preppers-and-doomsday-bunkers-tv-reality-shows .html?pagewanted=all&_r=0.

46   Augustine, *Confessions*, trans. Henry Chadwick (Oxford: Oxford University Press, 1991), 1.4, 2.18.

47   C. S. Lewis, *The Great Divorce* (1946; San Francisco: HarperSanFrancisco, 2001), 90.

48 Kevin Smith, *Green Arrow: Quiver* (New York: DC Comics, 2002), 169.

49 Ibid., 172.

50 A similar storyline from 2004 brought Ben Grimm, the Thing, back to earth in a *Fantastic Four* storyline written by Mark Waid; happy as he was to be safe and secure in paradise, the Thing misses his family. How can it be heaven without them?

51 Hannah Lockley, "Matt Damon Was Covered in Poo While Filming Elysium: 'We Literally Ate S**t'," *Enertainmentwise*, August 17, 2013, accessed at http://www.entertainmentwise.com/news/123896/Matt-Damon-Was-Covered-In-Poo-While-Filming-Elysium-We-Literally-Ate-St.

52 Jeph Loeb, *Batman: Hush*, vol. 1 (New York: DC Comics, 2003), 75.

53 Jeph Loeb, *Superman for All Seasons* (New York: DC Comics, 1999), 122.

54 Suzanne Collins, *Catching Fire* (New York: Scholastic, 2009), 122.

55 Ibid., 128.

56 Suzanne Collins, *Mockingjay* (New York, Scholastic, 2010), 47.

CHAPTER FOUR

1 James Joyce, *A Portrait of the Artist as a Young Man*, 1916 (Boston: Bedford Books, 1993), 113.

2 "Into Everlasting Fire," *Economist*, December 22, 2012, 25.

3 Thomas Keneally, *Schindler's List* (1982; New York: Touchstone, 1993), 130.

4 Thomas Harris, *The Silence of the Lambs* (New York: St. Martin's, 1988), 345.

5 Cormac McCarthy, *The Road* (New York: Vintage, 2006), 90.

6 Richard Bauckham, "Hades/Hell," *Anchor Yale Bible Dictionary* (New York: Doubleday, 1992), CD-ROM.

7 Matthew 18:8–9 (NRSV).

8 Matthew 25:41 (NRSV).

9 Qu'ran 2:119, 4:56, 22:19–20.

10 Gai Eaton, *Islam and the Destiny of Man* (Cambridge: Islamic Texts Society, 1994), 247, 249.

11 Augustine, *On the Trinity*, 13, 18, 518.

12 Augustine, *City of God*, 20.22.

13 Thomas Aquinas, *Summa Theologica*, supplement, 97.1, accessed at http://www.newadvent.org/summa/5097.htm#article1.

14 John Calvin, *Institutes of the Christian Religion*, 3, 25, 12, accessed at http://www.iclnet.org/pub/resources/text/m.sion/cvin3-31.htm.

15 Audrey Barrack, "Driscoll: Without Jesus, You Go to Hell," *Christian Post*, March 28, 2011, accessed at http://www.christianpost.com/news/driscoll-without-jesus-you-go-to-hell-49598/.

16 Roger E. Olson, *The SCM Press A–Z of Evangelical Theology* (London: SCM Press, 2005), 197.

17 Mark Galli, "Q&A: Francis Chan on Rob Bell and Hell," *Christianity Today*, July 5, 2011, accessed at http://www.christianitytoday.com/ct/2011/julyweb-only/francis-chan-hell.html?start=1.

18 Christopher Garrett, "Dostoevsky's Hell on Earth: Examining the Inner Torment of the Underground Man, Raskolnikov, and Ivan Karamazov," *Literature and Belief* 23.2 (2006): 53.

19 C. S. Lewis, *Surprised by Joy: The Shape of My Early Life* (New York: Harcourt, 1955), 232.

20 Karl Barth, *Dogmatics in Outline* (New York: Harper & Row, 1959), 118.

21 John Milton, *Paradise Lost* (Oxford: Oxford University Press, 2005), 61–72.

22 Ibid., 4.20, 73–74.

23 Ibid., 10.506–9.

24 John Casey, *After Lives: A Guide to Heaven, Hell, and Purgatory* (Oxford: Oxford University Press, 2009), 149.

25 Dante, *Inferno*, trans. Robert Pinsky (New York: Farrar, Straus, and Giroux, 1994), 5.37–41, p. 39.

26 Ibid., 7.98–99, p. 107.

27 Ibid., 34.98–99, pp. 37–40.

28 Iain Banks, *Surface Detail* (New York: Orbit, 2010), 47.

29 Ibid., 277.

30 Ibid., 132.

31 Ibid., 258, 59.

32 Ibid., 440, 445–46.

33 Facebook posts, October 13, 2013.

34 Roger Ebert, "Cool Hand Luke," *RogerEbert.com*, accessed at http://www.rogerebert.com/reviews/great-movie-cool-hand-luke-1967.

35 William Shakespeare, *The Merchant of Venice*, 1.3.93.

36 Peter Bradshaw, "A Time to Kill," *Guardian*, September 13, 2001, accessed at http://www.theguardian.com/culture/2001/sep/14/artsfeatures3?INTCMP=SRCH.

37 Susan Dominus, "Suzanne Collins's War Stories for Kids," *New York Times*, April 8, 2011, accessed at http://www.nytimes.com/2011/04/10/magazine/mag-10collins-t.html?pagewanted=all.

38 Suzanne Collins, *The Hunger Games* (New York: Scholastic, 2008), 18.

39 Ibid., 19.

40 Suzanne Collins, *Mockingjay* (New York: Scholastic, 2010), 370.

41 Ibid., 379.

42 Keith Phipps, "The Cabin in the Woods," *AV Club*, April 12, 2012, accessed at http://www.avclub.com/articles/the-cabin-in-the-woods,72287/.

43 "'Fear Factor': Unaired Episode with 'Donkey Semen' Stunt Had Hefty Price Tag," *Examiner*, February 5, 2012, accessed at http://www.examiner.com/ article/fear-factor-unaired-episode-with-donkey-semen-stunt-had-hefty-price-tag?cid=PROD-redesign-right-next.

44 Dave Siebert, "A Closer Look at the ACL as Tears Continue to Run Rampant in the NFL," *Bleacher Report*, August 7, 2013, accessed at http:// bleacherreport.com/articles/1729646-a-closer-look-at-the-acl-as-tears-continue-to-run-rampant-in-the-nfl; "ACL Injuries Ravaging NFL Rosters," *FoxSports.com*, August 8, 2013, accessed at http://msn.foxsports.com/nfl/ story/torn-acl-knee-injuries-ravage-nfl-training-camps-jeremy-maclin-bryan-bulaga-dan-koppen-adrian-peterson-robert-griffin-080713.

45 Erik Matuszewski, "Rob Gronkowski's Knee Injury Spotlights NFL's Surge in ACL Tears," *Bloomberg News*, December 9, 2013, accessed at http://www .bloomberg.com/news/2013-12-09/gronkowski-spotlights-nfl-s-60-surge-in-knee-injuries-from-2011.html.

46 Stephanie Smith, "NFL and Ex-players Reach Deal in Concussion Lawsuit," *CNN.com*, August 30, 2013, accessed at http://www.cnn.com/2013/08/29/ health/nfl-concussion-settlement/.

47 Rick Margolis, "Suzanne Collins's 'The Hunger Games' Has Plenty of Blood, Guts, and Heart," *School Library Journal*, September 1 2008, accessed at http://www.slj.com/2008/09/authors-illustrators/a-killer-story-an-interview-with-suzanne-collins-author-of-the-hunger-games/#_.

48 Dominus, "Suzanne Collins's War Stories for Kids."

49 Tertullian, *De Spectaculis*, 1, accessed at http://www.newadvent.org/ fathers/0303.htm.

50 Augustine, *Confessions*, 6.7.11, accessed at http://www.newadvent.org/ fathers/110106.htm.

51 Ibid., 6.8.13.

52 Dante, *Inferno*, 5.124–27, 6.1–5, pp. 37–40.

53 Tertullian, *De Spectaculus*, 30, accessed at accessed at http://www .newadvent.org/fathers/0303.htm.

54 Augustine, *City of God* 20.22; Aquinas, *Summa Theologica*, supplement, 94.1, accessed at http://www.newadvent.org/summa/5094.htm.

55 Aquinas, *Summa Theologica*, supplement, 94.2.

56 George Marsden, "Jonathan Edwards, American Augustine," *Books and Culture*, November–December 1999, accessed at http://www .booksandculture.com/articles/1999/novdec/9b6010.html; Roger A. Ward, *Conversion in American Philosophy: Exploring the Practice of Transformation* (New York: Fordham University Press, 2004), xxii; Avihu Zakai, *Jonathan Edwards's Philosophy of History: The Reenchantment of*

the World in the Age of Enlightenment (Princeton, NJ: Princeton University Press, 2003), 1.

57 Jonathan Edwards, "The Eternity of Hell Torments," *The Wrath of Almighty God* (Morgan, PA: Soli Deo Gloria, 1996), 356–57, 373.

58 Marsden, "Jonathan Edwards."

59 Dante, *Inferno*, 20.10–21, pp. 37–40.

60 Ibid., 20.27–28.

61 Benedict XVI, *Caritas in Veritate*, accessed at http://www.vatican.va/holy_father/benedict_xvi/encyclicals/documents/hf_ben-xvi_enc_20090629_caritas-in-veritate_en.html.

62 Mike Carey, *John Constantine: Hellblazer: The Gift* (New York: DC Comics, 2007), 79.

63 Ibid., 148.

64 Harris, *The Silence of the Lambs*, 354.

65 Ibid., 366.

66 Paul Asay, "In 'Gravity,' Finding Spirituality in Space," *On Faith*, October 7, 2013, accessed at http://www.faithstreet.com/onfaith/2013/10/07/in-gravity-finding-spirituality-in-space/25080.

67 Scott Snyder, *Batman* 24 (New York: DC Comics, 2013), n.p.

CHAPTER FIVE

1 Stephen King, "*Lost*'s Soul," *Entertainment Weekly*, February 1, 2007, accessed at http://www.ew.com/ew/article/0,20313460_1100673,00.html.

2 Public interview with Damon Lindelof, Austin Film Festival, Driskill Hotel, Austin, Texas, October 20, 2012. This interview was also edited for the PBS television show *On Story*; the episode entitled "A Conversation with Damon Lindelof" may be viewed at http://video.klru.tv/video/2365017581/.

3 Interview with Lindelof, Austin Film Festival.

4 Ryan Lambie, "Simon Beaufoy Interview: *127 Hours*, Danny Boyle, James Franco and More," *Den of Geek*, January 4, 2011, accessed at http://www.denofgeek.com/movies/16822/simon-beaufoy-interview-127-hours-danny-boyle-james-franco-and-more#ixzz2lYr6vBWz.

5 Ron Messer, "Danny Boyle Exclusive Interview *127 Hours*," *Collider*, n.d, accessed at http://collider.com/danny-boyle-interview-127-hours-paani-frankenstein-olympics/#BBohFyQQvyom2MqI.99.

6 Jacques Le Goff, *The Birth of Purgatory*, trans. Arthur Goldhammer (1981; London: Scolar Press, 1984), 346.

7 Peter Brown, *The Rise of Western Christendom*, 2nd ed. (Malden, MA: Blackwell, 2003), 258.

8 *Vision of Fursa*, 9.9.

9 Thomas Hoccleve, *How to Learn to Die*, 491–501.

10 Le Goff, *Birth of Purgatory*, 334.

11 Jeffrey T. Schnapp, "Introduction to Purgatorio," *The Cambridge Companion to Dante*, ed. Rachel Jacoff (Cambridge: Cambridge University Press, 1993), 192–93.

12 Dante, *Purgatorio*, trans. Robert Pinsky (New York: Farrar, Straus, and Giroux, 1994), 1.4–6.

13 Ibid., 2.120–23.

14 Ibid., 3.77–78, 23.5–6.

15 W. H. Anderson, ed. and trans., *Purgatory Surveyed* (London: Burns & Oates, 1874), 5, 8, 9.

16 C. S. Lewis, *Letters to Malcolm, Chiefly on Prayer* (1964; San Diego: Harvest, 1992), 108.

17 Ibid., 109.

18 Paul J. Griffiths, "Purgatory," *The Oxford Handbook of Eschatology*, ed. Jerry L. Walls (Oxford: Oxford University Press, 2008), 428.

19 Stephen Greenblatt, *Hamlet in Purgatory* (Princeton, NJ: Princeton University Press, 2001), 54.

20 Job 1:8–11 (NRSV).

21 Job 42:5–6 (NRSV).

22 Job 42:17 (NRSV).

23 Shane Black, "*Kiss Kiss Bang Bang*: Script to Screen," lecture, Austin Film Festival, Intercontinental Stephen F. Austin Ballroom, Austin, Texas, October 25, 2013.

24 *The Joker: Death of the Family* (New York: DC Comics, 2013), n.p.

25 Ibid., n.p.

26 Ibid., n.p.

27 Frank Miller and David Mazzucchelli, *Daredevil Legends*, vol. 2, *Born Again* (New York: Marvel Comics, 2003), 95.

28 Thomas Zaillian, *Schindler's List*, accessed at http://www.imsdb.com/scripts/Schindler's-List.html.

29 Thomas Keneally, *Schindler's List* (New York: Touchstone, 1982), 372.

30 Wesley Morris, "My Top 10 Best (Favorite) Movies of 2013," *Grantland*, December 19, 2013, accessed at http://www.grantland.com/blog/hollywood-prospectus/post/_/id/95932/my-top-10-best-favorite-movies-of-2013.

31 Griffiths, "Purgatory," 428.

32 "Interview with Danny Rubin," *Big Think*, July 20, 2010, accessed at http://bigthink.com/videos/big-think-interview-with-danny-rubin.

33 Roger E. Olson, "Protestant Purgatory," *Patheos*, September 7, 2010, accessed at http://www.patheos.com/blogs/rogereolson/2010/09/protestant-purgatory/.

34 Matt Fraction, *Hawkeye*, vol. 1 (New York: Marvel Comics, 2013), n.p.

35 Ibid., n.p.

36 Martin McDonagh, *In Bruges*, accessed at http://ubuntuone.com/5D8G1VlHOo1ebSNgKQZpOX.

37 Anderson, *Purgatory Surveyed*, 81.

38 M. Night Shymalan, *The Sixth Sense*, accessed at http://home.online.no/~bhundlan/scripts/TheSixthSense.htm.

CONCLUSION

1 C. S. Lewis, *The Great Divorce*, 1946 (San Francisco: HarperSanFrancisco, 2001), 29.

INDEX